Journey to Hell:
The Fiery Furnaces of Buchenwald

JOURNEY TO HELL

The Fiery Furnaces of BUCHENWALD

J. RAY CLARK

Pentland Press, Inc.
USA • England • Scotland

PUBLISHED BY PENTLAND PRESS, INC.
5124 Bur Oak Circle, Raleigh, North Carolina 27612
United States of America
919-782-0281

ISBN 1-57197-024-X
Library of Congress Catalog Card Number 96-68135
First Edition

Cover idea by Tim Maudlin.
Front cover photo courtesy of U.S. Army Signal Corps
Author photo courtesy of Joyce Wilson

Copyright © 1996 by J. Ray Clark
All rights reserved, which include the right to reproduce this book or portions thereof in any form whatsoever except as provided by the U.S. Copyright Law.

Printed in the United States of America

*I dedicate my book
As I have dedicated my life
To my beautiful and talented wife
Audrey Lovell Clark*

Contents

Chapter I	While the Storms Gather	1
Chapter II	Citizen Soldiers	7
Chapter III	This is the Army	16
Chapter IV	The Hardening Process: Learning to Kill	21
Chapter V	Separating the Men from the Boys	30
Chapter VI	Comrades Always; Close Friends Never	37
Chapter VII	Trained for Combat and Ready to Fight	44
Chapter VIII	Patton: "We Are Here"	50
Chapter IX	"Call Me Knobby"	54
Chapter X	Foxholes and Firefights	61
Chapter XI	Tigers and Dragon's Teeth	71
Chapter XII	Sights, Sounds and Tastes of War	77
Chapter XIII	A Combat Soldier Earns His Pay	83
Chapter XIV	Welcome to Hell: The Liberation of Buchenwald	93
Chapter XV	Pockets of Resistance	104
Chapter XVI	"Report to Russian Army Headquarters"	115
Chapter XVII	Patton's Best General: Horace L. McBride	120
Chapter XVIII	Respite	124
Chapter XIX	Munich: Beautiful But Dangerous	128
Chapter XX	Military Policeman On Duty	133
Chapter XXI	"Tarnish on the Blade"	138
Chapter XXII	Tourist in Switzerland	147
Appendix A	Prison Camps Established in Nazi Germany	153
Appendix B	Timeline	160
Appendix C	Nuremberg Tribunal— Major War Criminals	161
Bibliography		162
Index		163

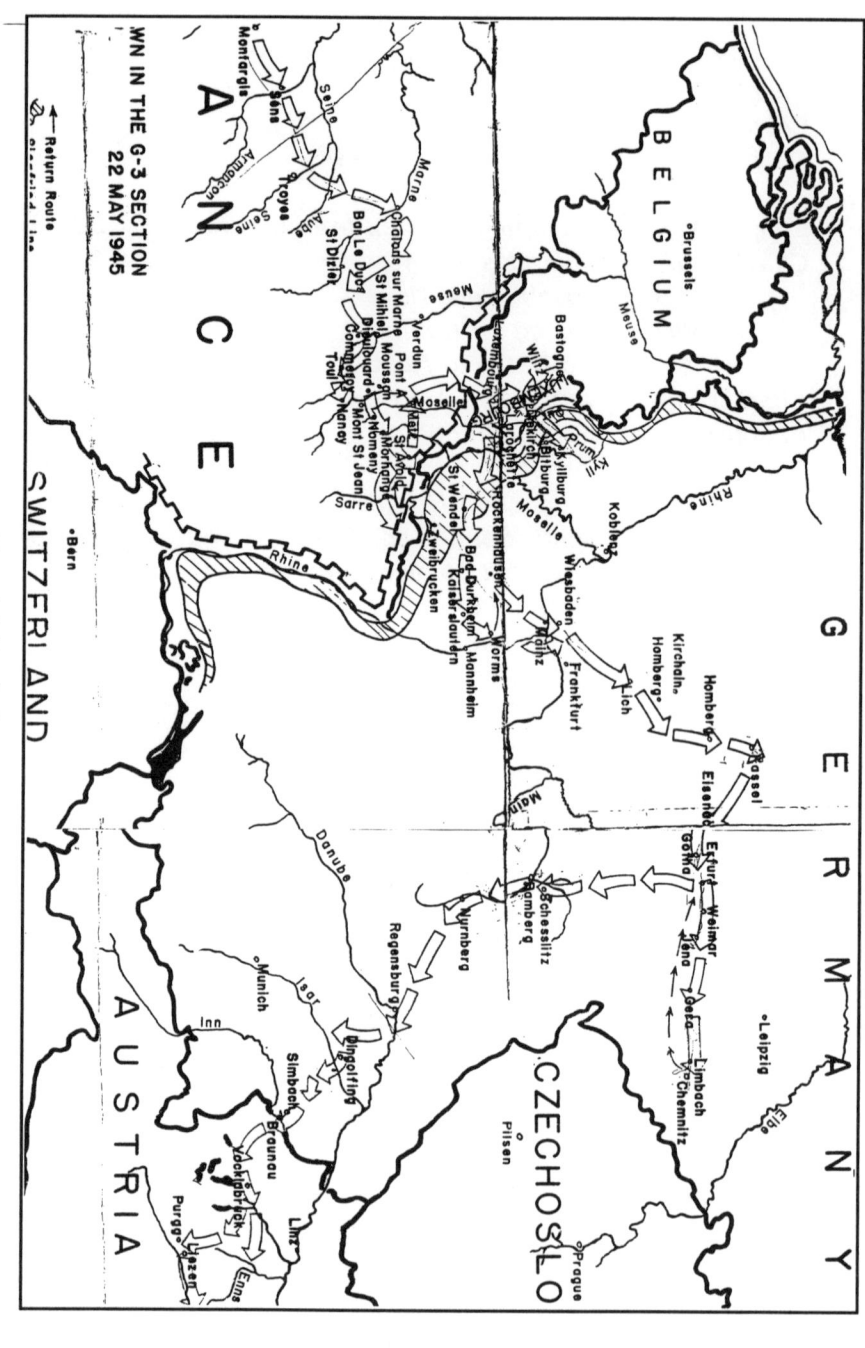

Map of Action in Europe

Chapter I
While the Storms Gather

The oath of allegiance was a quick and simple ceremony that was short and easy to understand. Any remaining doubt concerning our status was immediately removed as the sergeant commanded:
"Repeat after me."
"State your name."
"Take one step forward."
"Welcome to the United States Army!"
While the transformation from civilian to soldier was accomplished in an instant with this ceremony, it would take the horrible lime pits and fiery furnaces of Buchenwald Concentration Camp to convert an eighteen-year-old boy into a man far past that age.

For well over a decade, our generation had been groomed for our destiny and conditioned to accept the fact that we were growing up to become combat soldiers. Hatred of the enemy was instilled in us from a very early age by newspapers, radio, and the movies.

Our blood boiled as newsreels dramatically showed the Japanese attack that sank the United States gunboat *Panay*. This little warship was repeatedly bombed and strafed on 12 December 1937, while on routine patrol protecting American civilians and diplomats near the city of Nanking, China. The Japanese were proud of the fact that they had sunk a United States vessel, killing two American sailors and wounding forty-three others. Their purpose in releasing film of this deed was to prove to the United States and all other nations that the "Land of the Rising Sun" was now a world-class power to be reckoned with in the Orient.

The same month (December 1937), newspaper reporters and film crews gave us eyewitness accounts of the horrible atrocities committed by the Japanese military during and after the capture of Nanking. In a month long bloody rampage in that city, the Japanese Imperial Army killed more than 350,000 innocent Chinese civilians. Press photographers and film cameramen from Germany, France, England, and the United States documented this massacre, as power-crazed officers and soldiers used sabers and bayonets on thousands of helpless women and children.

Known as "The Rape of Nanking," this wanton destruction of the beautiful city equaled or exceeded many such occurrences of the past. In fact, it is comparable to the sack of Rome by the Vandals in 455 A.D., a destruction so hideous that even today (1,500 years later), any senseless crime is referred to as "vandalism."

From Nazi Germany, we were bombarded with scores of propaganda films. Exciting scenes burst on the screen, presenting dramatic torchlight parades, enormous rallies, goose-stepping soldiers, and thousands of twisted cross flags. In almost every newsreel, boys and girls our own age (Hitler Youth and Deutsch Madels) were spotlighted, dressed in fancy military uniforms, and marching in regimented precision under banners proclaiming "Strength Through Joy." These were, according to the English-speaking commentator, "Pure Aryans" who were "The Master Race."

During the Spanish Civil War (18 July 1936—28 May 1939), we were treated to live action pictures of screaming *stukas* (German Junker 87 dive-bombers) strafing and bombing unprotected cities. The poor Spanish peasants provided a fertile training ground for Mussolini's Italian Fascists and Hitler's German Nazis, as they perfected the art of killing defenseless civilians.

From Poland in September of 1939, we saw black-uniformed SS storm troopers demolish beautiful cities and towns with monstrous tanks and guns, leaving only dead civilians (mostly women and children) in their wake as they passed. From cameras mounted in tank turrets and fighter plane cockpits, we were thrust into the midst of actual war.

Seldom did a day pass that we did not learn new words and their meanings. Baseball, movies, and music as topics of conversation were replaced by more serious subjects. Our vocabulary was expanded to include *blitzkrieg* (lightning-fast movement of the German armies across Poland and France), *dive-bomber* (a streamlined two-engine fighter bomber that appeared to dive straight down, emitting a screaming sound as it released bombs with deadly accuracy), and *storm troopers* (stern-faced, hardened German soldiers in solid black uniforms, decorated with iron cross, SS, and death head emblems).

Geography was no longer a dull, dry subject and history came alive in the classroom. Far away countries became more than mere names or various colors on an old metal globe and even elementary school students could recognize a picture of Hitler or Mussolini at a glance.

Our world grew much smaller in May 1940, when the most formidable defense line in the world, the great Maginot Line, collapsed. This massive system of pillboxes, tank traps, and enormous artillery emplacements was constructed in the years following World

War I (1919-1939) for the purpose of containing the German army. These fortifications stretched from the Belgium border to Switzerland. However, when the Nazi blitzkrieg struck, the British and French armies on the continent of Europe were destroyed in six short weeks. The world shuttered as one army of victorious German troops marched into Paris and another stood on the Normandy coast, only twenty-two miles across the English Channel from British soil. Suddenly, we realized that the Atlantic Ocean, which for so many years had separated the United States from warring European nations, was no longer an insurmountable barrier to our enemies.

Newspapers, with daily war maps, made it easier to follow the progress of the German, Italian, and Japanese armies as they conquered more and more territory in Europe, Africa, and Asia. Reporters with sensational stories from the war gave us graphic descriptions of men and events all over the globe. We were fascinated as real people and real countries emerged from what had previously been only in our history and geography books.

In the press, we followed the Italian Fascist Forces as they invaded Ethiopia on 3 October 1935. From all accounts, everyone fully expected the American, British, and French governments to immediately honor their solemn treaty obligations and to step in on the side of Haile Selassie's African country. However, as Dictator Benito Mussolini's modern army—equipped with planes, tanks, and poison gas—slaughtered barefoot natives, armed only with spears, the prevailing attitude in the "civilized" world seemed to be, "Who cares about a few thousand African savages?"

The United States Congress passed the Neutrality Act of 31 August 1935. This was quickly signed into law by President Franklin D. Roosevelt making it illegal for anyone in our country to sell or transport arms to either nation. President Roosevelt's action, along with the Hoare-Laval Pact (an English and French deal with the Italian dictator) effectively sealed the fate of the uncivilized natives.

Flushed with victory, the king of Italy, Victor Emmanuel III, assumed the magnificent title, Emperor of Ethiopia. Of course this pompous act made headlines in all the major newspapers. However, this was an empty gesture to satisfy his vanity because everyone was well aware that, since 1922, Benito Mussolini and his Fascists had ruled Italy with an iron hand.

Radio played a large role in preparing our minds for the inevitable war. Speeches by Chancellor Adolph Hitler were broadcast into every city and town in the United States. Naturally, the tirades of the German Fuehrer brought a wide range of reaction from the American public.

Fritz Kuhn, head of the German American Bund, and Colonel Charles A. Lindbergh's America First organization applauded Hitler's programs with vigor. In fact, Lindbergh, who gained fame as the "Lone Eagle" after crossing the Atlantic alone in May 1927, became infamous only a decade later. Speaking to enormous crowds from coast to coast, he attacked President Roosevelt's policy of aid to England. As a reserve colonel in the United States Army Air Corps, he expressed delight that Nazi Germany was developing the most modern military air force in the world.

Lindbergh's numerous trips to Germany were reported by newspapers across the country and many published his picture on the front page as he accepted a Nazi medal from Hitler's deputy, Reichmarshal Hermann Goering. The Nazi government was not in power at the time of Lindbergh's historic flight, thus explaining the belated honor. Finally, President Roosevelt became so angered he recalled Lindbergh's army commission. Then, in one of his nationwide "Fireside Chats," he called the cashiered colonel a "copperhead."

Immediately following the Japanese attack on the United States at Pearl Harbor, Hawaii on 7 December 1941, Mr. Lindbergh offered his services to the military, but was promptly and publicly rejected by President Roosevelt. However, he was allowed to join Ford Motor Company as an advisor on military aircraft. In this capacity, he later visited bases in the Pacific War Theater evaluating the performance of planes and tactics of pilots who were fighting the Japanese.

The "Lone Eagle," as Lindbergh was called, took no part in the war against Germany. However, immediately after the conflict, he again visited old friends there, offering comfort and assistance, especially to aircraft industrialist Willie Messerschmidt. Through his friends in the United States Government, Lindbergh was able to obtain Willie's release from custody as a major Nazi war criminal. Messerschmidt did, however, go through the process of being de-Nazified and was found innocent of any wrongdoing. The Allied War Crimes Tribunal ruled he was a "reluctant beneficiary" of Adolph Hitler's twelve years in power. Lindbergh and these judges completely ignored the fact that Messerschmidt had personally requisitioned workers from occupied countries, then worked them to death in his factories. Also, Nazi pilots, flying Messerschmidt planes, wreaked havoc on the American Air Force during World War II, destroying aircraft and killing many young pilots. His V-I and V-2 rockets unleashed death and destruction on innocent civilians beyond the realm of civilized warfare. There is little doubt, without Charles A. Lindbergh's assistance, Willie Messerschmidt would have stood at the dock in Nuremberg with Hermann Goering, Albert Speer, and the other major Nazi war criminals.

On the other hand, the Roosevelt Administration and pro-British factions in the United States used every means possible to promote a war policy toward Germany. Mr. William Allen White's organization, The Committee To Defend America By Aiding The Allies, attacked Germany at every turn. Mr. White, a Kansas newspaper publisher, was no doubt sincere in his fight against Nazism, but he and his cohorts were over zealous in their support of the British cause. One of their greatest accomplishments occurred in September 1940 when President Roosevelt, with their assistance, was able to give England fifty United States destroyers. This unprecedented, unconstitutional action left the American Navy with only eighty-three of these essential vessels with which to protect our Atlantic and Pacific coastlines, and our bases at Pearl Harbor, the Panama Canal, and the Philippines.

Also in support of President Roosevelt, the movie industry in Hollywood produced many propaganda newsreels for the American public's consumption which were paid for by the United States Government. On the screen, we saw large flights of fifty or more Flying Fortresses (Boeing B-17s), four-engine bombers flying over New York, Chicago, and Los Angeles on the same day. Years later, we learned that these films had been shot in Hollywood studios using models, mirrors, and photographs. In fact, while we thought we were seeing hundreds of B-17s, only seven existed in the entire country. Films of the same nature depicted the United States Navy in action: battleships, cruisers, destroyers, and other ships of our fleet appeared to command vast areas of the Atlantic and Pacific Oceans.

The art of stirring our emotions was not confined to the movies, radio, and newspapers. School assemblies became patriotic rallies with speakers stressing we were "the arsenal of democracy" and that brave English pilots protected us from the horrors of war. Germans were referred to as *krauts, huns,* and *jerries* and, in a popular song of the day, Japan was "that yellow heathen land." The American public was thoroughly fooled into believing that, if we joined England in the European war, Germany would be defeated in less than one year. Then our mighty military machine could be turned against Japan in order to free China and the Far East.

Ample evidence appeared in the American press to verify the brutality of the Nazi regime against their own countrymen in Germany. As early as March of 1933, a courageous reporter, Pierre von Paassen, was thrown into the still unfinished concentration camp at Dachau, nine miles northwest of Munich, Germany, for a minor infraction of Nazi law. His release was obtained by the American Ambassador but only after ten days of repeated beatings. Mr. von Paassen's gruesome eyewitness account of torture and murder of German and Italian citizens appeared in the *New York Times* and other newspapers across the country. He also told of savage treatment to others in the camp whose only crime was that they had been born Jewish. On his release from Dachau, Mr. von Paassen was escorted by the Gestapo, or German Secret Police, to the Swiss border, expelled from Germany, and barred from that country for life.

Mr. von Paassen and other truthful reporters were labeled liars by Paul Joseph Goebbels, the Nazi propaganda chief, and by pro-Nazi groups in the United States. In fact, after a trip to Germany, Mr. Clifford M. Utley, Director of the Chicago Council of Foreign Relations, came to the aid of Goebbels stating, "Heinrich Himmler (Chief of the Secret Police) is a completely honest and upright man." Describing his visit to the concentration camp, Mr. Utley remarked, "The concentration camp at Dachau is well organized. The discipline of the inmates is excellent and their health is apparently satisfactory." Although the American public could not be absolutely sure which source was true, it was later learned from Ambassador Dodd's Diary, published in 1941, that the United States ambassador to Germany had, since 1933, reported eyewitness accounts to President Roosevelt of street beatings, concentration camps, and brutal crimes by the Nazis.

In July of 1934, the civilized world was shocked to learn that on the night of 30 June 1934, Hitler and his henchmen murdered between 2,000 and 4,000 prominent German citizens. Among those killed in this "blood bath" (Hitler's words) were Kurt von Schliecher, the former Chancellor, and his wife Elisabeth, Ernst Rohm, Hitler's personal bodyguard, Erich Klausner, the Catholic Action leader, Gustav von Kahr, a retired Bavarian Government official, and Willie Schmidt, music critic of the largest daily newspaper in Munich. Ironically, these depraved murderers showed a perverted sense of compassion. A few days later, they returned Willie Schmidt's ashes to his widow with condolence and an explanation that her husband's death was an unfortunate mistake. They had intended to shoot a Munich police officer named Wilhelm Schmidt.

In the course of this rampage, Hitler, Goering, Frank, Hess, and others settled many old scores, eliminating many long-standing personal enemies. However, not all were enemies; some were just friends who knew too much. The most notable of these was Adolph Hitler's personal confessor, a Catholic priest, Bernard Stempfle. His body, with a broken neck and three bullets in his heart, was left in the forest of Harlaching, near Munich, by a murder gang led by Emil Maurice.

Chapter II
Citizen Soldiers

As future soldiers, we became very excited when President Roosevelt, in his capacity as commander in chief of the armed forces, mobilized the National Guard and ordered it into active service for a period of one year. The United States Congress concurred with President Roosevelt by approving his action with a joint resolution on 27 August 1940.

One of the first units called to report for duty was the Thirtieth Infantry Division. Elements of "Old Hickory" left Nashville, Tennessee for Camp Jackson, South Carolina, on 16 September 1940. As the officers and men boarded the troop train in Union Station, singers on the Grand Old Opry stage lamented their parting with the first of many war ballads, "I'll Be Back in a Year Little Darling." However, shortly before that year of duty expired, Congress, by only one vote, extended their enlistment for "the duration of the emergency plus six months." Consequently, only a few would return in five years; most would fall in battle, in places they never knew existed, before the year 1940.

The Thirtieth Infantry Division was typical of units from all over the United States that answered the call to the colors. These modern day "minutemen" gave an excellent accounting in World War II as they wrote many brilliant pages in American history on every fighting front.

On 15 June 1944, "Old Hickory" went into action on Omaha Beach on the coast of France, near Cherbourg, relieving remnants of the first wave of assault forces that had stormed ashore on 6 June—D-Day. The Tennesseans crossed the Vire Canal on 7 July and, on 25 July spearheaded the breakthrough at St. Lo. Then, at 1:00 A.M. on 7 August, they caught the full force of a powerful German counterattack near Mortain, where the enemy threatened to split the Allied Army in half. Casualties were high, as five German panzer divisions supported by SS made one violent attack after another for seven critical days.

In this battle, the valiant men of the second battalion of the 120th Regiment were surrounded by the German Seventh Army for six days. As the fighting increased, the battalion ran so low on medical supplies that Major General Leland S. Hobbs ordered his long-range artillery to fire shells, stuffed with morphine and sulfa drugs, over the German lines into the area held by his troops. This lost battalion was finally relieved on 12 August by other units of "Old Hickory." For their valor and courage, the men of the second battalion were awarded a Presidential Unit Citation by President Roosevelt.

As the war progressed and casualties mounted, more and more replacements from every state in the union filled the ranks of the division. By the war's end on 9 May 1945, very few of the original guardsmen remained with the unit.

President Andrew Jackson, from whom the Old Hickory Division took its name, would have taken great pride in its achievements: six Medals of Honor, fifty Distinguished Service Crosses, twelve Legion of Merit Awards, almost 1,800 Silver Star Medals, and many unit and individual citations. However, many reaped only the nation's oldest award, the Purple Heart and a white wooden cross. For their grieving wife or mother, there was a tri-folded flag with forty-eight stars and a letter of regret.

In the fall of 1941, a large contingent of the United States Army came to middle Tennessee for maneuvers. Divided into the "Red" and "Blue" armies, the troops engaged in full-scale war games. Not yet fully equipped, most ground units used trucks designated as tanks and the Army Air Corps was represented by a small number of single engine airplanes. Flying at three to five hundred feet above the ground, these small aircraft, serving as bombers, would drop small bags of flour as bombs. One speck of this white dust and a man or piece of equipment was ruled out of action.

The maneuver referees were everywhere with their little white flags. When one zealous referee halted a squad of men who were crossing a bridge that was clearly marked as having been destroyed, the squad leader explained, "It's O.K. sir, these men have been dead for two days." One very important function of the referee was to make absolutely sure every action conformed with war department rules and regulations, properly executed in the prescribed manner taught at the Army War College. Consequently, in one major battle, the First Armored Division from Major General George S. Patton's Corps was declared "out of action" because it breached the enemy's, or Lieutenant General Hugh A. Drum's, main line of resistance (MLR), thus creating havoc in Drum's rear areas. (This very successful tactic later made Patton's armies famous.) Because of the embarrassment suffered by General Drum in the incident, General Patton was reprimanded by Major General Walter C. Short of the War Department for "operating independently and without regard for other members of the team."

General Short and his superior, Lieutenant General Herbert J. Brees, were reprimanded a short time later by General George C. Marshall, army chief of staff, for releasing a highly critical report to the press regarding the First Army's commanding general and his staff. In the *New York Times* story, Brees and Short were quoted as saying, "The First Army (Drum's) showed poor performance in reconnaissance, intelligence, liaison, and road discipline." From that date forward, all press releases were censored by General Headquarters in Washington D.C., and all observers were forbidden, by order of Chief of Staff Marshall, to find fault with any of the commanding generals in the field.

These war games had very little in common with actual combat. Troops in the field near the front line maintained a semblance of garrison life. The enlisted men slept in pup tents, were fed from field kitchens, and were segregated from their officers. Equipment was carefully preserved, tanks were limited to four hours running time each day, and trucks were restricted to good roads. Ammunition, both blank and live, was issued under strict guidelines and fired only on proper authority.

Visitors were welcome to visit the troops in their bivouac areas between battles and soldiers were given passes to cities and towns near the maneuvers when they were not on duty. They were really snazzy in their khaki uniforms, shiny leather-billed garrison caps, and "Sam Browne" belts. Although Uncle Sam was paying them only twenty-one dollars a month, there was no shortage of girls or beer in the many taverns and dance halls in middle Tennessee.

Enemy spies from Germany, Italy, and Japan had no trouble at all photographing the maneuvers; they simply joined themselves to the hoard of radio and newspaper reporters (approved by Army General Headquarters) and were welcomed by the press-hungry military brass in the field. Stories and pictures were so numerous that mistakes were common. In fact, one young officer pictured with General Walter Krueger was identified as Lieutenant Colonel D. D. Ersenbeing. Later, when President Dwight D. Eisenhower showed this photo to friends, he would remark, "Well at least they got my initials right."

When the Thirtieth Division returned to Tennessee and joined in the war games, we visited our relatives in the field. One of my brothers, Corporal Alva D. Clark, was a heavy machine gunner and my nephew, Private Arthur Eugene Lomax, was the bugler or messenger in Company H of the 117th Regiment. Corporal Clark served only a short time with the division. Later, during World War II, he served with distinction in the United States Merchant Marines. After a few months in the field, the army recognized Private Lomax's qualifications, and the former Eagle Scout was chosen to attend

Officers Candidate School at Fort Benning, Georgia. On completion of the three-month course, he was commissioned a second lieutenant. On 6 June 1944 (D-Day), having been assigned to the Twenty-ninth Infantry Division, he crossed the English Channel and led a rifle company ashore on Omaha Beach under heavy enemy fire. In 1973, Colonel Lomax retired from the United States Army with a chest full of medals attesting to his thirty-two years of devoted service to his country in three wars—World War II, Korea and Vietnam.

To visit the army in the field was the thrill of a lifetime. We were awed by real tanks: most mounted two .30 caliber machine guns and some even had a "large" 37 mm cannon in the turret. We were fascinated by the heavy 81 mm and the light 60 mm mortars. We had seen the 75 mm cannons before in the Tennessee War Memorial Museum. They were relics of World War I. The sight of the heavy artillery—105 mm Howitzers and 155 mm field guns—was terrifying. The antiaircraft gun crews enjoyed showing off their skill. In a simulated air raid drill, two soldiers stood inside a full circle steel ring on which was mounted a .50 caliber machine gun. Two others ran back and forth carrying blank ammunition from a nearby truck. The gunner grasped the gun with both hands and pressed the trigger with his thumbs, while the assistant fed an ammunition belt through the gun. A short distance away, a large searchlight, forty-eight inches in diameter, beamed toward the sky, occasionally following an imaginary enemy across the heavens. It was an impressive and exciting sight, but, like most of our high-ranking military officers and our 75 mm cannon, these tactics belonged to former wars.

By federalizing the National Guard, President Roosevelt left individual states without a force to deal with riots, strikes, and disasters. In order to fill this void, the United States Congress authorized, on 21 October 1940, the formation of troops for this purpose. Therefore, the governor of Tennessee, the Honorable Prentice Cooper, activated a state militia. The militia, commanded by Brigadier General Thomas A. Frazier, was called the Tennessee State Guard.

On reaching sixteen on 2 May 1942 I, like most young men at the time, volunteered to serve in the United States Navy. I was promptly rejected because my left eye tested 20/400. At age seventeen (the minimum entrance age), I attempted to join the army and the marines; again I was flatly turned down. Finally, I gave up and enlisted in the Tennessee State Guard.

At the Nashville armory, we were issued uniforms and equipment. Our rifles, World War I German Mausers and Spanish-American War Krags were heavy and hard to handle. We were required to train two nights per month, but were on call and subject to service anywhere in the state on one hour's notice. Instruction consisted of military courtesy and discipline, manual of arms, close order drill and, most important of all, riot control.

One particular exercise consisted of two squads (sixteen men) in a "V" formation, marching with the point of the "V" toward an unruly mob with bayonets gleaming on unloaded rifles. This formation was called a "flying wedge." This was a very appropriate name because a few well thrown rocks would have sent us flying. We were repeatedly reminded that we would never be issued live ammunition because we might, in the excitement, kill or wound an innocent civilian and the resulting bad publicity could hurt the governor in the next election. Fortunately, we did not experience race riots in Tennessee like those that occurred in Detroit, Chicago, and other northern cities in 1941 and 1942.

Our Tennessee State Guard uniforms were identical to those worn by the United States Army, with one exception—their neckties were khaki and ours were black. This distinguishing feature was only important to girls on the prowl who were out looking for dates with "real" soldiers.

Civilian industry began converting to war production in late 1941 and early 1942. The work force also took on a different look; as thousands of men left for the armed forces, women and girls replaced them in the factories. Gray and Dudley Manufacturing Company, where I worked, switched production from kitchen ranges to hand grenades. Many companies expanded or built new plants for the production of airplanes (the Vultee Vanguard was built in Nashville), ships, tanks, gunpowder, and all the other necessary weapons of war.

In my opinion, the most remarkable of these war plants was the Nashville Bridge Company. This firm, which before the war built river barges and bridge spans, began producing a small sea-going vessel that was not as large as a destroyer. For want of a better name, it was simply called a subchaser. Hundreds of these little warships were launched into the Cumberland River at Nashville. Once in the water, a United States Navy crew took charge and proceeded down the Cumberland to the Ohio, thence on to the Mississippi, and south to the Gulf of Mexico. Watching these little "men of war" hit the water, I could not resist thinking of the old nursery rhyme, "rub a dub dub, three men in a tub." However, as a nemesis to enemy submarines, the brave American sailors in these "tubs" proved their worth. In fact, many historians appropriately called the subchaser "President Roosevelt's secret weapon."

The war effort affected the lives of all Americans. The E. I. DuPont Company plant at Old Hickory, Tennessee, which had produced synthetic material for ladies lingerie, retooled for war. Many Old Hickory employees were relocated to a new, prefabricated village in Charlestown, Indiana, where a new DuPont gunpowder plant was put into operation. One of these transplanted Tennesseans was my brother-in-law, George Walter Hunt. George, a DuPont employee for many years, had been a member of our family since I was six years old. "Little Man," as he was affectionately called by sports writers, pitched for DuPont's baseball team, which consistently won the City League pennant. The team played almost every Saturday and Sunday afternoon during the spring and summer months. DuPont, Nashville Bridge, and other local firms paid players their regular wages for games. After each successful season, DuPont rewarded the players with an expenses-paid trip to the World Series. George and many of the other players were of professional caliber. In fact, one banner headline in the *Nashville Tennessean* proclaimed, "Little Man turns an iron man trick." In the story, the writer explained, "George Hunt, DuPont's star pitcher, had the previous afternoon pitched a seven inning and a nine inning game, without allowing a base hit by the other team, an almost impossible feat."

In the first year of the war, our unprepared military forces suffered defeat after defeat. The Stars and Stripes no longer flew over the Philippines, Guam, Wake, or the Aleutians; United States battleships, cruisers, aircraft carriers, destroyers, and submarines were sunk in record numbers; Japanese submarines shelled oil storage tanks on the west coast and German and Italian saboteurs were landed on the eastern seaboard. Eight of these agents were caught and hanged, but others joined enemy spies already in this country. Together they went about their deadly tasks of blowing up munition plants, starting fires in navy yards, and sabotaging military aircraft. Their actions were especially damaging because their targets were handpicked. In one incident, Major General Frank Mahin's plane was blown out of the sky over east Tennessee as he flew to take command of an infantry division in Arkansas. (General Mahin was the first of twelve general officers to be killed in action in World War II.)

Good news was sparse. General Douglas MacArthur finally halted his retreat in Southeast Asia and formed a defense line; General Jimmie Doolittle's squadron of B-25s took off from the aircraft carrier *Hornet* and bombed Tokyo, Japan; the United States Navy scored victories in the Coral Sea and at Midway; then, on 8 November 1942, just one month short of a year after the Japanese attack on Pearl Harbor, Major General George S. Patton landed an American Army on the coast of North Africa.

The war had not improved the social environment of Nashville; in fact, just the opposite was true, morality sank to an all-time low.

There were more soldiers, and therefore more taverns, houses of prostitution, and gambling dens. I saw very little promise in store for a young man who chose not to be a part of this scene, so shortly after the Hunt family settled in Charlestown, Indiana in 1943, I joined them and thus became a Hoosier.

There were many good jobs available in the area. I chose the Colgate plant in Jeffersonville, Indiana, and promptly went to work. Colgate was classified as nonessential (all men eighteen to forty-five years of age subject to military service) production, even though much of the product (soap) was shipped to the military. Therefore, every few days, another young man left for the service. This left more and more of the hard factory jobs to the women and girls. In fact, the girls we left behind were the unsung heroines of World War II. Many worked in war plants; farm mothers sent their sons to war, then went out and worked long, hard hours in the fields alongside their husbands. Others became angels of mercy and were of great assistance to overworked doctors and nurses by attending the sick and disabled at home.

As luck (or fate) would have it, one of the new employees at Colgate was a beautiful, young lady, Audrey Lovell, from Pekin, Indiana. When we met at the water fountain in the Super Suds building, she was just one day short of her eighteenth birthday. I fell head over heels in love with her at first sight. (After three children, ten grandchildren, and almost a half century, we do not regret one hour of our life together.)

Because I had been rejected for military service so many times in the past, I fully expected to be classified 4-F (unfit for active service), destined to remain a civilian throughout the war. When I registered with the Selective Service Board on my eighteenth birthday on 2 May 1944, I was assured, "The army won't take you." So I did a very foolish thing; I believed them. Consequently, Audrey and I were married on 25 July 1944.

My "Greetings," from the President of the United States, commanded me to report for my pre-induction physical examination on 3 August 1944. Along with a number of other young men, I duly complied and reported to the corner of Court and Spring Streets in Jeffersonville, Indiana. On the sidewalk next to the bus, we were each assigned an army serial number (mine was 35905849), handed our official travel orders, and loaded aboard the chartered Greyhound bus. After a two and one-half hour trip, we arrived at the Century Building, 36 South Pennsylvania Street in Indianapolis, Indiana.

Our physical examination was, to say the least, not very thorough. It consisted of two doctors who examined about fifty men in less than two hours. Of course, their job was made easier because we were all running from room to room stark naked. Believe it or not, we all passed as "fit for duty."

Since that time, many have expressed amazement that I was accepted and served as a combat rifleman with sight in only one eye. They do not, nor did we at the time, realize how dangerously close we came to losing World War II in 1944. The American citizens were kept in the dark by the United States Government Office of War Information (OWI), which controlled all the news media. In fact, on 7 November 1944, after being briefed on the imminent invasion of North Africa by Allied troops, reporters at the White House discovered that they were locked in the briefing room—where they were forced to remain until word was received that Patton's troops were ashore.

Through releases by the OWI, the American public was misled by radio, film, and the newspapers. We learned years later of training accidents off the coast of England, where an entire tank battalion of over 3,000 men was lost. Also, we were not told that the landings on the French coast on D-Day were a disaster. The campaign in the hedge rows that followed was extremely costly. In one particularly serious incident on 25 July 1944, U.S. planes of the Eighth and Ninth Air Force flew too high and released their bombs too soon, practically wiping out the front line troops of two American divisions. Among the casualties of this blunder was Lieutenant General Leslie J. McNair, Commanding General of the United States Ground Forces. The loss of General McNair, a brilliant officer, was a devastating blow because all available, capable high-ranking officers were already committed to essential tasks. The United States Military Academy (USMA) at West Point could graduate a fully-trained second lieutenant in three years and the Officer Candidate Schools were churning out combat infantry platoon leaders with the rank of second lieutenant every ninety days. But the army was woefully lacking in men like General McNair, who could measure up to the stature of Ulysses S. Grant, William T. Sherman, and John J. Pershing.

In Italy, the United States Army had taken heavy losses against stubborn resistance in the mountains and the II Corps under Major General John P. Lucas received a severe beating for five months at the Anzio beachhead. In the Southwest Pacific, General Douglas MacArthur's forces were paying a high price in American blood for each yard of advance in the jungles of New Guinea. Also, German submarines and the Imperial Japanese Fleet were inflicting enormous losses on the United States Navy. Allied losses in the air, at sea, and on the ground were occurring faster than they could be replaced. The Joint Chiefs of Staff in Britain and America were well aware of the situation and could surmise that the worst was yet to come. But neither the Chiefs of Staff nor the President would tell the truth to the American people.

When General George S. Patton's United States Third Army was committed to battle on 3 August 1944, in Northern France, the high command knew casualties would be extremely high because of Patton's audacious tactics. Actually, his army suffered more than 350,000 casualties in the nine months and five days that elapsed before the fighting ceased at midnight on 8 May 1945. In August 1944, the projected casualty figure for the war against the Japanese was in excess of one million men. However, that amount was reduced considerably by the dropping of the atomic bomb on Hiroshima on 6 August 1945 and Nagasaki three days later.

Chapter III
This is the Army

We dressed in civilian clothes, for the last time, shortly before noon on 3 August 1944. Suddenly, before we even had time to tie our shoes, we were ordered into a large room where we stood our first formation and answered the first of many military roll calls. To say the least, it was a very sobering experience. The sergeant commanded: "Answer with the last four numbers of your serial number, when I call your name." Then he barked sharply, "Take one step forward." This ceremonial procedure completed, we were transported a short distance to Fort Benjamin Harrison. Although we scarcely realized it at the time, our cares and worries of civilian life were over; we were now in the army.

At the fort, we were assigned bunks in a large, bright yellow, two-story barracks. Our new home was a room about twenty feet wide and forty feet long with beds along either side. There were two khaki blankets folded neatly on top of a rolled mattress at the foot of the bed. Later that afternoon, we would make and remake this bed several times before the sergeant was perfectly satisfied every one of us understood the importance of a properly made bed. Also, we learned everything in the army has a specific purpose. The bed is to provide a place to sleep. You can sit on a chair (though we had none), the floor, or your barracks bag, but your bed is to be ready for inspection at all times.

We only got a quick look at our new home, then rushed to the mess hall for our first "free" meal. After a big lunch, we went straight to the supply building where we were herded through for our basic government-issue clothing. From large bins and tables came everything: socks, shirts, shoes, pants, even two pairs of long underwear.

From the supply room, we rushed back to our barracks, expecting to rest until supper. This was a reasonable assumption considering we had reported in Jeffersonville at 7:00 A.M., which meant we had been up since before 5:00 A.M. However, just as we laid our new clothes down, we were blasted out of the building with another whistle. We learned quickly on that first day that the trusty old army bugle had been replaced by a small (but louder) army whistle. The express purpose of this assembly was to instruct us in the proper way to change clothes. The sergeant's orders were very specific, "Strip, dress from the skin out in GI clothing. Make a neat pile of your civilian clothes on the foot of your bunk." Then we were each issued a piece of brown paper, with instructions on how to properly wrap and address our civilian clothes. These were to be mailed to our next of kin.

Our next lesson concerned our new wardrobe and was that everything that we were not wearing went into a large, round, canvas container with a carrying handle and shoulder strap. When properly packed with the extra pair of shoes on the bottom, long underwear next, etc., this sack weighed approximately seventy pounds. For some unknown reason, the army called it "the barracks bag." Actually, a better name would have been field bag, travel bag, or something like that because it was, in fact, our home away from home.

In the next ten days at the Induction Center, we became aware of some fundamental facts about the military. First, and foremost, there are three ways to do everything: the right way, the wrong way, and the army way. Occasionally, we had to be forcefully reminded that we were now a part of the army, and therefore, we would do everything the army way. Second, as long as we remained in the army, we would always be expected to "hurry up and wait." From the first day, a sergeant's voice or a blasting whistle would summons us to rush to an assembly. After a quick roll call, the sergeant, fully aware that we could not march, would command, "route step, march" which, in army language, simply means walk. So we would walk to a designated point where we waited in line to eat, be inoculated, sign papers, receive orientation in Standard Operating Procedure (SOP), or just take a quick shower.

Roll call was usually accomplished in one of three ways: formal, or when your last name is called and you answer with the last four numbers of your army serial number; informal, to any sound resembling your name, you respond with a noise indicating you are present; and casual, on the command "count off," the man on the far right yells "one," then each man in turn from that point calls out the next highest number. With this process, a sergeant charged with a certain number of men always reports with enough men even if they are not the right ones.

At times, we felt like we were being shuffled like a deck of cards. Actually, whether we enjoyed it or not, we were being sorted. Those with mechanical ability were assigned to the tank and engineer corps. If by chance an exceptionally bright prospect was discovered, he would be offered Officers Candidate School. (I still wonder how they missed me.) By the time we left Fort Harrison, our original group from Jeffersonville was completely dispersed. As nearly as I can determine, none of us ever served together again.

Many of the units at Fort Harrison were highly classified and their areas were restricted. (Later, after the war, we learned that our spies and propaganda units were trained at Harrison.) However, there was a lot of open ground and, while we were there, we had to serve a useful purpose; every spare hour was spent on police duty. Police duty, to the army, meant clean up detail. At the sound of the whistle, we had to scour every inch of lawn for gum wrappers, cigarette butts, and bits of paper.

Another word found to have a very different meaning in the army was volunteer. Every sergeant considered you always ready and willing. Therefore, he would walk in and announce, "I need three volunteers, you, you, and you." Also, very early we learned to never admit we knew anything. If the sergeant asks, "Anybody here know how to drive the general's car?" and you answer in the affirmative, you will quickly discover that, if you are smart enough to drive his car, you are surely intelligent enough to push a wheelbarrow full of garbage.

It did not take very long for every one of us to figure out that the sergeant was the most important man in the United States Army. The sole purpose of every man in a unit is to keep the sergeant happy. If the sergeant is happy, the captain is happy, and if the captain is happy, everyone in the unit is happy. However, if for some reason the sergeant is provoked, the captain becomes unhappy. When this unfortunate event occurs, the life of every soldier in the unit becomes miserable. In fact, it does not take very much to provoke a genial, good-natured sergeant: an unmade bed, a pair of unshined shoes, a straggler reporting late for roll call, or a sassy answer. Furthermore, no matter how right you are, never tell a sergeant, "You can't make me do that." You may be absolutely right; he can't, but he can make you wish you had.

Fort Benjamin Harrison was a garrison camp; that is, a permanent military installation with an assigned body of troops in garrison. Troops on such posts were in many cases regular army soldiers who fully intended to make the military a lifetime career. In peacetime, these men were allowed to choose a specific post for their term of four to six years of enlistment. In contrast, troops assigned to temporary camps were a combination of regular army, Selective Service Draftees, and federalized National Guardsmen. The officers and enlisted men for these camps were assigned on an as needed basis and were not on permanent status.

Because the army was made up of many factions, assignments and promotions were often political in nature. Also, exile to an undesirable post was frequently used to keep both officers and enlisted men in line. A most notable example of this occurred during General Douglas MacArthur's tenure as chief of staff. Perceiving that Colonel George C. Marshall, a member of his staff, was getting too much attention in Washington General Headquarters, MacArthur reassigned him to the Illinois National Guard in Chicago. Marshall never forgave MacArthur for this insult and enacted his revenge on 16 December 1944 when he received his five-star rank two days before his adversary, thus becoming the highest ranking United States Army officer in World War II.

With war clouds gathering from 1939 to 1941, few choice assignments were available at garrison posts such as Fort Harrison. Men who sought advancement were quick to realize that promotions would come faster to those serving in field commands. Lieutenant Colonel Dwight D. Eisenhower gave up his coveted position as aide-de-camp to Field Marshall Douglas MacArthur in the Philippines. Returning to the United States mainland, he assumed command of an infantry battalion of 800 men stationed at Fort Lewis, Washington. Colonel George S. Patton Jr. relinquished his envious post as head of the United States Army Ceremonial Troop at Fort Myers, near the nation's capital, and stabled his polo ponies for the duration of the war. Reporting to Fort Benning, Georgia, he activated the Second Armored Division. Neither of these officers ever regretted their career decisions. Eisenhower rose to chief of staff of the army, then went on to become the thirty-fourth President of the United States. Patton eventually commanded the most illustrious unit in World War II, the United States Third Army.

There are basic differences in garrisoned troops and combat soldiers. Garrisoned troops are, first and foremost, trained soldiers and, when the need arises, they can and do become combat soldiers who are second to none. On the other hand, it is virtually impossible for a combat soldier to return to normal once he has been trained to act independently, without regard for consequences. For his purpose, the army exists to support him, whereas the garrison soldier exists to support the army in the field.

After World War II, many combat soldiers who returned to garrison duty were court-martialed for offenses that were perfectly normal and legal during combat. When the fighting ceased, it once again became necessary to account for equipment, stand formations, and conform to regulations. Combat officers were expected to be gentlemen once more and enlisted men were to become civilized. Many excellent combat soldiers were dishonored simply because they were mentally unable to conform to directives from Washington General Headquarters.

The garrison soldiers in the Pentagon made no exceptions. In September 1945, four months after the German surrender, with winter approaching, General George S. Patton ordered officers at his Third Army Depots to feed all hungry German civilians—contrary to War Department Regulations. Yellow journalists, newspaper publishers, and broadcast executives, motivated by greed, attacked the famous general. They alleged he was coddling Nazis, because they would also receive food. False reports actually accused Patton of comparing Nazis and non-Nazis to Republicans and Democrats. For this act of compassion, General Patton was reprimanded and removed from his Third Army Command.

Chapter IV
The Hardening Process: Learning to Kill

Though we were not aware of it at the time, our short stay at this beautiful fort was one of our most pleasant tours of duty. After breakfast on 16 August 1944, we departed Fort Harrison with our barracks bags for an unknown destination. Transportation was a troop train, which meant it carried only soldiers and consisted of coaches, no sleeping cars. We were assigned to certain cars, but not to specific seats. Our movement was not restricted and we were allowed to get off the train to buy hot dogs and snacks when it stopped at stations along the way.

Progress was slow and rumors were many. When we started south, the word was we were going to Camp Hood in Texas; if so, we would be tankers. Then someone heard it would be Camp Polk in Louisiana, an Infantry Replacement Training Center (IRTC). When we reached Chattanooga, Tennessee, we knew all our rumors were false. At daybreak on 17 August, we found ourselves moving slowly through a barren landscape, which turned out to be Georgia. When we proceeded south of Fort Benning near Atlanta, we thought the engineer surely must have missed a switch somewhere along the way, for the only possible place left to go was the swamps of Florida.

Quite often our train would stop on a siding in order to allow other trains to pass. Usually these were freights loaded with tanks, trucks, or other equipment, but others were troop trains going in the opposite direction. We later learned that these were IRTC soldiers who had completed their training cycle and were on their way to combat. We would take their place in training camp and soon follow them overseas.

We finally arrived at our destination, Camp Blanding, Florida, forty hours after we left Fort Harrison, Indiana. Our speed for the nine hundred miles had averaged less than twenty-five miles per hour. Slow as it was, the army was surprised to see us. Apparently they were expecting the new cycle to arrive a week or so later, because they were still loading out the soldiers who should have been gone before we left Harrison.

After considerable initial confusion, we were separated into groups of forty. Later that day, we discovered this was actually a platoon. From the train siding (an open field) we walked carrying a seventy pound barracks bag to a camp of wooden buildings. Each building was about twenty by forty feet and contained sixteen beds; for the next three and one-half months, we would call this home. Actually, the little building was where we kept our barracks bag; our home was out in the sand and swamps of northern Florida.

Camp Blanding was thirty-eight miles southwest of Jacksonville, Florida and about eight miles from the town of Starke. On a relief map, the camp appears to be located on the edge of the Okefenokee Swamp, but this is not accurate. Blanding is built on two or three feet of loose sand that covers the swamp.

According to a 1970s tourist guide, "Okefenokee is the home of over 389 wildlife species, including the most ancient of reptiles, the American alligator." The same guide also states, "The swamp prairies abound with egrets, herons, ibis, and sandhill cranes, while the pine uplands feature deer, wild turkeys, and an occasional black bear." It is very obvious to anyone who served at Blanding, that the person who wrote the guide book has never set foot in Okefenokee. Although we did not see any alligators or black bears, we did have more than enough varmints to write home about. There were wild boars, coral snakes, and thousands of big blue racers, to name a few.

Coral snakes are beautiful little things, but are deadly poisonous. A large one is only six to ten inches long and about as big around as a lead pencil. Their mouths are so small that they can only bite in very thin areas, such as between the fingers or, as on one occurrence, in the corner of the mouth. We were repeatedly warned not to attempt to pick them up. Big deal! I had no intention of getting within fifty feet of one. We were aware of incidents of coral snake bites, but none were in our immediate area.

The blue racer snakes were anything but pretty, be it in looks, actions, or general disposition. They were our biggest aggravation and would bite anybody, anywhere, anytime. We did not like them and they detested us. These enormous snakes were up to seven feet in length and five inches in diameter. Also, they were not at all like most other snakes in that they did not attempt to avoid contact with humans. When we went after one with a stick, it would run. However, as soon as we turned our back to walk away, the snake would reverse its course and chase its pursuer. The outcome usually depended on the size of the stick and the nerve of the soldier. Scientists who declare that these snakes do not stand up and run on their tails when you chase them, or when they chase you, have never properly provoked a blue racer.

Occasionally, one of these big snakes did add a little excitement to an otherwise dull day. On one particular exercise, we marched out to a remote area, set up our pup tents, then proceeded on a night combat patrol. We returned to the bivouac area about midnight under combat conditions (no lights or noise). But, combat or no combat, one man in the squad had to have a cigarette. As soon as he got the upper half of his body into his pup tent, he cupped his hands and, though it was against the rules, lit a match. Lucky for him he did, because right there coiled up on his blanket was no doubt one of the biggest blue racers in Florida. In a split second, he raised straight up, screamed like a banshee, and tore out down through the woods with his tent flying in the wind like Superman's cape. After the instructors caught him, he spent the rest of the night sitting atop a table in the field kitchen. For certain, that was one soldier who never again crawled into a pup tent.

The wild boar is one of the ugliest animals alive and, as near as I was able to determine, serves absolutely no useful purpose. However, it has a good sense of smell and will eat almost anything. The boars at Camp Blanding were especially fond of apples and candy bars that had been hidden (against regulations) in field packs. Therefore, it was not unusual to return to a bivouac area and find the packs that had contained food torn to shreds. Field kitchens were always secured against these pests. However, on one occasion, when we returned from a field problem, we found the guard, a city boy, standing on top of a table while the pigs wreaked havoc on the garbage cans. This would have been funny except that we had to clean up the mess before we could eat supper.

Florida is famous as the "Sunshine State." The tourist guide proudly proclaims, "Two hundred and eighty-five days of sunshine a year." This was not true of the year I trained at Blanding! In fact, in the area of northern Florida where Camp Blanding is located, it seems to rain at least part of every day. As the United States Army daily weather forecast consistently stated, "Dress for inclement weather."

General George Washington wore a cape back in 1775. Therefore, the powers that be in the army have always insisted that soldiers be issued protection against the elements. So every day we were required to carry one of the most useless pieces of military equipment ever invented, the army raincoat. When dry, it weighs about four pounds and is carried folded across the rifle belt in the middle of the back. In theory, it can be easily removed and put on while marching. However, when you are wearing a field pack or carrying a forty-five pound piece of the mortar or a machine gun, your raincoat stays on your belt until you are halted for a rest. Showers in Florida are apt to occur suddenly and without warning. Therefore, you are usually soaked to the skin before the raincoat can be put on at a rest stop. About ten minutes after the march is resumed, the rain stops and the hot Florida sun pops out; now you will wear an eight pound wet raincoat over soaked clothing for approximately four miles to the next scheduled rest stop. I still do not understand why the army did not just issue us umbrellas. We would have looked silly, but at least we could have stayed dry.

I was assigned to Company B, 217th Infantry, Sixty-seventh Training Regiment at the Infantry Replacement Training Center (IRTC). All men in B Company were to be especially trained as heavy weapons crewmen. At the end of our training cycle, we would be expected to take the 81 mm mortar and .30 caliber heavy machine gun into combat, in support of front line riflemen. In addition, we were, in thirteen short weeks, to become experts with the .30 caliber M-1 Garand rifle, the .45 caliber Colt pistol, the Browning automatic rifle, the Thompson submachine gun, explosives, grenades, rocket launchers, bayonets, compasses, and, of course, the entrenching tool or shovel.

In his welcome to Camp Blanding, Brigadier General Edwin Fales spoke to a restless, coughing, sneezing, whispering and, for the most part, inattentive bunch of raw recruits. A few long hard weeks later at our graduation, he bid Godspeed to a troop of trained, disciplined, and well-mannered soldiers. I have never envied him his task, nor have I quite understood how he accomplished it in such a short period of time.

The cadre or staff was a mixture of combat veterans and non-combatants who were too old for combat or had too many children, physical disabilities, etc. They had only one purpose: training soldiers who could go into combat and come out alive. The officers and non-commissioned sergeants and corporals were not considered friends, but they were always ready to help when a problem arose. Nit-picking inspections were few, and in our free time, seldom as it was, we were allowed to do as we pleased. First-run movies were shown on weekends at the post theater and in each company area we had a small recreation building called a day room.

Passes to the town of Starke were available and trips to resort areas like Crystal Lake and Jacksonville were arranged two or three times during our cycle. Many trainees took advantage of them but one Saturday afternoon in Starke was enough for me. It was typical of many small towns that developed near army camps in wartime. The main street was lined with gyp joints and souvenir shops. The side and back streets were reserved for beer halls and other establishments of that sort. Later, I was glad I did not play the tourist. I saw many who took their training too lightly make mistakes in combat that cost them dearly.

Neither we nor the cadre were garrison troops at Blanding. Our purpose was not the maintenance or security of the post; they were to train us in the art of modern warfare, we were to follow instruction, and in less than 100 days, be transformed from peaceful, law-abiding citizens into crafty, hardened, fighting soldiers who would be able to survive in combat.

Much of the first few weeks was spent in what we thought were dry, dull, unnecessary lectures. We received many hours of instruction on general orders.

—Take charge of this post and all government property in view.
—Keep always on the alert and observe everything within sight or hearing.
—Report all violations of orders I am instructed to enforce.
—Talk to no one except in line of duty.
—Quit my post only when properly relieved.

We were also taught military law and order from the U.S. Army code of law. These "Articles of War" would govern our every action for every minute we remained in the service of our country. Sitting in a crowded unair-conditioned theater we were indoctrinated on "Why We Fight." These propaganda films had only one theme: the United States and England are the good guys and the Germans, Italians and Japanese are the bad guys. Then there was military courtesy and discipline—a course on how to act and behave around civilized people. Later, we discovered that these lessons under the hot Florida sun had indeed been very valuable. Their principles became second nature in carrying out our duties, especially when we were the only law and order in a city as large as Munich, Germany.

Of course, from our first day at Blanding, we were constantly reminded that our Garand rifle was our best friend and, as such, should be treated kindly. It was, we learned from a 365-page manual, a .30 caliber M-1 gas-operated, clip-loaded (with eight rounds), air-cooled, semiautomatic, self-feeding shoulder weapon. The book gave its weight at nine and one-half pounds, but in those first few marches, it seemed much heavier. After a few drills, we were expected to field strip, clean, and reassemble our rifle in less than three minutes. Actually, this can be accomplished while lying on your stomach with your head down, in considerably less time—when it jams in combat.

With the rifle came a whole new vocabulary. Soon we were using words like *nomenclature*—the name of each piece and its function; *armor artificer*—the rifle repairman; *dry firing*—the simulated action of loading and firing the rifle; and *manual of arms*—the proper way to handle and present your weapon. I had an advantage in the manual of arms due to my Tennessee State Guard training; many of the other trainees were big city boys who had never handled a rifle before arriving at Blanding. They did very well with the commands "left shoulder arms" and "right shoulder arms," but when the sergeant barked, "port arms," they could not remember where their port was. (It is diagonally across the chest.)

The manual of arms was used only on special occasions, such as interior guard mount, inspection, and dress review. Therefore, we had very little opportunity to put into practice what we learned, either in training or in combat. However, after the war, when our comrades who had been killed in action were returned home, we became skilled in this art. From Attu in the Aleutians, from Normandy in France, from the Islands in the South Pacific, and from places not even on the map, they came back to Martinsburg, Borden, Olive Branch, Pekin, Mount Washington, and every other neighborhood resting place. Then, we as veterans formed into honor guards to give them a hero's farewell. As taps sounded, we snapped to present arms in a final salute, with tears in our eyes, vividly remembering the camaraderie we had shared.

Learning to fire the rifle was almost as much fun as becoming proficient in the manual of arms. First, we would hike about four miles to the firing range, wearing a twenty pound, light field pack. On arrival, we would place our packs in neat rows where they could be inspected by the wild boars. Then, we would report to the firing line and assume a number of positions. They were appropriately called standing, kneeling, squatting, sitting, and prone. Although we spent hours peering through the sights of an empty rifle in each of these positions, the prone position is most memorable.

According to the United States Army Field Manual (FM-23-5), "When the rifleman assumes a position, there is a point at which the rifle aims naturally and without effort." This never occurs when you are in the prone position, lying flat on your stomach, with both legs spread, toes pointed outward, heels flat on the ground, and your left elbow digging into the sand under the weight of a ten pound rifle. All the while, you are being encouraged to improve your posture: "Your feet are too close together," "Bring your elbow up," "Squeeze the trigger," and most emphatically, "Keep your hips down." Lying in the wet sand and being scolded by an irritated sergeant was not my idea of spending a pleasant day.

Finally, on 19 September 1944, after forty-eight days in the army, we were actually issued ammunition (one round at a time) and were permitted to fire the M-1 rifle. The range was a large, flat, open field with the firing line at one end and a trench at the other. In the trench, appropriately called the pits, were men who raised and lowered the targets by rope and pulley. For every hour on the firing line, we spent four hours in the pits. At the end of the pits were large white flags that were controlled by the range officer. As long as these flags remained up, no firing was to take place.

Here again, we lay flat on our stomachs and everything was done "by the numbers." Over the loudspeaker came the range officer's first command, "Keep your weapons up and down range." With a blank stare every one of us looked up at our instructor and asked, "What did he say?" We were informed that even an idiot would understand he meant, to point your rifle up in the air and down toward the pits. Other commands made a little more sense:

"lock and load," or put the safety on and a round in the chamber; "the flag is up," or do not fire; "ready on the left," "ready on the right," or clear the range; "the flag is waving," or prepare to fire; "the flag is down," or the range is open; and finally, "commence firing."

After each round of fire, the target was lowered and a marker placed over the hit. The target was then raised and your score was recorded by the location and number of hits. If, by chance, there was no hole in your target, the pit crew would wave a red flag (called Maggie's drawers) in front of it, indicating a miss. There was intense competition between companies, so every sergeant made sure that all of his men qualified as an expert or sharpshooter. Actually, I did very well at two hundred to three hundred yards, but at any greater distance I could not see my target. Therefore, I just fired at will and, as near as I can determine, I did not even hit him. At the five hundred yard range, the sergeant who marked my score card used what was commonly called "an M-1 pencil."

Qualifying with the pistol was a simple matter. Reporting to the pistol range, we were pleasantly surprised that we did not have to lie on our stomachs and the instruction was much less complicated. In fact, five minutes after we arrived, we stepped to the firing line and the instructor handed us a full clip of .45 caliber ammunition and what appeared to be a small cannon. Actually it was a Colt .45 caliber, 8.6-inch long, 2.44-pound weapon with a five to six pound trigger pull. We fired, by turns, at targets about eighty-five feet distant. Even though we were outside, the noise was deafening; the army was not yet aware of the necessity of hearing protection. After a morning of firing, we were given the afternoon to learn the pistol manual of arms and care and cleaning of the weapon.

The following day, we stood pistol inspection. Watching the drill instructor, it appeared so simple that anyone could master it. However, it was not that easy. Standing at attention with the pistol firmly held in your right hand, you take your left hand and push the receiver back until it locks into place. Then you raise the pistol to a half salute position in front of your right shoulder. Then, take a fully loaded magazine from your belt and extend it in your left hand palm up. After the captain and first sergeant pass in front of the ranks, the platoon sergeant commands, "order arms." On this command and in this exact order you first release the lock holding the receiver open with your right thumb; this causes the receiver to slide forward closing the empty chamber. Then, place the loaded clip into the handle of the pistol. With the pistol pointing toward the open sky, squeeze the handle and pull the trigger. The hammer falls on the firing pin with a distinct click and the pistol is ready to be placed in the holster.

There is only one problem with a pistol inspection. There is absolutely no margin for error and, almost without exception, one man in the platoon will make a simple mistake. He will place the loaded clip into the handle of the pistol *before* he releases the lock on the receiver. When this is done, a live round is fed into the firing chamber. Then, when he squeezes the handle and pulls the trigger, he (and everyone else) hears a loud bang instead of a distinct click.

The immediate reaction from the captain is always the same. He roars, "Who fired that shot?" The platoon sergeant moves quickly to remove the pistol from the hand of the startled soldier, because he is aware that being gas-operated and semiautomatic, the weapon has reloaded and is ready to fire again as soon as the trigger is pulled.

As the model number (M1911A1) indicates, the Colt .45 caliber automatic pistol had been the United States Army's basic hand-held weapon for many years. No doubt, it had the best stopping power available and compared favorably with the standard issue, 9 mm Luger of the German Army. As combat weapons, both pistols left a lot to be desired. The .45 was too big, too heavy, and had to be reloaded after only seven shots. The 9 mm Luger also held only seven shots; it made a good souvenir, but was very difficult to load and was not very accurate. In my opinion, the best pistol for combat was the German Walters P-38, a magazine-fed .38 caliber gas-operated, semiautomatic. It could be fired fourteen times before reloading, double the firepower of the United States Army Colt .45 and the German 9 mm Luger. The P-38 was easier to hold and aim because the grip was wider and it had much less recoil than the larger caliber .45.

In combat, we were constantly discarding pistols of various types. My first one was a Czechoslovakian 7.65 mm (about .32 caliber six shot semiautomatic). It would have made a nice little gun for a ladies handbag, but it had very little stopping power. It is indeed bad judgment to shoot an enemy soldier six times and just end up making him angry. I replaced the 7.65 mm at Kaiserslautern, Germany, with a standard German army-issue 9 mm Luger. Ten days later, during the fight for Weisbaden, Germany, I obtained (from an SS officer) a beautiful F. B. Radom, Belgium Browning .38 caliber, seven-round semiautomatic. It had all the features of the United States Army .45, including the hand grip safety, but it had less recoil and was much quieter. This is the hand gun I used from Weisbaden, Germany to Leizen, Austria. When I returned to the United States, I brought it home as a souvenir. I really wanted a P-38, but the only available ones I saw were lying on the ground and the most important lesson you learn in combat is never pick up anything that looks tempting on or near a battlefield. The Germans were excellent at mining (setting booby traps) and an Iron Cross medal, an SS dress dagger, or a P-38 were many times attached to trip wires that set off explosives or grenades.

For hand grenade training, our platoon of about forty men was marched out to a baseball field and seated in the bleachers. Our instructor, a combat veteran, must have been a comedian in civilian life. He began by explaining how dangerous and deadly the fragmentation grenade—a baseball-sized, steel container filled with explosives—was as a weapon. Then he proceeded to warn us about careless handling. We were told that, once the firing pin is pulled and the handle pops up, the grenade is armed and cannot be disarmed; "It will explode in seven seconds," he said. All this time, he is holding a live grenade. Suddenly, he accidentally drops it and the handle pops up, he falls to the ground, in his nice clean uniform and yells, "Grenade!" We are frozen in fear, there is no time to move, and all eyes are on the grenade. Then, it goes, spew-pop. It was the first practice grenade we ever saw. After this incident, we never trusted our instructor again, but we never quite trusted fragmentation grenades either.

The first few weeks at Blanding, we were gradually toughened up with short three-to-five mile hikes, carrying light, twenty pound field packs. Physical exercise included push ups, straddle jumps, and of course, the duck walk. Push ups and straddle jumps are self explanatory, but the duck walk must be participated in to be appreciated. First, you squat and grasp your ankles behind your back, then waddle around on your toes for fifteen minutes quacking at the top of your voice. It was almost as much fun as crawling, in wet sand with coral and black snakes, under machine gun fire, on the obstacle course. Needless to say, the weak, sickly, and careless were soon eliminated from our ranks. We received healthy meals and excellent medical care. We were never coddled, neither were we cursed or abused. In addition to our basic weapons, we were taught to swim, read maps, drive a truck, and how to hide in an open field.

Chapter V
Separating the Men from the Boys

Beyond any doubt, the most important officer in the United States Army is a full colonel. Although generals are above him in rank, the colonel, like the sergeant, is significant in his own right.

A favorite pastime of all colonels is the surprise inspection. Of course, everyone in the unit has been aware of it for days; otherwise, the captain and the first sergeant might look bad. Then the inspection would not serve its intended purpose. The colonel's little visit must do three things: make the sergeant look good, make the captain look good, and most importantly, make the colonel feel that his outfit is on the ball and first rate.

However, in order to show his eagle eye, he must point out a few discrepancies. On our first full field inspection by the regimental commander, a full colonel, I was right in the front rank with all my equipment spotless and in perfect order. When Colonel C. G. Banks, Captain George J. Dover, and the first sergeant stopped in front of me, I felt ten feet tall. The colonel's eyes went up and down, every button was polished, shoes shined, hat straight, and not a whisker out of place. Then, he took a good hard look at my equipment and saw everything laid out according to army regulations.

Suddenly, I went to two feet tall as he roared, "Soldier, where is your other tent peg?" Luckily, I remembered that there are only three proper answers to a colonel: "Yes Sir," "No Sir," and "I don't know Sir." So with a straight face I said, "I don't know Sir." I could have been perfectly honest and replied I did not have the faintest idea how many tent pegs I was supposed to account for. I would have enjoyed giving him my opinion of pup tents in general, with or without pegs.

I am sure he could guess my thoughts, so he retorted, "What do you mean, you don't know?" He knew full well I could not give one of the proper answers to that question so naturally, I offered the best excuse I could think of at the moment. Innocently I said, "I must have lost it." This put him in fine form. In effect, he informed me and everyone within one thousand yards, "Soldier, nothing is ever lost. You have been negligent and misplaced a valuable piece of equipment. You will be required to replace it!" Colonel Banks then turned to Captain Dover and intimated that I must be an example to all the men in his company. Then he turned on his heel and marched down the line. I thought I was in trouble, for sure, because the first sergeant had been writing on a clipboard during the entire incident. However, I never heard another word about the missing tent peg.

After we became proficient (an army word, meaning we could name them on sight) with our hand-carried weapons, called small arms, we received our heavy weapons. It really does not require any imagination to understand why these were called heavy weapons. The 81 mm mortar consisted of three parts: the forty-two pound plate (base), the thirty-eight pound bipod (legs), and the forty-two pound firing tube (barrel). These parts were carried by the three-man crew. I always tried to get the firing tube because it could be shifted from shoulder to shoulder while hiking and was easier to wipe clean after a Florida downpour. The army insists, and some sergeants can be downright nasty in requesting, that each man keep his weapons and equipment clean at all times. The .30 caliber water-cooled machine gun consisted of two parts: the forty-two pound tripod (legs) and the forty-two pound gun (receiver, water jacket, and barrel). Again, these parts, along with water cans and ammunition boxes, were carried by the crew. As with the mortar, the legs were carried on the back and the gun was switched from shoulder to shoulder during the hike.

On the four mile route step march to the weapons range, every man would alternate with another in the platoon. In this manner, each man carried a piece of the heavy weapon only half the distance. This does not sound so bad until you understand that for the other half, when you are not carrying the heavy weapon, you are carrying the other man's twenty pound field pack and his rifle, as well as your own.

At the range, the crew goes into action "by the numbers." In each dry run, or one without live ammunition, there are about thirty functions to be performed in each drill. Number one man (gunner) calls out each step; "base plate down, bipod in place, tube secure, sights in place, range, windage, ammunition H.E. (high explosive), increments in place, ready to commence firing!" At this signal from the gunner, the instructor will satisfy himself that the mortar is in the proper position for firing. If the crew passes inspection, he will command, "examine equipment before firing." At the time, we felt rather silly lying there in the wet sand, looking up at a 122 pound mortar. But later, in combat, we realized that last look could very well save your life. The mortar shell is very sensitive and explodes on contact. Therefore, if on leaving the tube it strikes an overhanging limb, the entire mortar crew can be wiped out.

After saying "examine equipment before firing," the instructor has a choice of two commands: "dig in" or "fall out one." On the first command, each man grabs his entrenching shovel and, as quickly as possible, digs a deep foxhole near the mortar. Then he assumes the position of a rifleman until he receives a new command.

But the more common command is "fall out one." When this command is given, the number one man crawls back about twenty-five feet and replaces the number three man. The number three man then replaces the number two man at the mortar, who moves into the gunner's position. This crew now takes the mortar out of action, moves it a few yards, and puts it back into action. This is accomplished quickly and as near to the ground as possible. So that we would not become bored, this drill was carried out on alternating days using the .30 caliber water-cooled heavy machine gun.

The next phase of our training gave us almost as much enjoyment as we had experienced in carrying the forty-two pound mortar tube. For want of a better description, the army called this little game chemical warfare. As Allied Forces approached the enemy homeland, the Axis Powers, Germany, Italy, and Japan, became more desperate. Therefore, with their vast supplies of poison gas, the possibility of chemical warfare was expected. In fact, we were provided with gas masks for a number of attacks late in the war.

Our order of the day, posted the night before, read: light field pack, field equipment, and dress for inclement weather. Depart 0700 for chemical warfare instruction in the field. This usually meant sitting for hours in the sun and rain listening to an instructor give a dry, dull lecture. Boy, were we mistaken! When the whistle blew for assembly, we fell in ranks and received our first of many surprises that day—a new piece of equipment called a gas mask. We detested it on sight because, to us, it was just five more pounds to carry.

We hiked out about four miles from camp to a group of isolated wooden buildings. Each building was without windows and had only one small door in each side, just large enough for one man to enter or exit at a time. We expected the gas mask to be air tight and, as with our other weapons, we thought we would receive hours of instruction on how to properly adjust and wear it. In a matter of a few minutes, we discovered that we were wrong on both counts.

First, we learned that our modern 1944 model United States Army gas mask was designated M1-1918. This meant it was identical to the old-fashioned one used in World War I. However, the instructor assured us that this one had an improved filter, because the Germans now had a more powerful gas. Next, to our surprise, we found that all our masks were the same size. Adjustments were made by loosening or tightening straps around the head. It was possible to make the mask snug—but not air tight—in about twenty minutes; but we were not given nearly that long.

After one drill, which consisted of removing the mask from the pack, putting it on, adjusting the straps, removing, and repacking it into the carrying case out in the open air, we went into the little building single file. As soon as we were securely packed in the door was closed. Suddenly, a canister of mustard gas was exploded and the sergeant yelled, "Gas!" At this signal we were allowed to unsnap the pack and remove and put on the mask. Three or four minutes later, the door opened and we staggered out, gagging and retching in the fresh air. We were allowed to recuperate for about an hour while other platoons went through. Then we assembled outside the building, put the mask on, and entered the building. After we were secured, a mustard gas canister was exploded, and on orders, we took the mask off and exited single file. Both times we got a good dose of World War I mustard gas. For the next four days, we went through the same drills using different, more powerful types of gas. This training gave every one of us a very healthy respect for the modern gas mask.

The next phase of our training sounded very simple. In fact, some of us thought it might be fun. The sergeant explained, "All you have to do is run through a little village, climb a rope, go over a wall, cross a small stream, then crawl 100 yards in loose sand." He called this game "the obstacle course." From his description, the exercise did not sound difficult, but the army always finds ways to make things interesting. We got a sobering clue when, for the first time, some men were given stretchers and designated as combat aid men.

To begin, the little village was booby trapped with trip wires everywhere. This meant every time you went through a door or window you set off an explosive charge. Our objective was to capture the village and kill as many of the enemy as possible. Bayoneting the sawdust dummy might have been fun but, as I said, the army has ways of making things interesting. Our "enemy" had been rigged so that when they were bayoneted their wooden arm swung around and tried to knock your head off. So you had to jerk the bayonet out fast and block the arm with the stock of your rifle. A few rifle stocks were actually broken by the dummy's arm and all of us got bruised hands and arms.

Later in combat, we discovered that the bayonet was a very useful piece of equipment. With it, you can dig a foxhole, open a C-ration can, kill a chicken or pig, and it can even be used to splint a broken bone. But never put a bayonet on the end of a rifle. The bayonet charge went out of style just a few seconds after Mr. Gatling's multi-barrel machine gun and Mr. Maxim's automatic rifle came into general use near the end of the 19th century (1865-1886). Fortunately, we were using blank ammunition. Every few minutes, someone would yell when they were struck by the wax plug from the end of a blank fired at close range. Under the watchful eyes of our instructors, we captured the village with only few minor cuts, bruises, mashed thumbs, and ringing ears. Before we entered our next stage, the sergeant ordered us to remove our bayonets from the rifle and case them, because, he said, "The rest of the course is very dangerous and we do not want you to be injured by your own bayonet." This did not sound like a very considerate gesture, taking into account they had just tried to knock our head off with the dummy.

We proceeded, at a run, to a nine-foot wall that was covered with rope netting. It resembled the side of a troop ship rigged so that assault troops can climb down the side into landing craft. Climbing down might have been easier, but climbing up with a ten pound rifle and combat equipment (canteen, shovel, first aid pouch, rations, and bayonet) was no easy task. On reaching the top, we jumped, or were pushed, into the loose sand. Then we quickly rolled out of the way so that the next man would not land on top of us. Now we understood why the bayonet was cased. The aid men stationed at this point were kept busy carrying off causalities. Most of the injuries were minor cuts, scratches, and bruises, but broken arms and legs were not unusual.

Those who were carried away from the base of the wall were lucky because, for the time being, they missed the next phase of the obstacle course. Regrouping, we marched about three miles to an area that resembled a World War I battlefield. Rolls and strands of barbed wire crisscrossed a wet sandy area that was covered with shell holes. On one side of the field were .30 caliber and .50 caliber machine gun emplacements. As we crawled on our stomachs, using our elbows to pull our bodies across the ground, the gunners fired live ammunition about twelve inches above our backs. Also, when we disturbed hidden trip wires, planted explosives went off with deafening noise. Here again, there was work for the combat aid men. Occasionally, one of the trainees would become so frightened by the noise or a stray snake, he would jump up to run and not be seen quickly enough by the machine gunners. Others were wounded when guns overheated and fired erratic patterns.

After our "baptism of fire" on the obstacle course, we were no longer soldier boys; we were now fighting men. Being shot at, and seeing our own men carried off the field, made us realize that, in a very short time, the Japanese, Italians, and Germans would be behind those machine guns. If we were going to survive, we would have to be better soldiers than our enemies. After the war, many combat soldiers, myself included, have been asked this same silly question, "Did you ever shoot anybody?" My answer has always been, "If I did not, then the United States Government wasted a lot of money teaching me how."

On our march back to camp in the pouring rain, we all agreed this had been our toughest day at Blanding. However, when we arrived in our company area, about two hours after dark, we received a surprise. Instead of being immediately dismissed by our platoon sergeants, we were held in ranks and issued C-rations. Then Captain Dover and the rest of our officers and non-commissioned cadre emerged from the company headquarters building. The Captain then began to read "the orders of the day." Big deal, we thought, our day was over. How wrong we were! Our orders were to shower, put on a clean field uniform, eat one C-ration, pack a full field pack, including three days ration, and be ready to move out in less than two hours. We should have known that this was not just another training exercise, when our platoon sergeant, a combat veteran, slipped us a word of advice; "Fill your canteen," he said.

At two hours sharp, the whistle blew for assembly and, in less than two minutes, we were all standing in the pouring rain in the company street. We then marched to the most secure building in the area, our mess hall. Only now did we understand why we had been given C-rations for supper. Our mess hall had been transformed into an assembly hall. All tables and counters had been piled up in front of boarded up windows and the kitchen was now our company headquarters.

First, we got the good news. We had been assembled in the mess hall for our own safety. According to weather reports, Camp Blanding was going to be hit with the full force of a dangerous hurricane. In all probability, our flimsy barracks would not withstand the storm. Then we received the bad news. As soon as the eye of the hurricane passed over land, we would march into Jacksonville, thirty-eight miles away, to clean up the mess and prevent looting. Now it made sense to have three-days ration and a full canteen of water. If Jacksonville's water supply was fouled, one canteen could be made to last two or three days. During the forty hours we were on alert, we ate C-rations, slept, cleaned our rifles, and prepared for the order to move out to Jacksonville. We became better acquainted by exchanging home addresses, discussing our civilian jobs, playing cards and singing "You Are My Sunshine" at least a hundred times. Sealed up in the confined space of the mess hall, we were all very happy that we had been given time to bathe and put on clean clothes, because the obstacle course had left us a stinking bunch of combat soldiers.

Luckily, the hurricane missed Jacksonville with its full force, and damage was not as bad as expected, so we did not have to go in. On the afternoon of the second day, we were allowed to return to our barracks, tired but happy. The hurricane made us realize we were no longer trainees. We were now full-fledged soldiers and the citizens of the United States had depended on us in a crisis.

Being alerted in an emergency taught us a valuable lesson. It made us understand that no matter how important a course of action might seem, that course can be changed in an instant. This is sometimes explained by the old military axiom, "Everything depends on the situation and terrain." In other words, if the situation or terrain changes, the response must immediately compensate for that change.

A classic example of this need for flexibility occurred on 16 December 1944, when the Allied Supreme Commander, General Dwight D. Eisenhower, was caught off guard by a major German counterattack. After fighting six months on French soil, Eisenhower halted six of his seven Allied armies. This was a necessary maneuver in order to allow them to refit and move their supply bases nearer to the front. These seven armies—two British in the Twenty-first Army Group commanded by Field Marshal Bernard Montgomery, three American in the Twelfth Army Group commanded by General Omar N. Bradley, and one American and one French in the Sixth Army Group commanded by General Jacob L. Devers—faced the enemy on a broad front, roughly along the western German border, extending from the North Sea to Switzerland.

In the north, the Second British Army commanded by General Miles Dempsey and the First Canadian Army under General Henry D. G. Crerar deployed along the Meuse River in Holland. Next, protecting Montgomery's southern flank, came General William H. Simpson's United States Ninth Army. At Aachen, Germany, General Courtney H. Hodges' United States First Army took over and faced the enemy until the line reached the southern tip of Luxembourg. General George S. Patton's United States Third Army, still attacking in force (he had not stopped to refit), began here and joined General Alexander M. Patch's United States Seventh Army near Sarreguemines, France. From there, Patch's army continued south to Strasbourg, France. From Strasbourg to the Swiss border, the line was held by the French First Army commanded by General Jean de Latte de Tassigny.

Suddenly, General Eisenhower's front was broken and breached near the Belgium/Luxembourg border. General Hodges' United States First Army became engaged in a fight to survive as a powerful German army completely destroyed one of his divisions (15,000 men), and advanced toward Antwerp, Belgium. General George S. Patton was the first to respond. He immediately ordered two of his most capable divisions, the Fourth Armored and the Eightieth Infantry, to disengage the enemy, withdraw across two rivers, then proceed 125 miles over snow-covered terrain to attack the southern flank of the German army. Patton's daring speed and flexibility turned defeat into victory.

Chapter VI
Comrades Always;
Close Friends Never

From the very first day, we lost those men who were weak, both mentally and physically; attrition had taken its toll. Now we were hardened and ready for our final weeks. There was a noticeable change in our officers and enlisted cadre. They were more relaxed and seemed to take pride in our performance. Night problems and combat patrols occurred more often and the hikes became longer, with more equipment to carry. However, there was less complaining because we all knew the real thing would be a lot tougher.

Every problem was under combat conditions. Therefore we had to assume we would not return to base camp. This meant we had to carry every piece of essential (and some non-essential) equipment on our back. This sixty to seventy pound load was referred to as a full field pack. Without a doubt, the most useless item in the pack is, in army language, a shelter half. We commonly called it, among other things, a pup tent. The pup tent consists of two pieces of thin canvas, approximately three by six and one-half feet, two tent poles, ten wooden pegs, and two short pieces of rope. For reasons known only to the army, someone in Washington General Headquarters decided the pup tent would be carried by two men, thus when it is time to bivouac, every two men will have a complete tent.

Usually after completing a night exercise we found ourselves in pitch-black darkness in an area we had never seen in daylight, searching quietly for a dry spot in the wet sand. That may sound like a simple task, but remember, it rains almost every day in the swamp and only about eighteen inches of sand covers this part of northern Florida. Once a spot is located, you unpack your shelter half and your tent mate does the same. Now you discover one does not have his pegs and the other has lost his rope. Then both of you scout around in the dark (no lights are permitted) for sticks to use as pegs and take off your belts to use as tent ropes. However, before the tent is put up, the field manual instructs, "Dig a trench around the tent, so that rainwater will be directed away from the sleeping area." This sounds like it makes good sense, so you try it, then you learn as soon as the water fills the trench it overflows into the tent. Quickly you realize that the officer who wrote the field manual never in his life occupied a pup tent in a Florida swamp.

Fully dressed and soaked to the skin, you finally crawl in out of the rain, ready for about four hours sleep. Guess again! Canvas drips and there is always a drip right in your face. Also, as you move, any spot on the tent that is accidentally touched will drip. Finally, you drop off to sleep with a smile on your face because you realize that everyone else in the company is just as miserable as you are.

Breakfast was C-rations, then after daybreak, our area was inspected. The sergeant never said a word about using sticks for tent pegs because our swayback effort looked as good as any of the rest. After conferring with Captain Dover, probably on whether to leave us there or take us back to camp, he blew the whistle and ordered, "Pack up and move out." When we arrived at our barracks, everything, including our bodies, had to be cleaned and dried. We were elated when one of the cadre, an old combat veteran, slyly told us, "After you leave Camp Blanding, you'll never see another pup tent." Later, we found out he failed to tell us that in combat you sleep on the ground without any covering at all, unless it snows, then you are covered with snow.

Near the end of our training cycle, we discovered that the two ordeals we had dreaded the most were not all that difficult. We had been told since the beginning that, in order to receive a certificate of completion, we would be required to spend two weeks on bivouac, camped out in the swamp, and to march thirty-two miles in eight hours with a full field pack.

The bivouac was a piece of cake. By this time, we had become accustomed to the snakes and pigs and they, in turn, tolerated us. We usually ate two hot meals a day, with C-rations at other times. Life was more casual in the field: no shoes to shine, no barracks to clean, and very few rules to follow. We trained in smaller, squad-sized groups of eight to twelve men. There were no more textbooks or classroom instruction. Instead, we were taken out in the swamp and left with a map and compass. Map reading gets a lot easier when you have been lost all day and supper time is approaching. You really have only two choices, find your way back to the bivouac area or sleep all night on an empty stomach in the swamp. Also, lessons in how to protect yourself come rather quickly when bullets from a concealed machine gun whiz overhead. We became experts in the art of camouflage and could spot a careless enemy's shiny canteen three hundred yards away. We learned, by practice, the importance of sanitary maintenance and could dig, use, and cover a slit trench latrine in a matter of minutes.

Naturally, we had brought along the pup tent. However, we soon discovered it was easier to roll up in the shelter half than it was to attempt to make a tent out of it. Usually we would just use our pack as a pillow and sack out under our raincoat.

Many of our weapons and pieces of equipment were referred to by name: Colt .45 pistol, Thompson submachine gun, Browning Automatic Rifle (BAR), Garand M-1 rifle, Sam Browne belt and, of course, the Lister bag. When we were introduced to one of these "gentlemen," we were skeptical because we always knew we were going to become better acquainted, sometimes to our sorrow. Browning and Garand made good weapons but the Sam Browne belt transformed the most common, friendly officer into a nit-picking Martinet and the Lister bag was the ruination of good drinking water.

Since arriving at Blanding, we had always filled our canteens from an ordinary water faucet but, on bivouac, out in the field, there were no water lines. Apparently the United States Army Medical Corps was convinced that Dr. Joseph Lister, First Baron of Lyme Regis (1827-1921), was correct when he made his brilliant discovery; there are germs in drinking water, but if you make the water taste bad enough, the germs will go elsewhere. Therefore, the Lister Bag is a large forty gallon bag suspended from the center of a teepee-like frame, filled with good clear water, which the army proceeded to ruin by tossing in a hundred or so water purification tablets. I am not sure these tablets had any effect on making the water purer, but they sure cut down on its use for drinking.

When we first arrived at Camp Blanding, not one of us could have completed a five mile hike, much less a thirty-two mile march. However, as our training progressed, four, eight, twelve, and sixteen mile distances became common. These were not parade ground type marches, but hikes in a loose formation called route step. Order was maintained with few, if any, commands. Rifles were carried by their slings, over the shoulder, leaving the hands free. Except for occasional simulated combat condition marches, we were allowed a ten minute relief break every hour.

We soon learned, with good reason, to try to stay away from the front of the column because we were our own traffic cops. As we approached a crossroad, the sergeant would bellow, "Scouts out!" On this command, the first two men would double-time to the crossing, come to port arms with an empty rifle, and traffic would courteously come to a halt. Then the scouts would fall in at the rear of the column. Of course, if the march was through the camp, where crossings were numerous, most of us served as scouts before we reached open country. (Later, as an MP in Munich, Germany, I did not dare to run out in the middle of an intersection to stop traffic, even though I was armed with a fully-loaded Thompson submachine gun.)

In preparation for the thirty-two mile march, we were given twenty-four hours off duty. The order of the day advised us to eat lightly, rest, and drink a reasonable amount of water throughout the day. As part of the full field pack, we would be required to carry a full canteen but not one sip would be allowed during the march.

Shortly after a supper of one C-ration, we "jumped off" toward Camp Blanding. The first two hours were the toughest; adjusting the sixty pound pack and shifting the rifle from shoulder to shoulder. Also some of the men had failed to heed the instruction concerning the intake of water and were miserably awaiting a "relief" break. After about four hours, a few men began to fall out. As soon as they sat down beside the path, they were checked by medics and either allowed to rest a few minutes, then resume the march, or, if they appeared to be ill, they were put on trucks and taken back to the aid station. I had neither the desire nor the intention of falling out, because this would have meant starting over at the thirty-two mile marker the following night.

We were tired but pleased with ourselves when we arrived back at our barracks. Now we knew we had only one more march to go in order to complete the training cycle. This happy event occurred just four days later, a full dress review on the parade grounds before the commanding general and his staff. We stepped off smartly as the regimental band saluted us with "On the Mall" and "I've Got a Sixpence." When we passed in front of the reviewing stand, Captain George J. Dover Jr. sang out, "eyes right" and, from the corner of our eye, we could see Brigadier General Edwin Fales proudly returning our salute.

That afternoon we assembled, once again, in the post theater—this time for our farewell address. It was hard to imagine that it had only been three months since we received our welcome to Camp Blanding in these very seats. As the general spoke, neither a cough nor a whisper was heard and he could sense that he had earned our respect. Under his direction, we had become soldiers in the United States Army and each of us could say with pride, "I trained at Blanding."

On completion of the training cycle, all new soldiers were scheduled to be given ten days leave at home before being shipped overseas. However, due to the serious German counterattack in Europe, men from the Replacement Training Centers at Fort Hood, Texas and Camp Polk, Louisiana, were flown directly to combat units. For once in my life, I was in the right place at the right time. The camps nearer to existing airports were able to supply enough troops for all available planes.

While waiting for travel orders, we engaged in what the army refers to as "interior guard mount." Surprisingly, "interior" to the army, means interior of the post, which, as everyone knows, is for the most part outside, and "mount," to the army, has absolutely nothing to do with riding a horse. A mount of guard duty usually consisted of twenty-four hours, two boring hours marching back and forth with an unloaded, bayonet-fixed rifle on the right shoulder, then four hours rest in the guardhouse. While you are resting, you must be ready at all times to respond to an emergency. Therefore, you are not allowed to remove any clothing or equipment and you do not step outside the guardhouse for any personal reason. At rest, you can play cards, sing, polish your shoes, or clean and re-clean your equipment, but with sentries coming and going every two hours and sergeants and officers issuing special orders every few minutes, you do not sleep.

As with everything else in the army, guard mount must be accomplished "by the numbers." Nothing is left to the imagination by a little brown book called a field manual. Every sentry is expected to memorize the eleven general orders, ten of which are not too difficult to understand. However, number four always gave us a little trouble. It reads, "To repeat all calls from post more distant from the guardhouse than my own." In a few rare cases, this was accomplished in the proper manner; however, more often the sentry would repeat what he heard, with a slight variation. For example, a sentry on post number six would request assistance, calling out, "corporal of the guard, post number six." This would be picked up by the next sentry and relayed as, "corporal of the guard, post number five." By the time the call reached the guardhouse, three or four sentries had repeated different post numbers. Therefore, the following day, we would all be required to sit in the hot Florida sun for four hours of instruction from the little brown book on how to properly mount an interior guard. These classes (and many others) were taught by "ninety day wonders," or second lieutenants who recently graduated from Officers Candidate School (OCS). Having absolutely no experience, they could only recite what they read in the field manual on any given subject. Therefore, when anyone asked a question on a point not covered in the book, the instructor would invariably look straight at him and say, "That's a good question, it shows you are thinking." Then he would proceed as though he never heard the question.

The best hours to walk post were from four to six A.M. because activity increases and time goes faster. On this tour, the sentry wakes the mess sergeant and cooks. Also, he is on duty when the milkman delivers the milk. Like everything else in the army, acquiring a drink of cold milk at 4:30 A.M. must be done by the numbers;

first, make sure the milkman is out of the area, then stack two or three cases off the top of the stack, remove and drink a quart of milk, replace the bottle and restack the cases so the missing milk will not be quickly discovered. Of course, if you are really daring, you can drink a quart from the top case, then when the sentry on the next post goes in the barracks to wake his cook, run over to the stack by his mess hall and replace your empty with a full one from his supply.

There were other tricks to relieve the boredom of pacing back and forth. Occasionally, one of the cadre would return after hours and, being fully aware that we were carrying unloaded weapons, would not halt when the challenge, "Halt! Who goes there?" was made. However, with a slight change in the challenge, you could quickly gain anyone's undivided attention: instead of going to port arms, the rifle was brought to a hip-firing position, then the bolt was released with a loud noise as though a live round was being loaded into the chamber. This never failed to work, although some old sergeants got very upset when stopped in this manner.

The strength of our training company (B-217-67) was about 150 men and I am not aware that any of us ever served together again. In fact, none of us really became personally acquainted because we realized any friendship made here would soon cease. As General Douglas MacArthur once said, "In order to remain unaffected by the loss of friends, treat them as though you both are always on travel orders." Comradeship and rapport were common in service, but lasting friendships were very rare.

Beginning about one week after our dress review, five or ten men would receive travel orders daily. Mine came as:

SPECIAL ORDERS NO 304 EXTRACT 8
20 DEC 44
Following EM (inf) atchd unasgd trainees orgns indicated TRFD in gr of PVT WP 23 DEC 44 AFG Replacement Depot #1 Ft. George G. Meade, Md. Reporting thereat to CG for overseas asgmt on or before noon on dates indicated below.
MOS (Heavy Weapons Trained)
No. Name Serial Days Delay Report
104 Clark, James R. 35905849 14 5 Jan 1945

Translated into civilian language, these orders read: The following named enlisted men, infantry trained are attached and unassigned to the organizations indicated and are transferred in the grade of private with pay on 23 December 1944 to the Army Ground Forces Replacement Depot #1 at Fort George G. Meade, Maryland. Reporting thereat on arrival to the commanding general or officer designated by him for overseas assignment on or before noon on the dates indicated below.

On the short trip from Camp Blanding to Jacksonville, we sat on wooden slatted seats in the back of an open truck over rough roads. To say the least, it was not very comfortable. However, this turned out to be the best leg of the trip to Nashville. When our group arrived at the railroad station, all the coaches on the last train north were full, so I rode on a stack of barracks bags from Jacksonville, Florida to Chattanooga, Tennessee. This, in itself, was not so bad, except that the bags were stacked on the platform between the coaches where all the cinders and coal dust settled from the locomotive. At Chattanooga, I managed to get a seat in one of the dirty coaches for the short, five-hour trip to Nashville.

Because our train from Jacksonville to Nashville was moving inland, north and west, we were not given any priority. Consequently, we were sent to the side tracks for all trains moving toward East Coast ports. As a result, I arrived in Nashville cold, dirty, and hungry, at the end of a twenty-five hour trip.

The ten days at home, with every possible minute spent with my beautiful wife, went by like a flash and remain a blur today. Suddenly it was time to say good-bye. Our world would never be the same, but neither would any of us who lived through the horror and loneliness of World War II.

Chapter VII
Trained For Combat and Ready to Fight

We really did not realize how important we were on 3 January 1945. Then suddenly police whistles began to sound all around us and the loudspeakers blared, "All military personnel will be boarded first. All civilians will clear the gates."

Union Station at Tenth and Broad Streets in Nashville, Tennessee was teeming with people. Many of the 6,000 to 7,000 civilians who were stranded had been waiting for available transportation since the day after Christmas. On that day, the United States Government had ordered that all military personnel be given first priority. This order was necessary because the Allied line in Europe had been under a severe German counterattack since 16 December 1944, and replacements were desperately needed to stop the enemy advance. The United States Army's 106th Infantry Division, commanded by Major General Alan Jones, was hardest hit, losing two of its three infantry regiments and many of its supporting units—nearly 10,000 men—in four days.

On this trip, I was one of the lucky ones who rode inside. As I boarded the train, I threw my luggage on the platform between the cars and made a flying leap for the first empty seat. We moved through Tennessee, Kentucky, and Virginia as a "green flag" special train; this designation cleared the tracks as all other traffic went to the side tracks so we would not be delayed. We made excellent time, stopping only to pick up more troops along the way. When we arrived in Washington, D.C. our train was surrounded by military police and members of the Washington Guards. Only those men with orders to the Washington area were allowed off the train and no passengers were allowed to board.

Shortly before noon on 5 January 1945, we arrived at Fort George G. Meade, Maryland. Here, we were assembled into company size units (approximately 200 men), fed, and kept overnight, then, early the following morning, shipped by truck to Camp Shanks, New York. Since that time, I have not been able to find such a place on any map, but that does not make any difference; I would not return to Camp Shanks even if I was absolutely sure of its location. First, it was cold, barren, and covered with at least ten inches of solid ice. While we were there, a blizzard occurred and it was almost impossible to walk or even stand up outside in the wind and blowing snow. In fact, many of us did not take advantage of the opportunity to attend a free boxing exhibition by Joe Louis, the Heavyweight Champion of the World, in the recreation hall across the street from our barracks. I really should have gone over and gotten his autograph, but at the time, I was not in the mood to be impressed.

The army referred to Camp Shanks as a staging area, which meant we were only there long enough to be equipped and assigned to units for overseas shipment. Our equipment included our first combat gear: a wool knit cap, plastic helmet liner, and a steel helmet. Also, we were issued two complete changes of clothing and an extra pair of combat boots. After we packed our barracks bag, it weighed slightly over eighty pounds. Little did we know that we would carry all that weight over 3,000 miles for someone else, whom we did not even know. On landing at Le Havre, France, a genial sergeant instructed us to pile our barracks bags in a designated area, and with a straight face assured us, "Your bags will be brought up to you by truck as soon as you reach your company." We never saw that sergeant or our barracks bags again. Some lucky Frenchman is probably still wearing my other pair of combat boots.

From the staging area, our unit moved to the first of many "undisclosed" locations on the way to the front lines. We were hauled in one and one-half ton canvas-covered trucks with wooden seats along the side. These trucks can carry fourteen soldiers with full field equipment. However, they are not built for comfort. Because these trucks had six wheels the army always referred to them as six-by-sixes.

After a cold, miserable, bumpy ride, we unloaded inside a large building that, at first glance, appeared to be a warehouse. However, on closer inspection, with a sinking feeling in the pit of our stomachs, we realized that one entire wall of the structure was the side of a ship. Actually, we were on a New York City pier and the ship, with a door in its side, was the HMS *Pasteur*. As we embarked, cadremen gave us tags to be tied in our top buttonhole. Mine read D-6 Port; the D designated the deck, D being four decks below the main deck, the number six indicated an area, and port meant the left side of the ship. Therefore my hammock was just forward of the center of the ship one deck below the water line on the left side of the vessel. In the event of a submarine attack, my little spot would have been the ideal target for a torpedo.

The HMS *Pasteur*, a former French luxury liner, was a beautiful ship. It had been seized by the English Navy after the fall of France in June of 1940, and impressed into their service as a troop carrier for the Allies. Built in 1938 (six years old at the time of my voyage), it was the seventh largest passenger ship afloat in the world. Only the below deck cabins had been altered in converting it to a troop carrier. On our trip, this majestic ship was able to accommodate nearly ten thousand soldiers.

Except for a few areas that were off-limits, we were allowed to explore the ship at will. Therefore, we spent many hours admiring the fine craftsmanship; the wide, circular staircase that ran from the main deck to the ballroom twenty feet below (with its fine polished brass hand rails) and the enormous, crystal chandelier that hung from the fifteen foot ceiling of the main dining room were especially impressive to our young eyes.

Some of our time was occupied by an attraction on the rear deck—the only gun, a British three-pounder, mounted on the ship. It was fully manned at all times, and the crew performed full dress drills (loading, sighting, and ranging) at least once every hour, but they never fired a shot. We were informed by one of the off-duty crewmen that more guns were unnecessary because the *Pasteur* was faster than the German submarines. This was not very reassuring, since we were all aware that enemy subs ran in packs and sometimes lay in wait along the sea routes so they could attack head on or from the side as we passed. We learned later that our ship had made contact with a number of subs but they were chased away by subchasers we could not see over the horizon.

We left New York harbor on a beautiful, bright, and sunny day. It was a sensation we had never before experienced and most likely never would again. Passing the Statue of Liberty gave us a distinct chill then, as we cleared the harbor and looked back, the lady with the torch appeared to wave good-bye. Up to this moment, we just thought we were homesick, now, with our hearts in our throats, we knew it for sure.

That afternoon the *Pasteur* was escorted by four destroyers which bristled with guns and depth charges and, although they were small ships, we felt safe and protected. However, the following morning, our destroyer escort was gone and we were out in the open sea, apparently alone.

All in all, it was a very interesting but casual trip. The *Pasteur* was so large, we barely felt any movement from side to side; it was almost like gliding on water. In fact, the motion was so slight that only a few appeared to have any symptoms of seasickness. During our voyage, we were not assigned any duties like KP or guard duty, though keeping the ship clean was everybody's job. Orders were few, but specific and strictly enforced: "No lights after dusk or before dawn!" "Do not throw anything overboard!" "Stay away from restricted areas!" Other than having to sleep in shifts in our hammocks, we were not crowded or inconvenienced. Actually, we were treated almost like paying passengers rather than a shipment of soldiers in transit.

The ship was kept spotless by the English crew who were very friendly and tolerant. No doubt our questions were the same ones they had answered many times before for other American troops: "Why are English sailors on a ship with a French name?" Their answer was, "We have not changed the name because this ship still belongs to the French Navy and will be returned to them as soon as France is free again." We asked, "How fast are we going?" and they answered, "About twenty knots." We replied, "What is a knot?" and this answer made no sense at all, something about knots on an imaginary rope that had nothing to do with speed in miles per hour. Then we asked, "How many trips have you made across the ocean and back?" and their answer: "About once a month for the past two years, but not always on the same ship." Then we asked a few questions that were never answered to our satisfaction: "Has the gun on this ship ever sunk a German submarine?" "What happened to our destroyer escort?" and, most important of all, "Aren't we sitting ducks?"

There were a few minor hazards to "landlubbers" adjusting to life aboard a seagoing vessel. We learned quickly to watch out for wet spots that made the metal floors as slick as glass. Also, there were so many low pipes in unexpected areas, we preferred to wear our steel helmet, even though it was not required. However, the one thing that caused us the most trouble was a strip of canvas. It was approximately two feet wide and six feet long, and was tied with a rope at each end to pipes that were secured at the floor and ceiling. These contraptions were referred to, by sailors, as hammocks; we called them by many other names. In the sleeping area (D-6 Port) they were hung five feet high and in rows about two feet apart. There were no ladders; we simply climbed from hammock to hammock to get to our assigned spot.

Getting into and out of bed was especially awkward when one or more of the lower hammocks was occupied by someone who was trying to sleep. In this case, you were left with two choices; you could pretend the hammock was empty and step on the occupant, or you could step on the rope or canvas. The latter method usually turned the hammock upside down, tossing the sleeping person on the metal floor. After the second day, most of us accepted being stepped on, which we much preferred to the sudden shock of being unceremoniously dumped onto the cold, steel deck.

The person who coined the phrase "getting there is half the fun" obviously never tried to nap in a hammock wearing full field dress, including a steel helmet and combat boots. Even after feeling securely snug, a person was not completely out of danger, because the slightest movement could and did dislodge various objects from the upper tiers. Steel helmets were the most common missiles that came crashing down to the metal floor. Usually, the wayward item, weighing from two to four pounds, bounced off a foot, a knee, a shoulder, or in many cases, a head, on its path to the deck. Someone would always be nice enough to retrieve your property and return it with grace and a few "kind" words. Most of us soon learned how to nap with our helmet on our chest and our arms folded through the fastened chin straps. This was awkward and uncomfortable, but it was satisfying to know we were not going to accidentally "bomb" a fellow soldier on the head before he even got to the front line.

The weather was ideal for most of our eight-day voyage. Daytime temperatures were in the forty to fifty degree Fahrenheit range, and from dawn to dusk, the sky was a beautiful, bright blue. Once or twice, we sailed through rain showers but even then, the sea was calm and we could see sunny skies only ten to fifteen miles away. Inside the ship, air circulation was extremely good and we were always warm and comfortable, even in our crowded hammock compartments.

We ate by units in one of the large dining rooms and were never rushed or crowded at mealtime. The food was United States Army Class A rations, which meant it was prepared from fresh meats, fruits, and vegetables and served the same as at any garrison post in the United States. Our meals were served on large metal trays and we were encouraged to take second helpings. The company grade officers ate with us, one or two at each table, and were very friendly. (Army officers are divided into three classes: lieutenants and captains are company grade; majors, lieutenant colonels and colonels are field grade; generals of all rank are called general officers. They were well aware that we were all headed for the same place, or as the old saying goes, "We were all in the same boat.")

At dawn, on the sixth day out of New York, we were pleasantly surprised to see that the United States Navy had returned to escort us in to port. However, this time we were only allotted two destroyers, one on each side of the *Pasteur*. We were elated to see them once more. They were fascinating to watch: darting back and forth, zigzagging, then steaming at full speed out in front of our ship, where they completed a very tight half circle and raced to the rear to begin to maneuver again. One of the farm boys in our unit remarked, "Those things remind me of my beagle hound searching a field for rabbits." Most of us stayed on deck all day hoping to see them go into action against an enemy submarine. Actually, if the truth were told, we were very happy that none were found in our vicinity.

The following morning we were awakened at 3:30 A.M. and ordered, by loudspeaker, to take down the hammocks and stack them neatly in one corner of the compartment. As soon as this task was completed, we naturally expected to hear mess call for breakfast. However, the next voice we heard said, "All troops will secure your equipment and remain in your compartments until you are ordered to debark."

We had no idea we were even close to land or what land it would be: England, Ireland, or perhaps France? Well, at least now we could stop heading our letters with "somewhere at sea."

Chapter VIII
Patton: "We Are Here"

The HMS *Pasteur* docked at Liverpool, on the west coast of England. However, due to the fact we were "buttoned up" below deck we were unable to see the city or the surrounding countryside. We debarked the same way we embarked, through the side of the ship, down a passageway, and into an enclosed train shed. Here we boarded a waiting train that appeared to be a relic of the First World War. The engine was approximately one-half the size of a modern (1945) American locomotive. The coaches were about thirty feet long and had an aisle down one side, with little enclosed compartments down the other. Six men with barracks bags were assigned to each compartment, which would have been crowded with four men without baggage. We had specific orders not to leave our "booth" except to visit a little room at the end of the coach, which the English referred to as the "water closet."

The train was sealed with guards at every exit. We were forbidden to disturb the blackout curtains because the sergeant said, "If you open the curtain, the German pilots will see the light and dive bomb the train." His reasoning did not seem to make any sense. First, we were traveling in broad daylight across open country and secondly, at this stage of the war (January 1945), the German Air Force had lost all its airfields in France. Therefore, the only enemy planes over England were occasional reconnaissance flights. In spite of the warning, or perhaps because of it, we did crack the blackout shade a couple of times. Once, I saw some cows in a field and the next time, some English women standing on a train station platform. Truthfully, I was not impressed by the women or the cows; neither, in my opinion, would have taken a prize in a beauty contest.

Actually, there was a very good reason that we were buttoned up. If we were captured later (as some were), we would not be able to give any details about, or locations of, installations in England such as gun emplacements, bomb damage, airfields, or depots.

After about twelve hours on the train, three of which were spent waiting in line at the water closet, we arrived at the city of Southampton on the English Channel. Here, in a rail yard, we stood our last formal formation for a long time. From this point until the end of the war, when we formed an Honor Guard for the Russians at Leizen, Austria, we moved in small groups such as squads or patrols and were given only general directions, not specific orders.

As we walked, carrying our eighty pound barracks bag through the streets from the train to the dock, we got our first real taste of destruction. The bomb damage in Southampton was awesome. We gazed in wonder at piles of rubble that had once been beautiful buildings. Suddenly, our faces reddened with fear and our hearts began to beat faster as we walked near holes in the street that displayed prominent signs reading "UXB" in large letters. It was a very sobering experience to pass within two feet of an UneXploded Bomb.

At the assembly area near the dock, American Red Cross ladies—one of whom, Jeanette Lyons Surina, later became the mayor of Greenwood, Indiana (population 30,000)—greeted us with free coffee and donuts. As combat soldiers, we were never asked to pay for anything at these canteens. However, rear echelon troops with barracks nearby were expected to pay a nominal amount.

Our landing at Liverpool, twelve hour train ride through the English countryside and walk through Southampton was, in less than twenty hours, our hello and good-bye to merry old England.

After about a four hour wait, standing in a cold, drizzling rain, we were embarked up a gangplank made of rotten boards onto a British Castle ship for the short, two day trip across the English Channel to France. The Castle fleet was built between 1926 and 1939. These ships were almost as large as the *Pasteur*, but they served an entirely different purpose. The *Pasteur* was a first class luxury liner, whereas the Castle ships were excursion ships for the second and third class tourist trade. At one time, these ships probably were presentable, but now their beauty had faded, and we saw no shiny brass or fine wood craftsmanship on board.

Our Castle ship looked and smelled like an oversized garbage truck. It was old and rusty and appeared to be falling apart. However, we had to agree with the British (who owned it) that, all things considered, it would be a waste of time and money to clean and repair a ship that was likely to be sunk at any minute. In fact, they had even removed all the guns and armament and placed them on newer transports in their fleet.

To the English crew, our crossing was routine. However, for us the rough trip was a once in a lifetime experience. As soon as we boarded, the ship began to roll front to back and pitch side to side at the same time. This movement made it almost impossible to stand up. However, we soon discovered it was even harder to keep anything down. The outside rail was packed with men and every one of them was trying his best to raise the level of the English Channel. The joke of the day was about a concerned sergeant who inquired of a pale faced young man, "Getting kind of weak, son?" to which the soldier replied, "Heck no, sarge, I'm throwing mine as far as everybody else." In our two days on the Castle ship, we had no trouble at all finding an empty hammock and there was never a chow line. In fact, very few of us even tried to eat. The only drinks on board were hot tea and purified water. The English tea was a concoction that tasted like burnt rags that had been soaked in syrup, then wrung out with greasy hands. But at least the tea was easier to drink than the purified water which smelled and tasted like kerosene. Any soldier on board would have gladly given a month's pay for just one twelve ounce bottle of Coca-Cola. However, a couple of weeks later, after drinking out of a few muddy shell holes, we would have welcomed a little English tea and the purified water was far superior to the French cognac.

Many times in training, we heard the expression, "Separate the men from the boys." Suddenly, we realized this had finally come to pass; there were no boys on this ship. Like it or not, we were all men and we were on our own. The English crew members were friendly and efficient and gave us the run of the ship. But, as our orders read, we were "unattached" and "unassigned." There were no rosters, formations, or units. Each man found his own place to sleep, eat, or write letters. The mess hall and sick bay were open twenty-four hours a day and no passes were needed to visit either place. Officers and enlisted men alike took care of their own bags and equipment. Actually, the ship was no different than a large truck. We were loaded at Southampton for transit, and would be unloaded (if we made it) at our destination somewhere on the coast of France.

Our first twenty-four hours on board the Castle ship were spent in port waiting for our escort ships. Naturally, we expected our little men-of-war destroyers. When the Castle ship began to move, we looked down and were surprised to see two very old tubs that appeared to be tugboats. Ugly as they were, we watched with intense interest when we learned that they were, in fact, warships and a vital part of His Majesty's (King George VI) battle fleet and very few ships ventured to cross the English Channel without their assistance.

They were minesweepers. Warships were divided into certain classes, according to their characteristics. For example, the United States Battleship *Missouri* is 887'3" in length, displaces 45,000 tons, and is armed with nine sixteen-inch and twenty five-inch guns. Therefore, it is referred to as an *Iowa* Class ship. While crossing the Channel, we saw boats and ships of all sizes and descriptions from the smallest Infantry Landing Craft (LCI) to the largest, a British battleship called the *Lord Nelson*. The *Nelson*, formerly a King George V Class ship, was now in a class by itself. Earlier in the war, it had suffered heavy damage and as a result was altered in a very odd way. The British, pressed for time to return it to service, had simply cut off the rear third of the ship. This kept all its big sixteen-inch guns intact without impairing the ship's fighting ability. However, now the *Nelson* looked like a heavyweight boxing champion with his big chest, broad shoulders, and mighty arms attached to a small waist and tiny hips.

Chapter IX
"Call Me Knobby"

When we arrived at Le Havre, France, on that cold, brisk January morning in 1945, we were surprised to discover there was no dock or berth for the ship. The Castle ship was just sitting next to an open pier which was forty to fifty feet lower than the deck. From the ship to the shore were a number of gangplanks that were held in place by ropes. Suddenly, before we realized our predicament, we were ordered to debark. After two days on the old "garbage scow," I thought I would be happy to get off. However, I held back as long as possible because it was an unforgettable experience to walk down a weak, swinging gangplank from a swaying ship, carrying approximately eighty pounds of clothing and equipment.

Once on land, we gazed at an awesome sight. On this spot less than six months before had stood the beautiful seacoast city of Le Havre (prewar population 164,083). Now all that remained were enormous heaps of rubble that served as a grave for the former inhabitants. The city was not simply damaged or destroyed, it had, like ancient Carthage and Troy, ceased to exist. On 10 September 1944, the British Army Commander, Field Marshal Bernard L. Montgomery, whose ground troops were advancing toward the city, called for naval and air support. In response, the United States battleships, *Texas* and *Nevada*, positioned off the French coast at the mouth of the Seine River, fired at point-blank range, while the British and American Air Forces pounded Le Havre with more than 5,000 tons of bombs. As we proceeded through the desolation, the only life we saw was a few American soldiers around an army Quonset hut and an engineer unit clearing more roads through the rubble with bulldozers.

Finally, after a ten to twelve mile walk, carrying our eighty pound barracks bag, we arrived at a tent city just outside the rubble of Le Havre. Here we were fed and supplied with rations, weapons, and ammunition. We expected to get food without any hassle, but were really surprised to learn that we were not required to sign for any supplies or equipment. Prior to this, we had always been responsible for a particular weapon; this time rifles were tossed to us from the back of one truck and from another we were given four clips of ammunition. Like well-trained soldiers, we promptly placed our ammunition in the proper pockets of our rifle belts. Not one man loaded his rifle. From boxes near the trucks, a supply sergeant suggested (not ordered) that every man take four grenades. Two of these were fragmentation types that we had trained with but the others were new to us. However, one of the combat veterans informed us that these contained a substance known as *thermit*. These, he said, were very useful when you capture an enemy's heavy gun. Before advancing (or retreating) and leaving the weapon unattended, you were to pull the pin which arms the grenade to explode in five seconds, drop it down the barrel, hit the ground, and listen for the explosion. Then, in less that a minute, you will see the thermit burn through the breech block—disabling the gun. I found thermit grenades more useful than the fragmentation type and they were not nearly as dangerous to the user.

At the tent city, we were not assigned any duties and name, rank, and serial numbers were not even used. In fact, we were only a number of bodies to be unloaded from the ship, fed, equipped, and transported to a replacement depot near the battle front.

About noon, our transportation arrived and we loaded into canvas-covered two and one-half-ton trucks, twelve to fourteen men per truck. There was no separation of officers and enlisted men and we were not loaded by name or serial number. As the old combat sergeant in charge explained, "Just get in, you are all going to the same place." However, shortly before loading, we were given time to neatly stack and tag our barracks bags that we had so carefully preserved over 2,500 miles. With a straight face, a kind, considerate supply sergeant informed us to "be sure that your bags are properly identified, so that the other truck can bring them to you when you reach your assigned unit." That other truck must have been blown to bits somewhere in France, because we never saw those bags or that sergeant again.

People often ask if I saw Paris. The answer is no, but had I been awake as we passed through on our way to the front, I could have gotten a glimpse. Truthfully, after standing in line at the water closet across England, two days at the rail of the Castle ship and a ten mile hike through rubble to the tent city, we were all exhausted. Therefore, uncomfortable as we were riding on rutted roads in the back of trucks with bad springs, we slept from Le Havre to Paris, across France and into Luxembourg.

However, just after dark, we were rudely awakened near the German border. Apparently our driver was unfamiliar with the area and had become separated from the rest of the convoy. Then he compounded his mistake; he stopped his truck, woke us, and asked if we knew where we were. Of course we did not have the slightest idea. However, because he appeared to be a non-commissioned officer, one of the men in the truck did have a question for him. In a meek and small voice, he said, "Sergeant, do you think we should load our rifles?" We all remember distinctly his exact words but they are not printable; in effect, he said, "Here I am all by myself out in the middle of nowhere with a whole truckload of idiots. Load them guns; we are probably surrounded by the whole German Army." Actually we were about ten miles from the German lines. Finally a rear echelon patrol jeep stopped and one of the soldiers in it directed him to the replacement depot where he seemed to be very happy to be rid of his charges.

The depot was located "somewhere in Luxembourg" in what appeared to be the town castle, which also housed nuns from a nearby bombed-out convent. Oddly enough, the slit trench latrine was located in the center of what had been the courtyard and was screened only at the sides. Therefore, the mayor, Catholic nuns, and everyone else above the first floor of the six-story building enjoyed a good view from the top.

In our short, six-hour stay we were sorted out. The combat veterans who were returning to duty with their units after hospital stays for wounds, pneumonia, and frozen feet were taken care of first. Then the balance of us were allotted to various units (armored, engineer, artillery, or infantry), according to our needs. The majority, including me, were assigned to rifle companies, no matter what training they had been given. Before leaving the depot, we were resupplied more rifle ammunition. When I left, I was carrying three bandoleers, a full rifle belt, and a clip in my rifle for a total of 216 rounds. This sounds like a lot of fire power but my thirty-two rounds from tent city lasted less than two minutes in my first fire fight.

Just after dark, our group of about forty riflemen moved out. We hiked, very quietly, for about three hours to a bombed-out building in what had been a small town. During our march there were no rest breaks, like Blanding, nor did anyone even think about falling out. There were no trucks to pick up stragglers and it was essential that we stay in the group for security. For the first time, we realized that our lives depended on each other.

At our destination, we were met by a soldier whom we first took to be a sergeant. However, as he began talking, we noticed a darkened silver eagle on his shirt collar. All of us were amazed that a full bird colonel would meet a group of buck private replacements. However, we soon learned that on the front line, bird colonels and buck sergeants are often interchangeable.

Colonel James H. Hayes was very sincere and honest. His first words were, "Welcome to the First Battalion of the 317th Regiment of the Eightieth Infantry Division." Then he gave us a sobering reminder, "Be alert and you will live longer!" He went on to say, "Take a good look at the man on either side of you, chances are in ten days one of you will not be here and in thirty days neither of you will be left." The colonel was almost 100 percent correct; after ninety-four days in combat, at war's end, 8 May 1945, I was one of three survivors of this group. The rest were casualties who were either killed or wounded in action or were captured while engaging in combat.

The battalion commander counted off so many men for each company in the battalion. No names were taken and no roll call was made. We were all riflemen and the company clerks could keep track of the assignments. My group of about twenty men were escorted by the "runner" from Company B to another bombed-out building that served as our company command post (CP). There, our names and serial numbers were taken by the company clerk and we were given our assignments. I was directed to the outskirts of town where, in a pile of rubble, I met my platoon leader, Second Lieutenant Frederick Knoll. His first (and last) order was, "Call me Knobby, everybody else does."

Knobby posted Freddy Howell and I at the foot of some stone steps at the edge of the town, which we later learned was Diekirch, Luxembourg. The lieutenant advised us to stay very still and stay alert for German patrols. Specifically, he said, "Shoot anything that comes over the top of these steps." Howell and I took turns at naps and everything was quiet until about four o'clock in the morning. Then suddenly I saw a movement about thirty feet away at the top of the steps which appeared to be someone crawling on their hands and knees, so I fired a full clip of eight rounds. After that everything was quiet and still, but neither of us took any more naps. At daybreak, we found a big dead dog on the top step; it had been hit three or four times. It was very sobering to learn that I had actually killed something and I was really amazed at the damage an M-1 Garand rifle did at short range.

After daybreak, we went back in small groups to a bombed-out building near the CP for a hot breakfast of bacon, eggs, and coffee. The food had been prepared in a field kitchen about one-half mile behind the front line and was brought up in insulated containers. With breakfast, we also received a clean pair of socks and extra ammunition. At the ammo pile, Sergeant Rampy held up a small yellow package and asked, "Any of you know what this is?" Naturally, I spoke up and said, "Sure it's a quarter-pound block of TNT." As soon as the words were out of my mouth, I realized I had given the right answer to the wrong question, for Rampy replied, "That's good! Now we have a new company demolition man." Nobody asked what had happened to the last one. Then he handed me four quarter-pound blocks of TNT, a hand full of detonator caps, and an eight-pound satchel charge of plastic explosives. I conveniently lost the satchel charge a few days later and left the use of plastic explosives to the combat engineers. However, these little blocks of TNT were very useful in blowing up pillboxes (concrete gun emplacements) on the German "Siegfried Line." For the record, that was the last time I ever recognized any weapon. In fact, a short time later, when Howell and I were given the rocket launcher, which I had qualified expert on at Blanding, I distinctly remember saying to Rampy, "What's this thing?"

To assist him, Lieutenant Knoll had three platoon sergeants: Rampy, Pilger, and Lund. Sergeant Rampy kept us supplied and made sure that our weapons were in good order. Pilger was usually responsible for directing our mortar and machine gun fire over our heads as we attacked or, as the situation warranted, retreated. Melvin S. Lund was the platoon guide; his job was to see that our platoon was always in the right place at the right time. Before we "jumped off," he would designate the point man (many times himself), who would lead the platoon into combat. All three of these brave men were wounded in action shortly after I joined the platoon, Rampy and Pilger by shrapnel and Lund by rifle and machine gun fire. We had other sergeants come and go as time went on, but I made it a point not to get to know them very well.

My first foxhole buddy was Freddie Howell. We dug in together when we could, then one could nap while the other watched for enemy movements. We became good friends in the short time we served together. He was from the small town of Owenton, Kentucky. Howell was quiet, almost shy, but was brave, even daring, when we engaged in a fire fight with the enemy. On the morning after the dog incident, Sergeant Pilger directed Freddy and me to the top of a nearby hill where we were to dig a hole that was to be used as an observation post. However, when we arrived at the designated spot, about 400 feet in front of our lines, we were elated to find a good hole large enough for two men already there. So we sat down, shared a D-Bar (hard dark chocolate) from our K-ration, and got acquainted. He had trained as a rifleman at Fort McClellan, Alabama, and had arrived on line only the previous morning. Neither of us had yet seen an enemy soldier. After an hour or so, we returned to the platoon and assured the sergeant that we had a good hole in an ideal spot.

Just after dark, Sergeant Pilger came over to our post, at the foot of the steps, and said, "Clark, you and Howell know where the outpost is so you two can go out and man it." This seemed like an intelligent order, but as we soon discovered, nothing on the front line is intelligent. As we proceeded out of Diekirch and up the hill, everything went fine until we got within sixty or seventy yards of "our" hole. Then, suddenly, a shot rang out, we hit the ground, looked at each other, and both of us realized, that was "their" hole. In fact, just before daylight we saw them get up and return to their lines.

Needless to say, after spending a cold night on top of the wet ground, watching for enemy patrols, we were a little smarter than the day before. After daylight, we dug our own hole about seventy-five yards to the right of theirs. Also, that afternoon, well before dark, we got permission from Pilger to man our observation post early.

In our first attack, we jumped off at Diekirch and cleared enemy resistance on the Luxembourg side of the Sauer River for about ten miles downstream. Then we crossed into Nazi Germany near the town of Bollendorf. When we entered the woods, just outside Diekirch, I saw my first of many battlefield casualties. This one was a German soldier and had probably been killed by artillery fire because he appeared to have been dead for at least two weeks. His skin was about as white as porcelain and he was very bloated and stunk. I started to vomit, but was looking ahead trying to keep the point man in sight and stepped right on another dead German body. After that incident, I tried to be more careful where I put my foot down. Suddenly, a fire fight started and all of us green replacements hit the ground. Unfortunately, I landed right between two more stagnant bodies. This fire fight lasted only about five minutes. I never saw anything to shoot at but I did fire eight to ten clips into the deep woods. There were no casualties in our squad and as we continued our advance, I did not see any German casualties other than old bloated corpses.

Colonel Robert S. Allen, in his book, *Lucky Forward: The History of Patton's Third U.S. Army*, gives a glowing account of our river crossing. The Colonel writes:

> *The Sauer is a small stream flowing generally north-south between Luxembourg and the Siegfried Line. Normally, it has a water gap of around 75 feet. At this period it was a flood-swollen torrent with deadly current. In addition, the Germans were powerfully emplaced on the heavily wooded shores in innumerable pillboxes and natural rock formations. Also, the steep banks were extensively barbed wired and mined and all approaches covered with direct artillery and machine gun fire. After furious fighting, the 80th succeeded in gaining a foothold on the east bank. The assaulting doughboys were savagely flayed with*

Nebelwefer fire, but they held their bridge sites. (Allen, Colonel Robert S. Lucky Forward: The History of Patton's Third U.S. Army. (New York: Vanguard Press, Inc., 1947), 290.)

With all due respect to Colonel Allen, he is a very descriptive writer, but he was nowhere near the place when we waded across the river in knee-deep water. The Sauer, at that point, was not much more than a creek. Also, our heavy artillery had silenced everything on the opposite shore. In fact, our big 155 mm "long toms" and 240 mm "railroad guns" had used a tremendous amount of proximity fuses, called time fire, which caused the shells to burst above the ground about treetop level. Consequently, we found many dead German soldiers that had been killed by wounds to the head and upper body.

Late in the afternoon, our platoon encountered resistance in a little farm village about three miles from the river on the German side. Surprisingly, this primitive place could have almost passed for the training village at Camp Blanding, right down to the muddy lane flowing through the center. However, this time the ammunition was live and the enemy was actually trying their best to kill us. Apparently, we had caught up with their rearguard or survivors of the artillery barrage who were retreating. The fire fight lasted about an hour, until it got so dark that we could not see. Finally, Sergeant Lund passed the word to for us dig in and to expect them to counterattack. Luckily, they were not so inclined. By morning, our machine gun and mortar platoon caught up to us so, at daybreak, we jumped off only to discover, to our joy, that the enemy had pulled out during the night.

Chapter X
Foxholes and Firefights

Since leaving Camp Shanks, New York, we had been "somewhere at sea," "somewhere in England," "somewhere in France," or "somewhere in Luxembourg." Now the Germans were aware that we had crossed their border, because Knobby informed us we could start heading our letters, "somewhere in Germany." This was quite a concession for the United States Army, but not a lot of help to our wives. At the very most, all they could glean was that we were inside the German border somewhere between Belgium and Switzerland. Also, in the ten to fifteen days it took for our letters to reach them, we had moved miles from where it was written. In fact, in this campaign our task was to breach the German defenses and to open the way for our tanks. In order to do this, we fought our way through the pillboxes and tank traps of the Siegfried Line three times in my first month of combat. After each seven- to ten-day battle, we would pull back into Luxembourg or France, replace our casualties and lost equipment, then reassemble on the German side of the border and jump off again.

Our outbound mail was always read and censored by an officer. We all, including the officer, thought this was a waste of time. Apparently, the United States Army did not want the Germans to find out where we were, even though we were shooting at them; how scared we were, even though they were shooting at us; or how little we knew about what was taking place. Actually, these things were about all we could write about. Perhaps our commanders had intercepted some letters written by German soldiers on the front line and had discovered some military secrets, like where they were (as if we didn't know), how scared they were because we were shooting at them, or how little they knew about what was taking place.

Very few things were ever cut out of my letters to "My Darling Wife." However, while, on the *Pasteur*, I did make the mistake of writing, "There is only one gun on this big ship." Naturally, an alert censor snipped it out and the Germans were none the wiser.

One man in our platoon could not read or write, so I enjoyed the privilege of carrying on the correspondence with his wife. His usual request was, "Write big so it will be at least three pages; she likes big letters." Like the army censor, I learned George loved and missed Loraine, and Loraine loved and missed George. In combat, George was all business, mean and gruff. His favorite weapon was the fragmentation hand grenade which made him dangerous to friend and enemy alike. However, when we sat down to write, he became kind and gentle.

Our mail was delivered with our rations, ammunition, and socks. Often we were not available for mail call. Occasionally we were behind the enemy's front line or lying on the cold ground fifty to seventy-five feet in front of him. Therefore, we usually received a handful of letters at a time about every two weeks. Packages from home were always shared, because we did not wear packs in combat and out pockets were full of necessities like TNT, ammunition grenades, and rations. All packages were welcome, but not everything was appropriate. Some men received the *Saturday Evening Post*, while others were shocked to find a can of Spam, which was always in abundant supply. Spam, a pressed ham packed in juice, did not have a bad taste. In fact, it really did not have any taste at all, except the slimy taste it left in your mouth for a couple of days. The Frenchmen we gave it to seemed to enjoy it but they washed it down with cognac that would have burned our tonsils out.

The best packages, by far, were filled with cookies, candies, and cakes. However, some cakes did not survive the long journey and others arrived slightly altered. The cakes from Audrey were always packed perfectly and, with the exception of one, arrived in the same condition that they left Pekin, Indiana. This particular cake was a beautiful pink angel food cake with green icing. On the way over, the icing had become moldy so, as with many things on the front line, we improvised. During the afternoon, we ate around the mold then after dark, we finished it off and nobody complained. Actually, we did not notice any difference in the taste.

The weather in early February 1945 was damp and cold. The ground was above freezing most of the time. Our clothing was designed to fight in, therefore, it was not well suited for winter comfort. We wore long cotton underwear, cotton pants and shirts, wool sleeveless pullover sweaters, light cotton jackets, wool knit caps, a plastic helmet liner, and a heavy steel helmet. Our shoes, called combat boots, were leather high tops with a four-inch hard leather band for ankle support, that replaced the old wraparound legging of the First World War. Cushioned with two pairs of cotton socks, the combat boots were not uncomfortable. Actually, only our hands, feet, and faces got cold enough to really notice.

In rear areas, the army issued wool knit gloves with leather palms to the troops. However, on the front line, they were useless to us. We could not fire a rifle while wearing them and you do not have time to take your gloves off when someone shoots at you. Except in rare cases we slept on (or in) the ground. I soon discovered that the best way to keep warm in a foxhole was to cup my hands on each side of my face and breath down my shirt front onto my chest. However, once I woke up in this position and found I had been lying face down in a puddle that had frozen and both hands were solidly encased in ice. The ice was not very thick so no real damage was done. The only after effect is that when my hands get very warm a pain reminds me they were once frozen.

One of our platoon sergeants had a very good sense of humor. Occasionally he would seriously inquire, "Would you men like to sleep in town tonight?" Naturally, one of the green replacements, which we always had, would respond, "I sure would." Then the sergeant would reply, "O.K., Captain Bettlinski says we can go take one" and off we would go. However, there was a catch; every time we routed the Germans from a little town, we would have to go beyond it and dig foxholes. If we remained in the town, we became sitting ducks for their artillery and mortars.

In the Eifel Hills near the little town of Nussbaum, Germany, Sergeant Lund put me on the point, about ten to fifteen yards in front of the platoon, as we advanced through dense woods. Suddenly we came to a clearing, called a fire break, which was about 200 feet wide. My task was to cross the open ground first and draw enemy fire. If I made it across, the rest of the platoon would follow. However, if I didn't, Lund would radio for machine gun and mortar support to move up so they could provide protective cover fire. Lucky for me, the Germans had chosen not to defend this particular fire break as they had others because we crossed without a fight. One thing is for sure: I left a raincoat, some excess ammunition, and my loot bag on our side of the clearing. I made that 200 feet in nothing flat. Later that day, we took Nussbaum and two or three other little villages, then dug in for the night.

During the night, shelling was intermittent. For the most part it was heavy artillery fire and counterfire; that is, one side fires, then the other side observes the muzzle blast and returns the fire. We soon learned how to determine which way an artillery shell was going and approximately where it would land. However, mortar shells are the exception because they make practically no noise at all until they explode, then it's too late to worry about them. As an old army saying goes, "You never have to worry about the bullet with your name on it, but you had better watch out for shrapnel addressed "To Whom It May Concern!"

Just after daybreak the following morning, we jumped off toward the Rhine River. Our objective was a hill (army map number 403) about one mile in front of us, but first we had to advance across open ground until we reached a sparsely wooded area at its base. As soon as we left our foxholes, we came under mortar and artillery fire. Of course, our cannon and heavy weapons answered with counterfire. In fact, we could see our shells and theirs bursting a short distance from us. Upon entering the woods, we encountered heavy machine gun and rifle fire. This was the most formidable defense fortification that we had made contact with since we crossed the German border. Our heavy artillery and P-47 fighter bombers had been blasting the Siegfried Line for days and had destroyed many of the pillboxes, dugouts, and machine gun nests. However, there were plenty of battle-hardened German troops between us and the Rhine and they had to be dealt with one at a time.

Many of the men in the first battalion were green replacements who had never been under fire. In fact, Company A had only fourteen men who had survived their last campaign. Therefore, we were repeatedly stopped, pinned down, and could not advance. After a number of attempts with heavy casualties, we got about half way up the hill. Finally, around two in the afternoon, we were ordered to hold in place. A while later, General McBride became impatient and ordered in the division reserves, a battle-hardened combat command from the Fifth ("bloody diamond") Infantry Division. Supported by tanks, they moved through our lines and fought their way to the top of the hill. In doing so, they lost a lot of men, but were never pinned down. Many times afterwards we were called on to move through green troops, but at hill 403, we were the novices.

Our commanding general, "Hairless" Horace McBride, firmly believed in the old adage, "If you fall off a horse, you have to get right back on." So about midnight, he ordered us to move through the troops of the Fifth Division who were dug in just over the crest of the hill. What a nasty night for an attack! It was very dark and a cold rain was pouring down as we waded through soft mud that was above the top of our combat boots. Green troops make far too much noise, so we advanced only a few yards before the Germans detected our movement. First came mortar and machine gun fire, then their artillery (88s) opened up on us. Suddenly, I heard what I thought was a German shell coming down right at me, although it was probably one of our 105s falling short, as they often did. I followed my instinct and training and dived right behind and into what appeared to be a pile of dirt. When I landed, the dirt went squash! I had actually made a running leap into a pile of manure covering some old German farmer's sugar beets so they wouldn't freeze. The shell landed about twenty feet away; luckily it was a dud and did not explode. I was covered with manure, but happy to still be in one piece. We advanced about 600 yards, then dug in for the rest of the night. Our artillery and theirs exchanged fire until dawn, almost shell for shell, with some falling among our foxholes. It was a very nasty night!

Apparently we lost our rocket launcher (bazooka) team on hill 403, because early the next morning, Sergeant Rampy gave Howell and me the honor of replacing them. One of us now carried the sixteen pound weapon and the other carried three five pound rounds of ammunition. The bazooka was a very effective weapon against small tanks at close (less than fifty feet) range. However, our shells would bounce or explode harmlessly when they struck a "Tiger" or "Royal Tiger" tank.

In addition to the bazooka, we each carried an M-1 rifle, eighteen to twenty-four clips (150 to 200 rounds) of rifle ammunition, two to four fragmentation grenades, two thermit grenades, a shovel, canteen, and a medical pouch. I also still carried the TNT and percussion caps. One jacket pocket was usually full of personal items: letters from Audrey, a candy bar, some writing paper, and a few German arm bands, medals, or other loot. We were not in combat very long before everyone had acquired a small pouch about the size of a ladies purse filled with souvenirs. This additional piece of equipment was referred to as a "loot bag."

We jumped off before noon and proceeded into the Eifel Hills. Sergeant Little was on the point, with Howell and me following him closely. Knobby and the rest of the platoon (thirty to thirty-five men) were spread thinly on a 200 foot semicircular front. Captain Bettlinski and Lieutenant Jones had moved up with their radiomen. Clyde A. Waldrip was carrying the SCR 300 and Stricker had the SCR 536 walkie-talkie. Neither of the radios were working, probably because of the iron in the hills. For the first two hours, we did not encounter any enemy resistance. However, we all knew the calm could not last very long, because we had heard firing on both sides of us since we started out. Then suddenly Little began firing at fifteen or twenty Germans who were in the process of placing a field gun in a clearing, about 100 feet away, at the top of the hill. Instantly, we joined in the firing and the enemy gun crew ran into a nearby woods.

We moved quickly up to the gun and discovered it was a multi-barrel mortar that the Germans called a Nebelwefer. However, it was better known to us as a "screaming meemie" because in flight the shells sounded like bombs from a dive-bomber. Lieutenant Jones told Stricker to destroy it immediately with a thermit grenade, but Bettlinski stopped him. The Captain said it would be better to have the platoon dig in right around the gun and leave it in perfect working order until he could personally turn it over to battalion headquarters. Then it would be on record that his company had captured this unusual prize. However, we soon found out that the Germans had no intention of allowing that to happen.

While Jones and Bettlinski were discussing the relative merits of the destruction or preservation of the captured Nebelwefer, the Germans apparently realized that there were not very many of us on their hill with their gun. Consequently, they decided to recover their property. So back they came, in force, with at least four Mark IV medium tanks and a company (about 150 men) of supporting infantry.

At the sight of the tanks, we left the clearing and tried to take cover. Bettlinski, Jones, and many of the platoon made it back into the deeper woods. Knobby, Little, and Lund kept two squads up near the gun, firing at the tanks in an effort to keep them "buttoned up." If we were successful, we could make them keep their turrets closed, giving them only a limited view. Freddie Howell and I went after the lead tank with the bazooka, but it was firing wildly with both machine gun and cannon. About fifty feet from our target, Howell was hit by cannon fire and killed instantly. I hit the ground and played dead as the tank passed within thirty feet of me. Then as their supporting infantry arrived, right behind the tank, seven of our men jumped up and yelled "kamerad," the German word for surrender. Corporal Birdwhistle, Sergeant Little, and I stayed flat on the ground and tried to look as dead as possible, which took very little effort considering how scared we were. Apparently Little and I appeared deader than Birdwhistle because one of the Germans gave the corporal a good swift kick, then picked up his rifle, and broke the stock against a tree. I could hear the Germans and our men who were now prisoners, but I could not see them because I was face down in the mud. My greatest fear was that I would be run over by one of their forty ton tanks.

After the Germans passed us, they went about 150 yards before they stopped at the deeper woods. Then they returned, right by us, to the top of the hill where they hooked the Nebelwefer on to a tank and hauled it off with them. When we could no longer hear their voices or tanks, Knobby, Birdwhistle, Little, and I went down the hill, the other direction from the Germans, and found what was left of the platoon. Lieutenant Jones had established a defense line and Captain Bettlinski had finally made radio contact with the rest of the battalion which was about a mile behind us. Jones easily convinced Bettlinski that it would be appropriate and show good judgment if we dug in right where we were and waited for reserves before we tried to go any further toward Bitburg. Knobby, Little, and I were in pretty good shape, but Birdwhistle was as white as a sheet for hours and could not speak a word for more than a week. This incident taught all of us a very important lesson. From that day forward, when we captured any piece of enemy artillery or equipment, we destroyed it immediately with a thermit grenade.

At our next engagement, we were a little more successful. After two days of pounding the German line with heavy artillery, we received replacements for our casualties and replenished our ammunition supply. Then about three in the afternoon, we again moved into the Eifel Hills. Around half past four, our platoon of thirty men was advancing in a skirmish line formation, with about thirty feet between each man. Little, the point man, had advanced forty feet in front of me. Suddenly, as we were nearing the foot of a good-sized hill, approaching a small stream at the bottom that ran between the hills, Little began firing. He had spotted eighty to one hundred Germans at the stream bathing and filling water containers. When the firing started, they dropped everything and started up the other hill toward their dugouts and machine gun emplacements. However, we were above them in the woods and they were below us in a clearing, therefore the advantage went to us. Also, they had no way of knowing how many of us there were on the wooded hill. We had only hit three or four, before all of them threw up their hands and yelled, "Kamerad." Knobby took eight of us down the hill, and Apmann ordered them to lie in the clearing face down with their hands clasped behind their necks. Gaddie and the German medics tended their wounded as though they were in the same army. Lund kept the rest of the platoon in the woods, covering the prisoners from there. If they ever found out how few of us there were, no doubt they would have made a run for their machine gun emplacements.

It was late afternoon and we did not have any idea how many more Germans were in the vicinity or how close our support troops were. One thing was for sure: we could not keep these prisoners fooled very long, even though Knobby told us to move around and make a lot of noise. Our walkie-talkie radios had quit working because of the iron in the hills, so Knobby sent two runners back in an attempt to locate the rest of the company. We were really in a bind; we could not move that many prisoners through the heavy woods and we knew we could not guard them after dark. Fortunately, at dusk the runners came back with a platoon from another company that they had found about a mile behind us. With their help, we were able to keep the prisoners guarded through the night. Early the following morning, with the assistance of the other platoon, we escorted our prisoners back to our lines and turned them over to Battalion Headquarters.

Later in the war, after we crossed the Rhine, it was not unusual to capture a large number of defeated German soldiers who were ready to give up. However, this was not the case in the hills. These

Germans were hard, surly, and mean with a lot of fight left in them. They had just made the mistake of all going to the creek at the same time, leaving all their defenses unmanned.

For the next two days, we were in battalion reserve, which meant Company A and Company C jumped off in the lead and we, Company B, would follow closely behind them. When either of the lead companies hit heavy resistance, we would move up in support. This turned out great because both companies took their objectives without our assistance. The first night, our squad was lucky enough to sleep in a barn and, the next night, in a half-destroyed house with an undamaged piano in one room. One of our men played for about an hour while we sang "You Are My Sunshine" and other army favorites. The most popular song at the time was "Don't Fence Me In" and I still live that night over every time I hear it played. There we were, only a few hundred yards from the enemy lines and could very well be blown to bits any minute. Yet we were, in our own minds, back in a day room at Blanding, singing off-key to an out-of-tune piano. Also, we were all aware that, by the law of averages, of the ten men in the room, only half or fewer would come through the war without becoming casualties. Actually, only two of us did.

On the third day, we moved back into the lead by taking over a position on the forward slope of a hill where C Company had been dug in. In front of us was the beautiful flat open country of the Rhine River valley. After we secured the area by occupying some of their foxholes, digging some new ones, and setting up light machine guns and mortars, we began to improve our home away from home. One man stayed on guard in the foxhole, while the other scoured the immediate area for small limbs and twigs to make the hole drier and more comfortable. On my turn to forage, I walked within ten feet of General McBride, who was talking with two other officers. I paid no attention to them because it was not unusual to see the general on the front line. When I returned to our foxhole, Apmann identified the other officers and asked, "What do you think of Patton." I was surprised and we both wondered why General Patton, the Third Army commander, and General Walton H. Walker, the XX Corps commander, were at our B Company position with our division commander. Beyond a doubt, something was going to happen close to this spot very soon and we would be involved in it.

A few minutes later, I was about forty feet from our foxhole looking for more sticks, when suddenly and without warning I thought the world had come to an end. It began with a loud "swish," then almost immediately a series of enormous explosions occurred a short distance away. This was repeated ten times before it ended. I could not tell whether the shells were going out or coming in, so

I started digging another hole right there. As soon as the noise stopped, I ventured a look around and was shocked to discover, right behind me less than fifty feet away, was the most unusual weapon I had ever seen. It was a medium tank, but instead of a cannon it had sixty tubes mounted on top of the turret. Later I learned to appreciate the rocket launching tank, but this first one scared the living daylights out of me.

Apparently General Patton and General Walker were there to observe the effect of the new weapon on the Germans, who were in the town about a half mile away. They should have been satisfied because when I returned to my position and looked down in the valley, the town was no longer there.

That afternoon, the generals wanted to get a closer look at the damage. So, we left our dry, warm foxholes by request, and began our advance across the valley. By dark, we had moved about five miles beyond the ruins of the town and were dug in on the west side of the Pruem River.

According to Third Army Headquarters, our next attack was routine. As we crossed the Pruem River and turned south toward Bitburg, Germany, the public relations officer (PRO) informed reporters, "Enemy opposition is at first light but becomes heavy later in the day . . . " Actually, Colonel J. T. Quirk had no idea how much resistance we were meeting, for in his very next message to the press, he admitted we were out of contact with the rest of the division. But to be honest, light or heavy opposition really makes no difference at all. It only takes one enemy bullet or a small piece of shrapnel to cause the secretary of war to send an "I regret to inform you" letter to your next of kin.

After a lively fire fight, we captured Niederweiler about noon, then around four in the afternoon, we evicted some stubborn Nazi SS troops from Liessem. To complete our day, we moved out just before dark and cut the main road from the north, leading into Bitburg, Germany. This blocked enemy units which were attempting to reinforce the city and bottled up German troops in Bitburg, who were under attack from the south and west. But due to the fact we were separated from the rest of the division by the Pruem River, we were under attack from all four sides.

Our roadblocks held and the following day Bitburg fell to the Fifth Infantry Division. We then turned east and, for the next six days, with the Fifth Infantry on our right and the Fourth Armored in support, we advanced toward the Rhine River. When we reached Kyllburg, Germany, on the Kyll River, the Siegfried Line was broken. So the Fourth Armored and the Fifth Infantry made a flying attack toward the Rhine, and we were pulled back into Thionville, France, for replacements.

As tough and realistic as the training at Camp Blanding had been, it was no substitute for the real thing. The more experience we had in combat, the less mistakes we made, and in turn, the fewer casualties we suffered. At hill 403, we learned when a fire fight starts, the best thing to do is stay up and keep firing. When you cease firing, you are a stationary target and the enemy can and will zero in on your position and you are a dead duck. At the Nebelwefer, we discovered how stupid it was not to destroy the enemy's field gun immediately and to fail to dig in the minute we stopped. For in the short ten minutes between the time they ran and their return, we could have established a defense line and prepared to give them a good fight with fewer casualties. However, at the creek we saw that even experienced enemy soldiers could make serious mistakes, such as leaving their fortified positions unattended and, in doing so, losing their entire unit.

Chapter XI
Tigers and Dragon's Teeth

During our first month of combat, we were not aware of the physical and mental changes that were taking place in our mind and bodies. However, when we arrived at the replacement depot and saw the green troops that had just arrived from the United States, we were shocked at their appearance. They were neat, well fed, and trim, with new clothing, equipment, and weapons. Their mood was very upbeat and some were actually excited at the thought of going into combat. In contrast, our clothes and our bodies were well worn. We were not gaunt, but in four short weeks of field rations and forced marches, we had lost all of our "baby fat." Our expressions were serious and we did not make any new friends. We now understood why Rampy, Pilger, Gaddie, and others were distant to us when we joined the company in Luxembourg. It just stands to reason, if you do not know the name of a fellow soldier's wife when he is killed in action, you won't feel as bad as you would if you were on a first name basis with his family. Therefore, the more personal distance you can keep from others in combat, the less pain you will feel when they are gone.

For the replacements' good, as well as our own, we helped them prepare for combat. First, we taped everything that made a noise, then, by using boot dubbing, we made every shiny piece of equipment very dull. Next, we advised them on what equipment they would not have any use for on the front line. Most would take one look at us to see what we were not burdened with and would lighten their load without question. However, a few were not convinced, some even carried their five-pound gas mask, a four-pound raincoat, and other useless junk for a week or two before tossing all of it into a convenient ditch.

On 13 March 1945, we left Thionville, France and moved back up into the front line near Saarburg, Germany. According to the *Official United States Army History*, on that date, "The 80th Infantry Division drives through the 94th and 26th Divisions and breaks through the enemy lines to block the one good road through the Wadern Forest at a point near the center of the forest; 317th (Regiment) captures Greimerath." (Greenfield, Kent Roberts. General Editor. *The United States Army in World War II, The Last*

Offensive. (Washington, D.C.: Department of the Army, ca. 1960)). If anyone was driving, I did not get to ride. Actually, we jumped off on our stomachs and, for most of the next three weeks, we crawled through a fortified line of trenches, pillboxes, tank traps (called "dragon's teeth"), and machine gun emplacements. This section of the Siegfried Line was nearly thirty miles across and the German Army fought hard to keep us from breaking it. They knew once their "West Wall" was breached, they could not keep us from reaching the Rhine River and, when we crossed the Rhine, there was no natural barrier between the Allied Forces and the Russian Army. Fortunately, the enemy could not man all of the pillboxes and field gun emplacements because of previous losses. However, in our section it seemed like they had plenty of men and ammunition, with some to spare.

On the first night, we crawled through their lines in small groups. In fact, we were so close to their foxholes we could hear them talking quietly. As soon as we got 200 to 300 feet behind their lines, we would begin firing and while they were busy with us, our combat engineers would move forward and clear a path for our tanks with high explosives. The tanks would then come charging through with the rest of our rifle company in support. In a short time, we would mop up the resistance, then move to the next line of obstacles, which were less than one-half mile away. The Germans we captured told us they were caught off guard because they never thought anyone would be foolish enough to attempt to advance through the dragon's teeth at night.

The second night we tried the same tactics, but this time they were wise to us and fired at everything that moved. As a result, my squad of eight men was cut off from the rest of the company. By two o'clock in the morning, we could hear orders being given in German on all sides of our little patch of ground, which was apparently a farmer's hog lot. It was impossible to dig in because the enemy would have fired at the noise, so we laid real still (well not real still, we were shaking a lot) in about six inches of smelly mud.

For most of the night we could see the outline of their tanks moving back and forth. In one sweep, a Tiger tank came within fifty feet of me, so close I could even smell it. A little before dawn they gave up the search and moved back behind their next line of pillboxes. Just after daybreak, P-47 fighter bombers from our XIX Tactical Air Force bombed and strafed their line between us and our army. Then the division artillery Piper Cub came over and spotted us and some other trapped troops. The forward observer (FO) in the cub immediately ordered our big guns to shell over our heads into their next line of fortifications. Some of our artillery used proximity fuses, which caused the shells to burst in the air as they had at Diekirch. Consequently, when we advanced we found many enemy soldiers killed from shrapnel that had fallen like rain. Some of the shells contained white phosphorous which burned right through their helmets and back packs. This was the most sickening sight we ever encountered on the battlefield.

The P-47s of General O. P. Weyland's XIX Tactical Air Force attacked the Germans from daylight to dark during the Saar Campaign. Every day, we found the road in front of us littered with destroyed equipment, dead enemy soldiers, and dead horses. This gave us an incentive to attack in order to get further away from the smell. But usually, just a short distance down the road we would find another German horse-drawn supply train splattered by bombs from our P-47s.

In our next engagement, as usual, we were a very small, but important part of a large battle plan against a stubborn section of the Siegfried Line. This "order of battle" is described by the United States Army's chief historian in these words:

> In (Lieutenant) General Walker's XX Corps, combat commands of the 10th Armored (Major General William H. H. Morris, Jr.) began passing through infantry of the 80th (Major General Horace L. McBride) and the 94th (Major General Harry J. Malony) Divisions before daylight on March 16, (1945). Although the Germans of General Hahm's LXXXII (82nd) Corps during the night had formed a new crust of resistance sufficient to deny genuine armored exploitation for another 24 hours, no doubt remained among either American or German commanders as the day ended that a deep armored thrust was in the offing. (Greenfield, Kent Roberts. General Editor. *The United States Army in World War II, The Last Offensive.* (Washington, D.C.: Department of the Army, ca. 1960), 68)

However, a short paragraph in an army history book cannot do justice to the brave men who were given the task of "breaking the crust" of the German Siegfried Line about thirty miles southeast of Saarburg, Germany. This is one of the few engagements where all of the details are still vivid in my memory.

After an all-day push, with sporadic fire fights, we—First Platoon of B Company—advanced about twelve miles into the Saar Region. Then just before dark, on 15 March, we captured the little village of Waldholzbach, Germany. Exhausted, we secured the village and posted guards in all directions, because we were well out in front of our supporting troops. About midnight, a German supply train, using horses and wagons, came into the village from the same direction we had entered; apparently our guard at that post was not alert. However, as the Germans tried to exit at the other end of the village, he saw horses, recognized the enemy troops, and began firing. Almost at once, everyone, both German and American, became aware of what had happened. In fifteen to twenty minutes, the fire fight was over and dead horses and soldiers were lying in the street from one end of the village to the other. The Germans who were not killed or seriously wounded escaped into the woods just outside the village in the darkness.

Shortly after daybreak, on 16 March, we were startled to see two large, Mark IV tanks about a half mile away. They were moving slowly forward, toward Waldholzbach without infantry support. When they were within about 1500 feet of our foxholes, two tank destroyers that had joined our unit before dawn went out to engage them. This gave us a ringside seat at the battle. First, both tank destroyers attacked the lead tank and, although their 76 mm shells could not penetrate its armor, they did succeed in setting it afire. Suddenly, the second enemy tank scored a direct hit on one of our destroyers, killing the entire crew. The commander of our other destroyer realized that alone he was no match for a Tiger tank. So he quickly returned to the village and took cover among the buildings. Wisely, the German commander would not risk advancing, unprotected by infantry. He stopped about 700 feet in front of our foxholes, fired ten rounds into Waldholzbach, then went into the woods where the Germans from the supply train were hiding.

A very short time later, we were ordered to jump off first squad of the first platoon in the lead, with Sergeant Melvin S. Lund on the point. We proceeded past a pile of twisted metal that had been our tank destroyer and their burning tank, into the woods where the second tank had entered about an hour earlier.

We moved slowly up the wooded hill; Balmer with a Browning Automatic Rifle (BAR) was on the far left of our line; Lund, the platoon sergeant, was about twenty-five to thirty feet to his right and slightly in front of the rest of us. I was twenty-five to thirty feet to the right of Lund, and Sergeant Little was about the same distance from me. The remainder of the squad, five or six men, were in a skirmish line formation to the right of Little. With the exception of Balmer, we were all armed with .30 caliber M-1 Garand rifles.

The Germans saw us first. They were dug in and began firing when we got within 100 feet of their line. Sergeant Lund was hit with one of their first shots. The bullet went clear through his right shoulder but he did not stop; I really believe he did not realize he was wounded. Then Little's helmet was hit; we later learned that the bullet went through his helmet, liner, and wool knit cap, without touching his head. Suddenly, two Germans came out of a dugout and started for an unmanned machine gun on our left front.

Luckily, Balmer, who was closer, killed both of them with a burst of fire from his BAR. Lund was hit again, this time across the upper back; he went down on impact but got to his feet and started up the hill again. We followed. Two more Germans attempted to man their machine gun. Again Balmer killed both of them with his BAR. However, at least two of their other machine guns now had us pinned down.

Our medic, Gaddie, tried to get up the hill to Lund, but enemy machine gunners and riflemen would not let him get within 100 feet. At this point, I was lying at the base of a small tree firing at five or six (or more) of the enemy directly in front of me. One, in particular, would shoot at me and, as I ducked, Little would shoot at him, then he would shoot at Little, giving me the opportunity to take a shot at him. However, this kind of games never lasts long. About fifty feet in front of me, there was a hole which appeared to be the entrance to a dugout. I really wanted to toss a grenade into it. But I realized I could not raise my head or shoulders because one of the German machine guns was cutting the bark off my tree just six to ten inches above my head. I have no idea how many of the enemy were in this dugout, but my guess is that a few of them are still there because I fired about every third clip, containing eight rounds, into the entrance.

By this time, we were all firing from the ground except Balmer, who was kneeling on one knee, and firing from the hip. His BAR magazine held only twenty rounds, but he was replacing clips so fast it sounded like a machine gun. The fact that they were higher up the hill made them a little more exposed than us. However, they were dug in and we were not, so they definitely had the advantage and if they could have manned the machine gun, which was only fifty feet in front of Balmer, they would have no doubt killed our entire squad.

Suddenly, Sergeant Lund decided to again try to lead us up the hill. He stood up and was immediately hit again; this time, across the bridge of the nose, blinding both eyes. Little called over to me and said he was hit. Then he crawled back to the medic. Gaddie checked and found that a bullet had gone through Little's jacket and shirt and had burned a blister on his shoulder, but did not break the skin.

Balmer killed two more who almost made it to their machine gun, and our line started to pull back. Little and Gaddie were attempting to make it back up to Lund, but were pinned down by machine gun fire. Only Lund and I were still on the point about 150 feet above Little and Gaddie. I left my rifle and crawled over to Lund, put a compress bandage (first aid pack) on his face, then pulled him by the feet down the hill to Gaddie. As I went up after

Lund, I saw two German machine gunners get up from their gun, about 200 feet to my right, and move toward the top of the hill. They were moving away from me and, even though they looked straight at me, they chose to ignore me, so I returned the favor and ignored them. Actually, I had no choice, since my rifle was at least fifty feet away. Apparently, they got the word to disengage about the same time we did. This fire fight had lasted less than one hour.

Sergeant Melvin S. Lund was awarded the Distinguished Service Cross, the second highest decoration, for his bravery and valor in leading us up the hill. He justly deserved the Medal of Honor, but there was no officer on the hill to attest to his actions. I received a General Commendation (Certificate of Merit) and a Bronze Star Medal for bringing him down the hill. My actions were not great; I was the nearest one to him and I am certain he would have done the same for me.

Back in the village of Waldholzbach, we were pleasantly surprised to see that our tanks had caught up with us. As soon as we replenished our ammunition supply (I had fired over 200 rounds), we piled up on the tanks and moved out. Our next fire fight occurred six hours later near Noswendel, Germany.

Chapter XII
Sights, Sounds
and Tastes of War

As we advanced into Germany, we liberated various types of Nazi prison camps (See Appendix A). The first of these was a slave labor camp near the city of Tholey, Germany, in the Saar Basin. The prisoners here, male and female, had been seized by the Nazis in captured countries and shipped to this, and other, industrial centers where they were forced to work long hours for no compensation. Most of the inmates in these camps appeared to have been fed sufficiently to keep them in reasonable health for hard labor. Their clothing was old and tattered. In fact, it was the clothing they had worn for two to five years, since their forced relocation. Living quarters in the camp were cramped and sparsely furnished and there were no medical facilities available to the prisoners. They were elated at being liberated and, although many showed signs of old injuries, they did not complain of physical mistreatment by their captors.

Luckily, near Tholey we captured a German supply warehouse full of civilian clothing, which had been looted from France for distribution inside Germany. However, when we opened it up to the inmates of the slave labor camp, they would not take anything until they were ordered to do so. Also, when we gave them the rations we were carrying, they were amazed at both the amount of food we had and the variety. It had been twelve years since they had seen chocolate candy, chewing gum, cheese, or American cigarettes. We were very impressed with these, and other prisoners, because they did not beg and were not greedy. When we gave them anything, they freely shared with others. In fact, they were so grateful that they even offered to go with us, to carry our ammunition and equipment. (Too bad we had to leave them there, I could have used at least three of them when the sergeant loaded me down for the Rhine River crossing about two weeks later.) As we progressed across Germany, we liberated other large slave labor camps near Kassel, Erfurt, Bamberg, and Regensburg.

East of Tholey, Apmann and I were on the point as we were clearing a woods. Suddenly, we both saw a German soldier crawl into a hole about forty feet in front of us. Neither of us fired, even though the target was broad and tempting. We approached very cautiously and saw that it was an elaborate dugout. Apparently, it was some kind of a command post but for some reason "our" German could not get very far in; he was still visible and was attempting to get turned around. Apmann, who spoke perfect German, commanded, "Comm uns see rous mitt de han de ho." Which, roughly translated, means "Come out with your hands up." The German, still trying to get into a position to shoot at us, replied, "Nien, nien." At this rude refusal, Apmann took two fragmentation grenades off his lapels, pulled the pins, and tossed them into the hole. We both hit the ground to avoid being wounded with our own shrapnel. After the explosion, we discovered why our "Kraut" was not able to get all the way in the hole. At least fifteen German soldiers came crawling out and a few dead and some seriously wounded were still in the hole when Gaddie and a couple of medics arrived to tend their wounds a short time later. It was our good fortune that we saw him when we did. If we had passed them up, as they intended, they would have come out after we passed and attacked us from the rear. In all probability, a unit that size, with the element of surprise on their side, would have wiped out our whole platoon.

Eric Apmann was a good soldier and a good man to be close to in combat. He was a full-blooded German who emigrated to the United States with his family in 1936. He never said why they left their homeland. However, he had great contempt for Hitler and the Nazis. Apmann was calm under fire and at night would crawl right up to an enemy foxhole, speaking calmly in German, until we got close enough to capture the enemy. Most of the time this ruse worked, but on one occasion, a German sentry handed him a live concussion grenade. Apmann gave it a good throw and as luck would have it, the grenade, like many of their "potato mashers," was a dud and did not explode. We took the prisoner back to our line, and turned him over to the battalion intelligence officer. I didn't think much more about the incident, but Apmann never did forgive him for the scare.

After we got through the "dragon's teeth" (concrete tank traps) we were usually supported by one or two tanks or tank destroyers. However, when armor moves through a wooded area, it must have infantry on both sides to protect it from enemy troops with rocket launchers. Therefore, when we were clearing (running the Germans out) a wooded hill near St. Wendel, I was right alongside one of our tank destroyers which was moving slowly down an old lane. The TD gunner was standing up in his turret firing the .50 caliber machine gun that is mounted on a ring above the turret. He would swing the gun first to one side of the woods, then to the other. Suddenly, two enemy riflemen came out of the woods on my side and started running down the lane right in front of the tank destroyer. The gunner in the turret and I saw them at the same time, but I was busy firing at two or three who were up in the woods to my left so I let him have them. However, instead of using his .50 caliber, he kicked his driver on the shoulder as a signal to fire the smaller .30 caliber machine gun that is mounted alongside the 76 mm cannon in the turret. The driver apparently got the wrong message and fired the cannon! What a noise and what a mess, because the Germans were not more than fifty feet in front of the cannon muzzle. Later that morning, after the woods were cleared, we stopped for a few minutes. I took out a can of C-rations and just as I started to sit down, two enemy soldiers jumped up and took off. I can only guess they thought my ration can was a hand grenade and I was getting ready to throw it. Also, they assumed I saw them first; not so, you can't shoot and eat at the same time. We were more careful the rest of the day. As the old saying goes, "The woods were full of them."

We engaged in a few more fire fights between St. Wendel and Kaiserslautern. Then, as our regiment approached the city of Kaiserslauten (population, 65,000) our battalion swung north to cut the main highway. However, while the rest of the division, supported by the Tenth Armored Division, was assembling to assault this "fortress," Sergeant Byron Hoover, a Hoosier, effected its surrender. Sergeant Hoover, with twelve to sixteen men of the Regimental Intelligence and Reconnaissance (I&R) Platoon, were on patrol with .50 caliber machine guns mounted on jeeps. At the edge of the city, they broke through an enemy roadblock and did not encounter any more resistance until they reached the center. In the main square, they met sniper fire. So, Hoover and his men began tossing grenades and firing right into city hall. The burgomaster, thinking that Hoover was leading a major attack and not wanting his city destroyed, convinced the German SS commander to surrender. When the First Battalion arrived in the town square six hours later, we found Sergeant Hoover and his little army guarding the burgomaster, one Nazi colonel, four majors, five captains, ten lieutenants, and over 100 non-commissioned officers and privates of the German Army. Turning his prisoners over to Colonel Hayes, Hoover said, "Here are the keys to this joint, who wants to be Mayor of Kaiserslautern? We've got places to go." Apparently, one of the Germans must have given him a clue as to what he would find in the next town.

We dug in, just east of Kaiserslautern, that afternoon and jumped off early the next morning. The Tenth Armored Division had joined us so most of us were riding on top of their tanks. We only engaged in an occasional fire fight with the enemy rear guard as General Hahm's defeated army withdrew toward the Rhine River, which was thirty miles to the east.

Historians have chosen to ignore the Eightieth Infantry Division's largest and most successful battle of World War II. This particular engagement, however, did not involve enemy troops. We rolled into Bad Durkheim, twenty miles east of Kaiserslautern, wet to the skin and chilled to the bone. But instead of the German Army, we found warehouses full of expensive Rhineland Champagne. After riding on top of tanks and sleeping in the mud for over a month, we combat men attacked immediately and tried to drink it all so none would be left for the rear echelon troops. According to the order of battle, we were supposed to take the town, regroup, resupply, and jump off in three or four hours. As it turned out, we occupied the wine cellars of Bad Durkheim for three days. Perhaps General McBride thought we deserved a much needed rest. The general was well aware that they did not have pure water in this area. We were supplied with water purification tablets, but they gave the water such a rotten taste we usually filled our canteens at a clean mud hole.

From Saarburg to Bad Durkheim, I became very adept at getting on and off moving tanks. Also, I found there were definite advantages and disadvantages to being the first man on or the last man to mount. If you are lucky enough to be the first to get on, you can climb up next to the escape hatch on the turret, go to sleep in relative comfort, and not worry about falling off because there are two or three other men between you and the side. However, when a fight breaks out, you are the last man off and ten or fifteen seconds is a long time when an enemy machine gun is spraying the other side or if your tank is hit by a rocket launcher. On the other hand, if you are the last man to mount the tank, you must stay awake and hold on to avoid being thrown off, but when the fight starts, you are the first man on the ground. I preferred to be first on and take my chances. However, once or twice I had good reason to wish I had stayed on the ground. Incidentally, you do not climb down off a tank when a fight starts, you fall off and scramble away from the treads.

In my first forty-five days of combat, I was out of action only three days. This was due to a temperature of 104°, which was caused by being wet and cold for days. Gaddie, our medic, sent me back to the Battalion Aid Station where the doctor took one look at me, tied a tag through my shirt buttonhole, and sent me further to the rear to a clearing station. Here I was treated with APC (All Purpose Capsule) and rest. (APC is a well-known civilian medicine, commonly called aspirin.) As soon as my temperature came down to 101°, I was sent back to the front line. If my condition had worsened, I would have been sent to a field hospital somewhere in France. However, I was not that lucky, so it was back to being shot at.

During this period—January, February, and March of 1945—we lost a number of men from our company due to viral infections and frozen feet. We received clean dry socks and ammunition with our rations almost every day, but it was still impossible to keep our feet dry in combat boots. A few units were fortunate enough to get winter shoes, called sno-packs, that were waterproof but these were very scarce and most were lost on the way to the front line. Therefore, we never got the chance to try them out.

One of the first things a combat soldier learns (after how to dig) is how to distinguish between friendly and hostile fire. In small arms, there was a noticeable difference in sound. Our Garand M-1 rifle was a gas-operated, semiautomatic; it went "pop-pop-pop" when fired. The enemy rifle was bolt operated, so it went "pop-click-pop." The German machine guns fired at a much faster rate than ours. We used an old 1917 model .30 caliber which had a very slow rate of fire and went "rat-a-tat-tat." They used a .31 caliber that had been perfected in the 1930s during the Spanish Civil War. It had an extremely fast rate of fire; so fast, the noise blurred into a "burp-burp." In fact, their hand-held machine gun, similar to our Thompson submachine gun was called a "burp" gun. Our Browning Automatic Rifle held a twenty-round clip and could be fired either semi or full automatic. But like our machine guns, it had a slow rate of fire.

In artillery, the German 88 mm field gun had a very high velocity; this caused its shells to whistle as they went through the air toward the target. The "88" was a most versatile weapon; it was used on tanks as a fixed emplacement gun, as an antiaircraft gun, and in many instances, fired point-blank at advancing infantry. Our supporting heavy artillery, 155 mm, 240 mm and eight inch guns, were not equal to the 88 in velocity; this, and the fact that they were larger, caused them to make a whining sound as they passed overhead. Close support was provided by our Battalion Cannon Companies, firing 105 mm howitzers that had a very slow velocity. In fact, on a clear day, you could actually see their shells in flight and the noise, as they flew overhead, was similar to the 155s. When they fell short, as they often did, we did not hear anything until we were jolted by a nearby explosion. Our cannon company usually fired a battery (three howitzers) at a time. Invariably, two of the howitzers fired on the target and one fell short, right on our line. After we survived a few near misses, our forward observer (FO) raised his fire order, causing them to fire deep; one shell on the

German front line and two behind it. The Nazi rear echelon probably did not appreciate the way we solved our problem, but better them than us.

Mortar shells, both theirs and ours, varied in size and were fired from tubes without rifling. Therefore, they traveled slowly and made very little or no noise at all until impact. Then the sound was more like a crunching than an explosion.

General McBride occasionally used twin 40 mm antiaircraft (pom pom) guns, firing just above our heads, into woods, and across streams. These were very effective against the enemy, but the noise and stray shells were unnerving to us. Another easily discernible sound was the noise made by artillery spotter planes. The German "storch" used a low octane fuel that caused the engine to make a rough, putt-putt sound. Our L4 and L5 "cubs" were very similar to the storch in appearance, but we used a high-octane fuel. So when we heard a smooth running engine, we breathed a little easier.

Both sides used artillery spotter planes. They flew at a very low altitude over the front line almost every night, hoping to spot a light off reflection on the ground. These were appropriately called "targets of opportunity." The slightest movement or smallest light would bring a barrage of artillery fire, then the other side would respond with counterfire. Naturally, we caught shells that fell short from both sides. Due to the hour of their flights, the spotter planes were referred to as "Bed Check Charlie." We learned very early to never fire at Charlie, because he could call on a whole battery of 88s, and all we had were M-1 rifles.

In addition to spotter airplanes, our cannon companies assigned a forward observer (FO) to the rifle companies and he directed artillery from the front line. Our FO, Lieutenant Lazar was short, stocky, and fearless. He actually liked to get as close to the Germans as possible. Many times, he would leave his radioman with his jeep at the battalion command post and go into action with our squad. When he did this, Waldrip, Stricker, or I would assist him on the front line. I really enjoyed working with him. First, he would give the cannon company distances and map coordinates, then call for two or three rounds. After observing these fall, he would correct the range and say three beautiful words, "Fire for effect." As soon as we heard the cannoneer reply, "On the way," we would put our heads down and hope that none fell short. Just three days before the end of the war, Lieutenant Lazar became one of our last casualties when his jeep turned over and he was thrown out. We were engaging die-hard SS units at the time, so I did not learn how seriously he was injured or whether he survived.

Chapter XIII
A Combat Soldier Earns His Pay

At Bad Durkheim, we received men and equipment to replace our recent losses. Then we loaded on trucks for a fifty mile trip to the Rhine River. Four hours later, we dismounted in one of the main plazas in the 2,000-year-old German city of Mainz. Apparently a large shell or bomb had destroyed a bank building in the vicinity, because the street was strewn with money. To a combat soldier, money is the most useless thing he can carry, so we did not bother to pick any of it up—even for souvenirs.

As soon as we assembled, Colonel Hayes informed us that General Patton was unhappy because we were on the west side of the Rhine and the German Army was on the east side. However, this would soon be corrected; in order to please the Third Army Commander, General McBride had volunteered our services. Now all we were expected to do was cross the river and rout the German Army.

About 5:00 A.M., we were herded into assault boats (Landing Craft Vehicle Personnel—LCVP) that the United States Navy had brought to Mainz for our short trip across the river. We were under the impression that we were fully armed and equipped before we reached the edge of the river because every man was carrying sixty to eighty pounds. However, just as we stepped aboard the boat, we were each handed an 81 mm mortar shell and instructed to carry it across. The shell was to be placed on the other bank so that when the mortars landed they would have a supply of ammunition on the east bank of the river. The man in front of me protested that he could not swim with a mortar shell in his hand. He was sharply reminded that if the boat sank, he would go to the bottom like a rock, weighted down with eighty pounds of equipment and ammunition.

General McBride had moved every weapon he could lay his hands on right up to the edge of the river. We saw and heard twin 40 mm antiaircraft pom poms, rocket tanks, 90 mm assault guns, 105 mm howitzers, 155 mm and 240 mm cannons, and various other guns we could not recognize. In addition to the artillery, .30 and .50 caliber machine guns were firing close support, twelve to twenty-four inches over our heads. As soon as I stepped off the boat onto the levee, the man in front of me was hit and started rolling back into the water, so I lay down my mortar shell, picked him up, and carried him about forty feet up the levee, to the street where the medics could find him.

My squad lay in the street for two or three minutes under German machine gun and rifle fire. I distinctly remember thinking how glad I was that a four-inch high street curb was affording me some protection. Suddenly, Knobby, who was about six feet from me, jumped up and yelled, "Let's go." That was all we needed. We got to our feet, firing from the hip, and started toward Weisbaden. It was reported that "the First Battalion of the 317th Infantry Regiment met 'light resistance' in crossing at Mainz." Apparently, that reporter was still in Bad Durkheim drinking champagne when we crossed the Rhine. I am absolutely sure he was not in the first wave of assault boats.

We advanced slowly until after daylight, then we moved at a good pace for a while. About mid-morning we received a big surprise. Two fighter planes that appeared to be our P-51 Mustangs flew over our column. However, when they recognized us as American troops they climbed, peeled off, and strafed us. As they came in low over the street, firing, we saw the German insignia and realized they were ME-109s. That was the first and only time we were strafed and rest assured, one such experience is enough to last a lifetime.

An hour or so after we crossed the Rhine, Knobby received word that Lieutenant Jones, the company executive officer, needed a radio operator. I was the nearest man to him when the request came in, so naturally, I got the job. Nobody said what happened to his last radioman and I did not ask. Jones was near the head of the column when I joined him. I soon learned that I was now one of the company headquarters three-man radio team. We operated in the same manner as a gun crew; one man carries a thirty-eight pound backpack SCR 300 radio and stays close (sometimes too close) to the company commander. The second man, also near the captain, carries an SCR 536 hand-held walkie-talkie. The third man, also with a SCR 536, is with the second in command of the company, who is usually with the forward platoon in an attack. The SCR 300 is used to maintain contact between the rifle company and battalion headquarters. At battalion headquarters, a vehicle-mounted SCR 610 is used to contact supporting units, such as air, artillery, and tanks. The SCR 536 maintains contact between units within the company. Each man on the radio team takes his turn carrying the SCR 300. Incidentally, when the man carrying the SCR 300 backpack is hit, one of the men with a SCR 536 has to go up and get the big radio. That is where the expression "It's a nasty job, but somebody has to do it" came from.

Entering the suburbs of Wiesbaden, Lieutenant Jones and I were about one city block from the head of the column. The first two squads were moving single file on each side of the street and German civilians lined the sidewalks watching us come into the city. The crowd revealed no emotions outwardly. We were greeted as neither conquerors or liberators. On the other hand, we accepted their presence as natural and made no gesture, neither friendly or threatening, toward them. Suddenly, we heard and saw a large explosion between us and the pointman. As the lieutenant and I ran toward the scene, Captain Bettlinski, who was somewhere behind us, called to Jones on my radio, "Stop the column, one of our men just stepped on a mine." The always calm and composed lieutenant almost lost his cool. In effect, he said, "That idiot would not know a mine if he saw one, our bazooka man just dropped an armed shell." Which was exactly what had happened. We were on the spot in less than one minute and it sure was a mess. We lost one or two men and some of the civilians nearby were wounded. It could have been much worse, but a number of civilian nurses responded from a nearby hospital and stopped many from bleeding to death before our medical personnel arrived.

In the early afternoon, we moved into the edge of Wiesbaden and, considering the size (population 200,000) of it, we secured our area as well as could be expected. I had switched radios with Waldrip and was now with the company commander. Needing a vantage point for observation, I went up to the second floor of the command post with the backpack radio and sat down on the balcony railing. From here I could see about three blocks in both directions. However, we had not slept in almost thirty hours and I was half asleep on my feet. Suddenly, I was wide awake. I glanced in the direction we had just come from and less than twenty yards away, thirty fully-armed German soldiers were marching down the street. There I was, a sitting duck. Then one of our men stepped out of our building and the German officer halted his men and informed the surprised rifleman, in perfect English, "I heard you people were here in Wiesbaden, so I brought my men up to surrender." Suffice it to say, I still do not like to sit on balconies.

During the afternoon, more Germans, many officers in full dress, found us and gave up. However, not all were quite ready to turn themselves in. As we were clearing (going from room to room) the house next door to the CP, I rushed in to find a fully-armed SS officer. He stared at me defiantly and said, in very proper English, "I will only surrender to an officer." My reply was, "Handy Ho," the only two German words I knew, which is roughly translated, "You have a split second to give up or be killed." In that split second I think he realized that an M-1 rifle makes an awful nasty hole when it is fired at point-blank range from about three feet. Incidentally, my grandson still has his SS dress dagger and my son is the proud possessor of his .38 caliber Belgium Browning Pistol. The United States Army let me keep them as captured weapons.

Another interesting incident occurred during our first night in Wiesbaden. I was asleep on the second floor in the room with the balcony. At about two o'clock in the morning, one of our men woke me and said, "It's your turn to go down and guard the front door." In combat you never question an order of this kind, so he lay down in my warm spot on the floor and I went down the stairs. Passing a dimly lit room on the first floor, I looked in and saw perhaps forty German prisoners. Many of them were officers who seemed to be discussing the war. After about ten minutes at the door, I realized that the only people on the first floor were me and a roomful of Germans. Actually, I suppose it was a little chicken of me but I decided to move my post to a spot halfway up the stairs where I could see both their room and the front door. That is where I sat the remainder of the night, wide awake, with my rifle across my lap. If three or four of those Germans changed their minds and decided to fight, I would have had a better chance above them in the dark stairwell than I would have had in the doorway.

The following morning, German civilians were ordered to turn in all weapons. Most were collector items and many were old and beautiful. I took one odd-looking .38 caliber pistol out of the pile and loaded fifteen rounds in it from the top like a rifle. Then, I stepped behind the building, aimed at a C-ration can and squeezed the trigger. What a shock! It made fifteen holes in the wall before I could turn loose of the trigger. The blasted thing was a fully automatic machine pistol, a relic from World War I. I threw it back in the pile and decided right then and there not to play with any more guns. I was fortunate I did not blow my head off with that pistol.

Luckily, we were not involved in the biggest fight at Wiesbaden. In fact, neither was the German Army. We, the Eightieth Infantry, came into the city from the southwest, the Sixth Armored advanced from the northeast, and the Tenth Armored moved north of us to enter from the northwest. Unfortunately, someone in corps or army headquarters failed to advise either armored division that they were on a collision course with the other. Therefore, when they suddenly got a glimpse of another army, they began firing. It was not until one side recognized the other that they realized their mistake. However, by this time, damage was done and some men were killed and others wounded. This error occurred many times after the American Army crossed the Rhine, due to the fact that German forces had been penetrated in many different places and there was no well-defined front line.

Leaving Wiesbaden after two days, we mounted up on tanks and proceeded north toward Kassel, Germany. In the next three days, riding the Sixth Armored tanks like cowboys, we captured thousands of prisoners. We encountered only light to moderate resistance on the way to Kassel. But when we were almost to the city, we had to jump on tanks and go back forty miles to break a roadblock the SS had established on the Autobahn.

On our return to the front line, we hit strong resistance in the Wilhelmshore (Kaiser Wilhelm Forest) just outside of Kassel. Of great assistance to the German troops were a large number of brand new Royal Tiger heavy tanks right off the assembly lines in the city. However, the enemy was hampered because he had to fight just outside the factory. Even though some of the tanks had diesel fuel, no motor oil was available, so as the motors froze, they became pillboxes. Our artillery had not caught up to us but we were in close radio contact with the XIX Tactical Air Force P-47s and when we spotted a tank they would respond and knock it out in a couple of passes.

We had to take Kassel house to house, or I should say rubble to rubble, because the city (population 175,000) was over ninety percent destroyed. As I started out of a building in Neidervellmar, a Kassel suburb, an enemy concussion grenade hit the door facing. I woke up hours later in a clearing station hospital. I could see a 155 mm artillery battery nearby and from the firing angle of the cannons, I guessed I was three to five miles behind the front line. No real harm was done except I was very groggy and unsteady on my feet for three days. Actually, I was fortunate to miss this period of action, because my platoon suffered a lot of casualties in those three days.

After we secured the city, we turned over to the Sixty-ninth Infantry Division, a green unit that had just arrived from the United States. We moved southeast to capture Gotha. In less than a week, the German SS recaptured Kassel, routing the Sixty-ninth. Then, with the assistance of two more divisions, the Germans were dislodged again and the "Fighting Sixty-ninth" made the cover of *Life*, in the United States, taking the city of Kassel, Germany.

We rode the Sixth Armored tanks from Gotha to the outskirts of Erfurt, stopping only for an occasional fire fight along the way. Then we were forced to come to a complete halt just outside the city so our supply units could catch up. Now for the first and last time, we had to establish a "main line of resistance"—the United States Army's term for a final defense line.

While we were securing the line at Erfurt, a serious problem arose about twenty miles behind us, at Gotha, Germany. As it happened, when we came through Gotha, we liberated a slave labor camp consisting of women only. Now that we, the combat troops had advanced, Quartermaster (supply) troops had moved in and the women were being molested. There were not enough military police in Gotha to protect the camp. Consequently, General McBride pulled our company off the line, moved us back to the camp, and ordered us to protect the women inmates. Apparently, the general failed to inform the rear echelon troop commander that the few military police had been replaced by a front line rifle company. Unfortunately, just after dark, the Quartermaster troops came out to the camp in force and were met with force. I think the United States Army learned a lesson that night and I am certain the Quartermaster did. You do not take fully armed combat soldiers off the front line and expect them to act like trained, civilized military police. Needless to say, early the next morning we were sent back to the front line at Erfurt, with specific orders from General McBride to shoot only Germans for the remainder of the war in Europe.

At Erfurt we learned the hard way that establishing an MLR defense line was not as simple as it had appeared at Camp Blanding. There we were taught to set out mines in loose sand, lay barbed wire with gloves on, dig a few outpost while standing up, then place our machine guns at each end of our line so that they fired across our front. First, you cannot lay mines in concrete sidewalks unless you have a jackhammer; as for barbed wire, we had not seen any in Europe, nor did we have any gloves. Also, we did not need outpost, we *were* the outpost. Finally, we not only had a front, we also had two sides and a rear to protect. Incidentally, they failed to tell us at Camp Blanding that the Germans and our old friend the blue racer snake have the same disposition. As long as you have either of them on the run, you have an advantage. But once you stop, you are at their mercy.

The German 88 mm field gun is about as accurate as an M-1 rifle and they had two 88s placed in concrete less than a mile away. In addition, four or five Royal Tiger tanks were prowling the area. We were sitting ducks, and to prove it, the Germans made direct hits on the command post building that I was in, more than once knocking big holes in the walls.

Another detail omitted at Blanding in regard to an MLR concerned patrols. We quickly discovered that once you go on the defensive, you must maintain constant contact with the enemy. The purpose of this tactic is to allow you to know where he is, how strong he is, and what he is capable of doing at all times. General McBride did not expect his division to be caught off guard by a surprise attack. Contact with the enemy is maintained in various ways, the most common being combat patrols, which vary in size and purpose. Some consist of only two or three men, while others might contain thirty to forty men. Patrols also differ in purpose: they are *reconnaissance*, or see what you can and return without fighting, if possible; *intelligence*, or capture one or more prisoners and bring them back alive for interrogation; *combat*, or see how much enemy fire you can draw so that his strength can be determined; or *penetration*, or see how far you can advance into the enemy line before you are pinned down and are forced to call for reinforcements to set you out. Penetration patrols are usually made a few hours before a major attack and these men are most vulnerable because, as the battle begins, they are often caught in a crossfire.

It was my pleasure to serve in one such penetration patrol at Erfurt. Just after dark, on the night before the division jump off from the MLR, Knobby assembled the First Platoon in the basement of the company command post. There, Colonel Hayes, the battalion commander, instructed us that we had been chosen to penetrate the German line. Simply put, we were to proceed through a line of enemy riflemen who were in one-man foxholes about 300 feet in front of our line. Then, at 800 feet, we would cross a railroad, advance another 300 feet, and set up a command post in one of the apartment buildings. From this point we could direct fire for the attack.

As we approached their line, Knobby sent Apmann through first so he could find and cut their communication wires. He was an ideal choice, because he looked, acted, and even carried his rifle like a German soldier. We waited a specified time, then Knobby and I (with a SCR 536 radio) proceeded through their front. The remainder of the patrol followed, one man at a time, about thirty feet apart. We passed within 100 feet of their one-man foxholes and could see their rifles follow us as we walked slowly forward. Later, we learned from prisoners that their plan was to let us in but not to let us out. Their commander thought we were a reconnaissance patrol.

About two o'clock in the morning, we finally reached a block of buildings near the field guns. Knobby chose the middle unit of a three-story townhouse. This afforded us some protection, because we only had to fire, and take fire, from front and rear doors and windows. Once inside, I switched on my radio and gave our patrol call signal, "zebra seven to zebra one." Colonel Hayes answered immediately with a few choice words: "Where have you been? Why have you not reported in? Have you met any opposition? Where are you now?" Knobby calmly ignored all of his questions and reported that we were in the buildings and had established a good observation post, from which we could report the enemy's movement after daylight. Actually, he could have honestly reported that we had no idea where we have been because after we passed through their first line we have been crawling on our stomachs for the past six hours. Also, we had not spoken to each other all night and we were not about to let the Germans hear us call him. The lieutenant knew that all the colonel really wanted to know was that we had accomplished our mission.

Luckily, the unit we entered was not occupied by German troops. As soon as we entered, Apmann asked one of the occupants, "Are there any German soldiers in this building?" Her reply gave us a shock. "Only about 300," she said. Then we received a bigger surprise; Apmann had to convince her that we were not

Germans dressed in American uniforms. It seems the civilians in this area had been told the day before that the American Army could not get across the Rhine. We had until daylight to make our unit secure, so we stayed as quiet as possible. Using the bathroom was out of the question because a lot of flushes would alert our next door neighbors. Therefore, we did the next best thing, we established a latrine in the corner of the living room, out on the line of fire from the windows. After we were discovered, it helped to have civilians in our part of the building. This kept the Germans from blasting us out. At daybreak we could see the German line so we radioed the location of strong points to the battalion commander. That afternoon, we were united with our company when the division broke through, supported by tanks. For once, we were happy to see Captain Bettlinski, because we did not like the "Heinie's" potato masher concussion grenades any better than they liked our sniping.

When we rejoined the company, I took the SCR 300 and gave Waldrip the 536 because he had been carrying the thirty-eight pound backpack for almost thirty-six hours. I really did not mind carrying the big radio except this meant I had to stay close to Captain Bettlinski. I felt more at ease and safer with Knobby and Jones. As we cleared the suburbs of Erfurt, house to house, the Captain sent a squad of seven men out on a reconnaissance patrol. Bettlinski told the squad leader to go around the first corner, down the side street for two city blocks, and return the same way. We waited about twenty minutes, then when they did not report back as expected, my squad followed their route. Just around the corner, less than 200 feet from their starting point, in the second house we found their helmets, broken rifles, and equipment. It was apparent that they had not followed orders. As soon as they were out of sight of the captain, they went in what they assumed to be an empty house, stopped to eat and rest, and were captured by German troops who were lying in wait. (A combat infantryman is like a boxer in the ring, he must protect himself at all times.)

The retreating enemy left behind quite a few snipers to slow our advance through this section of the city. With the large number of apartment windows, one sniper in particular was aggravating and almost impossible to spot. Captain Bettlinski was determined to locate the exact building he was in so he could direct tank fire on it. This was one of many times that I disagreed with the captain's judgment and tactics. First, Bettlinski would run across the street and the sniper would fire at him, then I would dash over, as it was my job to stay close to the captain, and the German soldier would fire at me. After four or five trips, I felt like a fugitive from the law of averages. Finally, Lieutenant Jones came up to the point and convinced Bettlinski to call for tank fire on all the buildings facing us. Actually, it required only a single blast from the 90 mm cannon for white flags (sheets) to begin flying from all the windows. One sniper surrendered. When he came up to the captain and me with his hands up he said, "Hello, I speak a little English." However, we were not in the mood to carry on a friendly conversation. He was sent to the rear under guard. I have always been glad I was not selected for his guard because, in my frame of mind, he probably would not have made it to the prisoner of war cage. I had good and sufficient reason to be upset. A number of our men had been hit that morning, seven others captured, and this Nazi had tried to shoot me personally. With the assistance of the Sixth Armored Division, Lieutenant Jones, now leading the company, decided to clear the remaining blocks the proper way; blasting every building with 90 mm shells, regardless of snipers or white flags. We probably killed a number of civilians with this approach. However, it sure served its purpose of discouraging snipers.

Just northwest of Erfurt, General McBride assembled the division for our next attack. We, Company B, were situated on high ground overlooking beautiful open country. Less than a mile away was an orchard with leafless trees. Just beyond the orchard was a medium-size town. I was carrying the SCR 300 for Lieutenant Lazar, our artillery observer, and was with him when the general outlined his textbook plan of attack to the company officers. I was elated to learn that, for once, Company B was lucky because we were placed in battalion reserve. This meant we would not be called on unless the other two (A and C) companies hit more than they could handle and that did not appear likely. Company A was to pass through our line and proceed to the edge of town; Company C was to follow as soon as Company A reached their objective. Everything went according to plan until Company C reached the center of the orchard. Suddenly, the enemy attacked in force. Now, we had Company A in town and Company C pinned down in the orchard by German tanks. This meant Company B had to jump off, down the open hill, and into the barren orchard to the aid of Company C. However, while we were advancing, the Germans could not give us their undivided attention, because Company A came out fighting. Their company commander, Captain James A. Woodside, was a gung-ho individual who enjoyed personally going after German tanks with a bazooka. By the time we reached Company C, he had put three tanks out of action and the enemy had dug in. About four hours later, Companies A and B were dug in facing the Germans and Company C was up in our holes at the top of the hill. After we covered their pullout, the general decided we could hold where we were until he got a few tank destroyers from Third Army reserves.

There were a couple of interesting sidelights to this action. First, the division and Third Army intelligence officers assured General McBride on the previous day that he could release all our tank and tank destroyer support. In their opinion, we would encounter only light resistance in this area consisting of stragglers and Volkstrum units which were too old or too young to put up much of a fight. Second, even worse than their report was the fact that Hairless Horace believed them and turned our armor over to another division.

As Company C prepared to jump off, Lieutenant Lazar spotted fifteen to twenty German tanks about 800 yards to our left front. So he (and I with the radio) walked over to General McBride and the regimental commander who were observing the attack. Lazar pointed out the Germans and requested that Company A be halted so he could call for artillery fire on the tanks. The general emphatically informed the lieutenant that the enemy had already pulled out of the area. Furthermore, if he saw any tanks they were American armored units, probably the ones we had released. Lazar then walked over to Colonel Hayes, our battalion commander, and pointed out the enemy threat to our flank. Colonel Hayes told him, in no uncertain terms, "If General McBride says those are our tanks, they are our tanks." Knowing he had done everything he could for the time being, Lazar shut up, took out his map, and called in a possible fire order. We did not have long to wait. As soon as the tanks began firing, General McBride yelled, "Lieutenant, can't you see those German tanks?" We already had the coordinates in to the Cannon Company, so after just one register, Lazar ordered, "Fire for effect." This caused the tanks to scatter, giving Companies A and B time to get to Company C. I think after that action, the general had a little more respect for his forward observer's suggestions. The following day, the battalion, with tank destroyer support, was able to clear the orchards.

In the Civil War, the American soldier took his trusty old rifle with him when he went off to war. Over four years later, he returned home with the same fine gun. This was not the case in World War II. The M-1 Garand was a well-built, accurate weapon, but it was mass-produced. Therefore, it could not withstand the punishment inflicted upon it by a combat infantryman. My rifle was far from trusty. I broke one stock in training, one in combat, and two M-1s failed mechanically in combat. By the same token, if I was rough on it, in turn, it was rough on me. An M-1 is loaded by placing an eight-round clip in the top of the open breech and pushing down with the right thumb. As soon as the clip is properly seated, the bolt slams forward sending a round into the firing chamber. This is a simple operation and can be accomplished in training without incident. However, when you are engaged in a fire fight and speed in loading is a matter of life or death, your thumb often gets caught in the breech. Consequently, most combat riflemen, myself included, can show a scarred M-1 right thumb for the rest of their lives.

Chapter XIV
Welcome to Hell:
The Liberation of Buchenwald

In our next attack, I had the point for the first platoon but I felt fairly safe. Lieutenant Jones and the second platoon had jumped off first and were already out in front of our supporting tanks. In fact, I was about three feet from our leading tank, ready to hitch a ride as soon as we reached the open country at the top of the hill. We were proceeding slowly up a sparsely settled street not expecting any enemy opposition. However, just as we crested the hill, the Germans, who were lying in wait for our tank, fired their emplaced field gun from only 300 yards away. At that distance, the German gunners could not miss. The 88 mm armor-piercing shell made a direct hit on the tank's gun shield. Being armor piercing rather than high explosive, it was deflected. When it hit, it sounded as though someone had clapped cymbals together in my head, then all I could hear was the shell screaming as it appeared to go straight up. If the shell had been high explosive, or had it hit a less vulnerable spot and penetrated the tank, everyone in or near the tank would have been killed, including me.

Our tank crew lost no time getting out of the tank and escaped before the Germans fired again. When they resumed fire (a minute or so later), their next two shells were deflected, then one penetrated and the tank immediately exploded and burned. By that time I was a good 200 feet away from it. (In looking for cover, I could not help recalling Sergeant Gaddie's remark concerning his experience with the German machine gunners at the Moselle River, "When I turned left at Pont-a-Mosson, their bullets just kept going straight." Truer words were never spoken.)

In putting some distance between me and the exploding tank, I somehow lost three of my four bandoleers of rifle ammunition, two fragmentation grenades, a raincoat, and my prize possession, my loot bag. My loot bag was full of German belt buckles which carried the inscription *Gott mit uns* and assorted medals. There were even some Russian and French medals that the Germans had acquired from their enemies. I really hope the person who later found my

The Fiery Furnaces of Buchenwald

U.S. Army Signal Corps Photo

Buchenwald Concentration Camp, 13 April 1945

This photograph shows the condition and the amount of sleeping space for the prisoners at Buchenwald.

When we arrived at Buchenwald on 10 April 1945, many of the inmates had been prepared for the ovens. Therefore, they were totally naked; others had on only the shirt of the prison clothing which was made of a light cotton material.

The barracks were unheated wooden frame buildings without insulation. There was no bedding of any sort on these racks which were used for sleeping.

Elie Wiesel, Nobel Prize winning author, is in this photograph. He is lying on the second bunk looking over the right shoulder of the seated man who is facing the camera. At the time, Wiesel was only fifteen years old.

J. Ray Clark

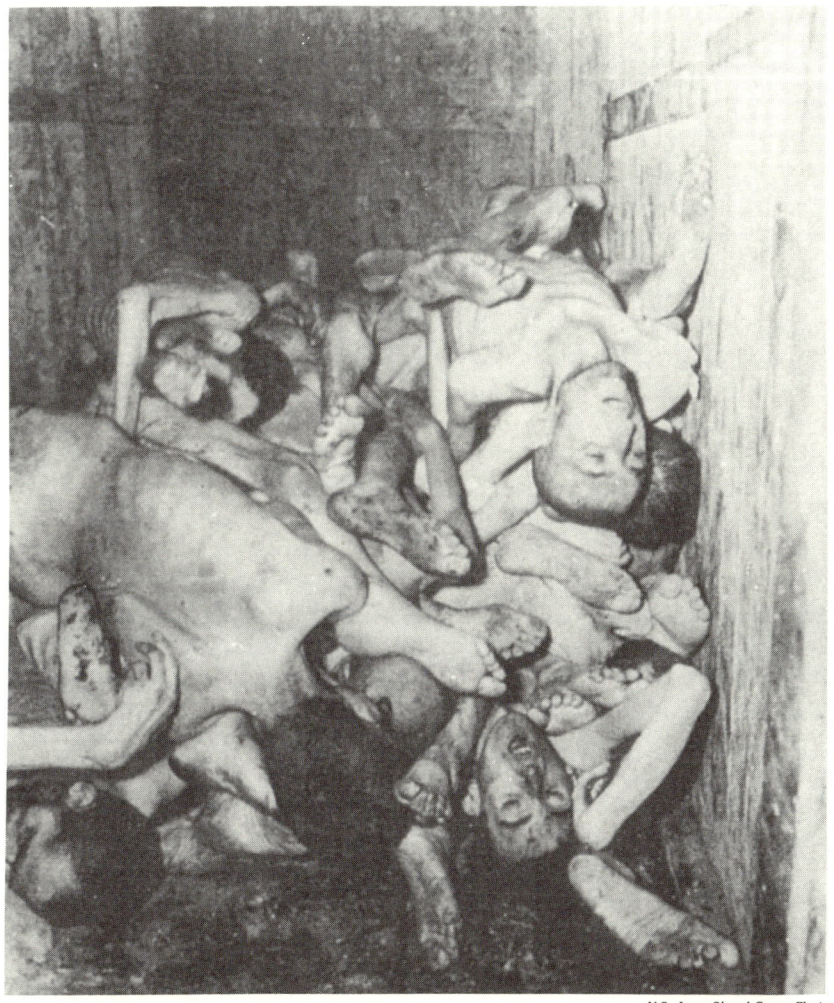

U.S. Army Signal Corps Photo

Buchenwald Concentration Camp, 14 April 1945

These bodies, dead and near death, are brought into the crematorium on carts by slave laborers and piled near the furnaces. Then, from there they are placed on a table in front of the oven and as other bodies are consumed they are shoved into the oven with a pusher tool. Other slaves removed the ashes with shovels and wheelbarrows.

I saw four ovens at Buchenwald and was told that each oven was capable of consuming approximately 200 bodies in eight hours. However, prior to our arrival the ovens had been operating twenty-four hours a day.

loot bag does not tell too many tall tales on how he acquired so many enemy medals.

Naturally, we had to regroup without the tanks (our Sherman tanks were no match for emplaced German field guns) and advance across the open field to put the 88s out of action. As we neared the dug in enemy, a rather brisk fire fight broke out. One of the first men hit was the radioman with Lieutenant Lazar, our forward observer. I began crawling toward Lazar so he could use my radio for artillery support. Suddenly, I heard a sharp ping on my helmet and thought I had surely been hit. I reached up and felt my face and neck but found no blood. Then I ran my hand over my helmet and discovered that my SCR 300 radio antenna was lying on my head. A German rifle or machine gun bullet had severed it about two inches above the back of my neck. The ping sound was the antenna striking my steel helmet. When we finally captured the field guns later that day, we discovered they had fired all of their ammunition. I would have been just as happy if they had not had any to begin with; that first shot scared me out of ten-years growth. The guns were laid for direct fire, which meant they were pointed straight across the field. When I reached the first one, I shoved a thermit grenade down the barrel and then watched it melt through the breech. (We learned our lesson with the Nebelwefer; always destroy every captured enemy weapon.)

Next, we jumped off toward the city of Weiner (population 50,000). As we approached the city, we were assured that the burgomaster (mayor) had surrendered the city to our regimental commander, Colonel Norman Costello. However, as we were moving into the suburbs, a die-hard SS unit opened fire with rifles, burp guns, and light mortars. This ambush killed and wounded a number of fine, young men who were respecting white flags of truce that flew from every window. Many innocent German civilians lost their lives as a result of this breach of faith. We simply called in artillery, tank, and air support, and leveled six or eight city blocks. The average German soldier was, for the most part, civilized and decent, but the black uniformed SS were arrogant and ungodly. Their favorite motto was, "We will die for the Fuehrer." Consequently, we did all we could to accommodate them in fulfilling their expressed goal.

As we moved into one of the better sections of the city, two jeep loads of OSS (Office of Strategic Service) men came roaring up and stopped right behind Apmann, who was on the point. I was only about twenty feet away when they (our counterintelligence men) burst into a house and came out with one of the major Nazi war criminals. Apmann recognized him immediately, as the former German chancellor, Franz von Papen.

Photo from the author's private collection.

War Criminals

Left to right: Hermann Goering, Hitler's Deputy. He committed suicide only hours before his scheduled execution for war crimes. Franz von Papen, Nazi diplomat who, due to the influence of his friends in Washington, D.C., was acquitted of his war crimes. Julius Streicher. Hanged at Nuremberg for war crimes. Arthur Seyss-Inquart. Hanged at Nuremberg for war crimes. These four criminals were responsible for more than half of the deaths that occurred in the Nazi Concentration Camps in World War II.

Photo from the author's private collection.

War Criminals

Left to right, beginning with the third man from the left: Paul Joseph Goebbels; a Nazi judge; S.S. chief, Heinrich Himmler; Otto Skorzeny. Skorzeny ordered the machine gun massacre of American prisoners of war at Malmedy, Belgium in December 1944.

The Fiery Furnaces of Buchenwald

U.S. Army Signal Corps Photo

Ohrdruf Concentration Camp, 10 April 1945
Bodies of victims stacked up like cordwood waiting to either be burned in the ovens or buried in a mass grave. The white substance is lime sprinkled over the bodies to keep down the odor.
   Germany refused to recognize the Geneva Convention as it pertained to the treatment of prisoners of war in World War II. For fear of retribution most American and British prisoners were treated humanely. However, some were maltreated and a number were actually sent to the death camps and executed in violation of this international agreement that had been signed by the German Government.
   From all appearances these are either French or Russian soldiers who have been captured on the battlefield. Notice their facial features and the size of their feet. Taking into account their muscle structure and bone size they are probably in their early twenties.

Actually, in this incident, our OSS men risked their lives for nothing, because von Papen was one of many Nazi leaders who had English and American friends in high places, including Eleanor Lansing (Dulles) Blondheim, wife of SS General David Blondheim. Mrs. Blondheim, an early supporter of Adolph Hitler and an ardent Nazi, was also the sister of Allen Welsh Dulles and John Foster Dulles. John represented New York banking interests in Germany in the mid-1930s and later (1953-1959) served as secretary of state. Allen, chief of staff of the OSS in Switzerland during World War II, was in constant contact with Nazi agents. Consequently, Mrs. Blondheim, serving under her maiden name, Dulles, was placed in

U.S. Army Signal Corps Photo

Buchenwald Concentration Camp, 13 April 1945

This photograph is a piece of tattooed skin which was removed from a man's back or chest and has been tacked and glued to a board. The dried skin is yellowed with age and to the touch feels like the sheepskin of an old diploma or early land grant deed. It was located in the office of Commandant Ilsa Koch, "the Bitch of Buchenwald."

In this office there were also some slightly larger and many smaller pieces of dried, tattoed human skin. In addition to the wall hangings, some of the skins had been crudely sewn together and stretched over wire frames. These frames were later referred to as "lamp shades" by people who only saw pictures of them. However the ones I saw and handled were simply ornamental and were not fitted to be placed on lamps.

charge of German-American affairs at the State Department in Washington, D.C., shortly after the fighting ceased. Therefore, it is not surprising that Franz von Papen was acquitted at the International War Crimes Tribunal in Nuremberg, Germany in September of 1946.

We jumped off early on 10 April 1945 and advanced north of the city, engaging in two or three fire fights as we encountered pockets of resistance. Then we lost contact with the enemy. About 10:00 A.M., we approached what appeared to be another slave labor camp. The machine gun guard towers did not return our fire and as we got closer, we could see prisoners at the fences. It was obvious

U.S. Army Signal Corps Photo

Burial Ground Near Nuremberg, Germany, 29 April 1945

When large quantities of dead bodies were found in the British or Russian sectors during the war, they were buried in mass graves without any ceremony. However, in camps liberated by his troops, American General George S. Patton gave orders for the Germans to bury the bodies in individual coffins and that religious services be held for both Christians and Jews.

General Patton also ordered that all available American troops be routed through the camps so that they would be eyewitness to the horrible acts performed by the Nazis.

Further he insisted that all civilians from nearby cities and towns be marched through so that they could not later deny that the camps existed. Some German civilians, including the Mayor of Ohrdruf and his wife, committed suicide shortly after viewing the crimes committed by their countrymen.

that the German troops had fled. On entering this camp, we received the shock of our lives.

We had liberated the infamous Buchenwald Concentration Camp. Inside the camp, we found a cadre of slave laborers, who were killing and burning other prisoners. Later, we learned that they had been threatened by the departing Nazis, "If you quit burning them, we will come back and burn you."

Buchenwald was not like any of the other prison camps we had encountered. First it was much larger, containing 25,000 to 30,000 inmates. Second, it did not serve a useful purpose, as a slave labor or prisoner of war confinement camp. It was simply an extermination camp established in June of 1937 (only Dachau was older) by the Nazi Government as an emigration camp for German citizens and subjects who "voluntarily" donated all their possessions to the Nazis and agreed to emigrate to other countries. However, in the year 1938, the United States accepted a total of thirty-eight of them and the British Empire barred them all. Therefore, thousands were condemned to the gas chamber and lime pits.

This camp was commanded by a woman, Ilsa Koch, "the Bitch of Buchenwald." In her office, we found polished skulls of various (adult and children) sizes used as paperweights, and lamp shades made of tattooed human skin on every desk. Also some tattooed skin had been stretched over boards and was used as wall hangings. You could almost see your reflection in the shiny skulls, and the skin looked and felt like parchment.

Combat infantrymen are accustomed to gory scenes and death. Many times in battle, injury and death are instantaneous. It is not uncommon to come upon enemy soldiers in a state of decay, who were killed by bombs or artillery two or three weeks previously. But hardened as we were, nothing we had experienced before prepared us for the carnage we discovered at Buchenwald.

To restore order and stop the killing and burning, we had to use force, even to the point of shooting some of the slave laborers. After this was accomplished, we secured the area against a possible counterattack by the enemy. Then, we were able to observe the entire camp.

First we saw the living dead. These were human beings who had been systematically starved to the point of death. There was no flesh on their bodies, only skin stretched over bones that were visible. Their arms at the wrist were no larger than one and one-half inches in diameter and the heaviest person I saw was no more than three inches thick at the waist. Even their slightest movement required great effort, and many died as they stood by watching us as we patrolled the camp.

Then we entered the crematorium. It was the largest building in the camp. Inside we found a number of ovens, which contained partially burned bodies, charred bones, and ashes. Nearby there were stacks of bodies (some were still alive) and piles of ashes. In front of each oven was a metal table piled with bodies, ready to be shoved into the roaring fire. Being so badly dehydrated, we were told, they burned extremely fast and left very few ashes. There was every indication that the ovens had been in continuous use day and night, as our army approached, in order to destroy as much evidence as possible. A conservative estimate of the dead we saw that first day would be between 5,000 and 7,000. The figure released by the newspapers was much higher, but it probably included those who died after liberation.

Outside the crematorium, we saw the pits. The largest of these was eight to ten feet wide and about 200 feet long. It was partially filled with layers of bodies (living and dead), sprinkled with lime or a similar substance. Nearby were bodies stacked like cordwood, about five feet high, awaiting interment. Surprisingly, there was not the stench of death present because of the absence of flesh. There was a smell, but it was not overwhelming; it was somewhat like a wet animal on a hot day.

We were most impressed by the attitude of the inmates. In contrast to those liberated in prisoner of war and slave labor camps, these inmates showed absolutely no joy in being liberated. In fact, they, like the slave laborers, fully expected us (the United States Army) to continue operating the camp in the same manner as the German SS. After all, both the inmates and the cadre knew that we, the American people and the American Government, had been aware of their persecution for many years. The conditions inside the concentration camps and the murder of inmates were reported in U.S. newspapers as early as 1933. Also, President Roosevelt, in his instructions to Mr. William Dodd, ambassador designate to Germany, on 16 June 1933, is quoted as saying, "The German authorities are treating the Jews shamefully and the Jews in this country are greatly excited. But this is not a (United States) governmental affair. We can do nothing except for American citizens who happen to be made victims." (Dodd's Diary, first edition. (Harcourt, Brace and Company, 1941) 5.)

The inmates of Buchenwald were calm and dignified, and even in their emancipated state, dressed in scant clothing or naked as many of them were, their composure was that of intelligent, civilized human beings. They did not beg, but graciously accepted that which was offered. However, we soon discovered that we could not give them anything to eat because their systems were too weak to tolerate even our K-ration cheese and crackers. Later in the day, our first medical corps units arrived and began feeding them a weak broth. The doctors and nurses did a remarkable job, saving about half of those who were alive when they arrived. We assisted by setting up cots and supplying blankets. The inmates had been sleeping on wooden slats without bedding and in unheated buildings for months, without medical attention of any kind.

General McBride ordered that everything (pits, stacks of bodies, ovens, lamp shades made of human skin, and the polished skulls) be left exactly as it was until the arrival of General Walton H. Walker, XX Corps commander. The following day (12 April 1945), we were relieved of duty at Buchenwald. Within hours after we left, General Patton and General Eisenhower conducted a contingent of United States Senators and Congressmen through Buchenwald so they could see with their own eyes the horror of the Holocaust!

The most appropriate description I can give of the concentration camp at Buchenwald, would be to say that it gave the appearance of an earthquake in a cemetery. At Buchenwald, many of the dead were walking among us. The commandant of Buchenwald, Ilsa Koch, well deserved her title, "the Bitch of Buchenwald." Her favorite sport was to turn her large dogs loose on arriving inmates and watch as helpless men, women, and children were torn apart. At the railhead, she also engaged in her hobby, inspecting naked inmates in search of tattoos. On finding a suitable specimen, she would have the individual killed in such a way so as not to damage the tattoo. Then, this human skin was stretched over a wire frame. After drying to a parchment, these "mementos" were used as lamp shades in her office and given as gifts to other Nazi officials.

After their capture, concentration camp commanders were tried by an International Tribunal for crimes against humanity. Rudolph Hess, commandant at Auschwitz, SS Captain Josef, "the Beast of Bergen-Belsen," and others were hanged, but Ilsa Koch played on the mercy of the court. She was found guilty and sentenced to life imprisonment. After serving only four years in an Allied (British and American) prison, her sentence was commuted and she was released to German custody. On 15 January 1951, a German court found her guilty of the murder of German citizens and sentenced her to life imprisonment. While serving this sentence in a German prison, she allegedly committed suicide in 1967.

Chapter XV
Pockets of Resistance

Jumping off from Buchenwald, we began cleaning out large pockets of resistance that had been bypassed by General Patton's Fourth and Sixth Armored Divisions as they raced to cut Germany in half. An Associated Press story in the *Chicago Tribune*, describing one of these pockets stated, "The 80th Division of the United States Third Army captured it (the city of Jena, population 60,000) easily in a brief, half-hearted 'battle of honor,' in which only a few shots were exchanged." If we had been given a choice, the "descriptive writer" correspondent who wrote the tripe could have enjoyed the "honor" of being shot at by the die-hard Nazis at Jena, who were determined to kill at least one more American soldier before they had the honor of dying for the Fuehrer.

With the city of Jena secured, we rested in our foxholes for the night. Then we advanced on foot, thirty-two miles to the next city, Gera (population 80,000). Here we encountered only enough snipers to remind us the war was still in progress. At Gera, General McBride received intelligence reports that the road to Chemnitz was lightly defended. So early on the morning of 15 April 1945, he gave the order and we mounted our tanks and headed east. In less than six hours, we moved forty miles and captured Glauchau (population 29,000). From there, we could see the city of Chemnitz (population 300,000), only eight miles away.

Beyond Chemnitz, it was open country to Dresden, about fifty miles to the east. However, as we regrouped, General Patton received an order from Supreme Headquarters Allied Expeditionary Force (General Eisenhower) to "Halt in place." Our new mission was to prevent the German troops and civilians caught between us and the Russian Army from escaping to the west.

Actually, Chemnitz was an undefended "open city" and could have been captured without firing a shot. However, at the "big three" meeting at Yalta in February of 1945, President Franklin D. Roosevelt of the United States, Prime Minister Winston Churchill of England, and Premier Joseph Stalin of the Soviet Union agreed not to advance beyond certain lines in Europe. This left Chemnitz, Leipzig, Prague, Berlin, and 14,000 American and British prisoners of war at Dresden to the mercy of the Russians. By 18 April we were pinched out of the "political" front line and replaced by the Seventy-sixth Infantry Division.

About two miles behind the line, we loaded onto trucks for the first time since Bad Durkheim, and proceeded to a depot at Amberg. Here, we were brought up to full strength and supplied with new weapons and equipment, including a raincoat. On our way south toward the battle front, we stopped for a day in the beautiful city of Bamberg (population 60,000). Due to its location and lack of war industries, Bamberg escaped much of the bombing and destruction that most German cities received. This was the first German city where we, the combat soldiers, were allowed to behave as tourists. Military government was in place, so we were free to walk around and observe civilians in a peaceful environment. However, fraternization (social contact) with German citizens was forbidden, under threat of court-martial. This rule, a farce from the beginning, was soon relaxed, then abandoned altogether by the United States Army.

Combat soldiers are not easily shocked and most can recognize a house of prostitution. Therefore, when we saw a number of big blond females beckoning to us from the windows of a large apartment building in Bamberg, we quite naturally assumed that it was a house of ill repute. However, on closer observation, we noticed that many of these women had three or four young children. Upon inquiring, we were informed that this was a German "mothers" home, a pregnancy camp. The Nazi Government had always encouraged families to have more children and even gave subsistence and medals to those who did. Then, soon after World War II began, pregnancy camps, such as this one, were established where women could have children by soldiers on leave from the fighting front. According to Rudolph Hess, Hitler's deputy, "Women should produce children while the men are fighting." Hess then named a number of great men whose fathers and grandfathers were of illegitimate birth, including Charlemagne and Leonardo da Vinci.

Official Nazi policy written by Hess and published in 1939 stated,

> With the child that you expect, you give and your fiancé has given in a way lasting beyond his own life, the highest thing that you can give for the further existence of our people—a young life. You and your child will be taken care of quite as if your marriage had been concluded and all young mothers in your situation will be treated in a similar way. The National Socialist movement views the family as the germ call of the people, particular measures departing from the basic rules may have to be taken. Above in war, which

calls for the death of many of the best men, every new life is of particular importance to the nation. If and when, therefore, racially unobjectionable young men going to the front leave behind children who transmit their blood to future generations, children from girls of equally good heritage and of a corresponding age, with whom marriage for one reason or another could not be consummated at once, care will be taken of this valuable possession. Hesitations which may have their justification in normal times must be put aside. The father of such a child will be called "war father" officially in the public birth registry; the mother, while retaining her maiden name, will be addressed as "Mrs." Whenever the mother wants wardens for her child, the (Nazi) Party will obtain these, though grandparents should fulfill this role.

In spite of Hess' fancy words and justification, the building in Bamberg, Germany, full of big blond females, was still what we thought it was when we first saw it, a house of prostitution.

As we loaded on trucks and said good-bye to Bamberg, we received "good" news. Orders from Third Army Headquarters read, "The 80th Infantry Division is designated as occupation troops for the city of Nuremberg, Germany." This meant, if it was true, that our shooting war was over. However, when we arrived to take possession of our prize, we discovered that the prewar city of Nuremberg, with its half-million population, no longer existed; it was just piles and piles of rubble.

Because I was an SCR 300 radioman, I was assigned to the company command post, which was a bomb-damaged building near the 1936 Olympic swimming stadium. Out first task was to run wire to battalion headquarters, because our radios would not work in most areas of the city due to interference from the steel in the rubble. Nuremberg had been captured only three days earlier, so we secured our area against enemy holdouts who were hiding in the ruins. After dark on the first night, Apmann and I were on guard near the entrance to our headquarters. When we attempted to check in with the battalion CP we discovered our phone was dead. I decided to check the wire and began crawling along the street. Suddenly, we heard *ping ping*; then we understood why the phone would not work. A German sniper had cut the wire and was lying in wait for it to be checked. Lucky for me, he was a lousy shot. Apmann and I, both brave but not stupid, decided that if battalion wanted to talk to us, they could check their wire.

General McBride immediately volunteered our division for combat duty in the Pacific War Theater. Consequently, the following morning we went into intensive Camp Blanding-type training.

However, this time we, the old men of the division, were the cadre. Waldrip and I were assigned to teach classes in the proper operation and codes for the SCR 300 and other front line radios. Actually we were good teachers, because we had learned under fire. The language was very similar to that used by police officers today. We used a phonetic alphabet: A-Able, B-Baker, C-Charley, etc. As for code, enemy soldiers were playmates, tank destroyers were red devils, etc. Units were lettered and numbered like such: Zebra one to Zebra seven could mean, command post to patrol seven. Also, there were certain things that were never said over a rifle company radio. First, you do not use rank (major, sergeant, captain) or unit (company, squad, division) designation. Next, do not give or describe your exact location, because the enemy can and will pick up your transmission. Finally, never say the word *repeat* over the air. Repeat to any artillery unit means, "Fire your last order." Therefore, if any supporting cannon company in the area happens to hear the word repeat at the wrong time, they might drop fifteen to twenty 105 mm shells right on top of your platoon.

Naturally, Waldrip and I thought (and still do) we were the best combat radiomen in the army. But, occasionally in the midst of a fire fight, our transmissions were not textbook perfect. Such was the case at Kassel; Captain Bettlinski was leading the company with Waldrip as his radioman, and I was with Lieutenant Jones and Colonel Hayes. Suddenly, the Germans counterattacked with tanks pinning down Bettlinski and his men. Waldrip immediately called for support, so the colonel ordered our tank destroyers to respond. In a very short time, Waldrip transmitted a message and I repeated it to Colonel Hayes. (The SCR 300 has a telephone handset, so only the operator hears the message.) The colonel frowned quizzically and said, "Ask him what he means." So I gave Waldrip, "Say again, say again, over." He replied, exactly as before, "Our red devils are having a field day." Not wanting to disturb the colonel with the same message, I prompted Waldrip with, "Able one to able seven, be more specific, over." This time he came back loud and clear with, "Our TDs are kicking their ———." I had only repeated the first three words, when the colonel said, "That's enough Clark, he just means that his support is having the desired effect."

In addition to the Olympic swimming stadium, the Nazis had built an enormous parade grounds at Nuremberg for their annual Party Day celebrations. It was about one mile square and had a raised concrete reviewing stand at one end that was overshadowed (until our tanks and artillery blew it to bits) by a large Nazi emblem.

Naturally, as soon as General Patton saw the parade grounds, he could not resist the temptation of showing off on Hitler's personal territory. Therefore, we, the Eightieth Division, were chosen for the honor of giving him a parade. At the end of our training cycle at Camp Blanding, we had been reviewed by Brigadier General Edwin Fales. This, however, would be a little different. In addition to General George S. Patton Jr., a four star, on the reviewing stand was Lieutenant General Walton H. Walker, the XX Corps Commander, three star, Major General Hobart J. Gay, Patton's two star chief of staff, ten to fifteen division commanders who were two star major generals, plus the Third Army's staff of seven one star brigadier generals, and twenty-seven bird colonels. No doubt, we were the sloppiest marchers in the United States Army, as we tried to keep in step wearing full field gear including steel helmets and combat boots. But Patton made up for our lack of luster by wearing his battle dress uniform with his pearl handle six-shooters and all his medals. Actually, we all shared his honors because he said, "You win them and I'll wear them for you."

Apparently General Patton thought we could fight better than we could march because, the following day, we were ordered back into combat. At 5:00 A.M., we loaded into trucks and were transported about fifty miles to a point just south of Regensburg. After we dismounted, we walked about eight miles, past almost every kind of United States Army unit. When we stopped to rest, Lazar, our forward observer, told us that our cannon company was already in position and waiting for us to attack.

A German SS "Werewolf" Division had stopped one of our green divisions north of the town of Dingolfing in the foothills of the Alps. We moved through the stalled division's supporting artillery and approached the MLR. Finally, we saw our cannon company's 105s pointing upward at a sharp angle. This indicated we would be advancing 200 to 300 yards behind their fire. (When a howitzer or other artillery piece fires almost straight up, the shells go high then come straight down.) The enemy was well dug-in and supported by emplaced artillery and a few medium tanks. However, when we jumped off, our corps artillery's big guns, 155s and 240s, joined our smaller 105s, so all we had to do was clean out a few machine gun nests and strong points, then move in and mop up the snipers in Dingolfing.

Many years later, in New Albany, Indiana, I overheard a German war bride from Dingolfing describing American soldiers to her friends. They were, she said, "so sweet and kind, except those who first entered our town and they were *mean* and *nasty*." She would have been mean and nasty too if she had been rousted out of a good warm building with a dry concrete floor and sent back to a cold, wet, muddy foxhole just because some hardheaded, fanatic Nazis wanted to die for their Fuehrer. Actually her description was very mild. Most Germans referred to us, Patton's Third Army, as "Roosevelt's Butchers." Of course they never said it to our face.

From Dingolfing, we moved southeast and on 2 May 1945, my nineteenth birthday, we captured Simbach on the German side of the Inn River. The following morning, we walked across a stone bridge into Branau, Austria, Adolph Hitler's birthplace, without firing a shot. In fact, I don't think any of us in the platoon knew, or cared, where any of the Nazis were born. Our concern was seeing that they died as soon as possible.

At Branau, our division was split into three Regimental Combat Teams (RCT). Our regiment, the 317th, teamed up with the Third Cavalry Group as a Task Force (TF) with orders to rapidly penetrate as far into Austria as possible in order to prevent fanatical SS units from forming a guerrilla force in the mountains.

To the north of us, other units of the Third Army happily advanced deep into Czechoslovakia, with glee, as liberators. The Czechs were not at war with the United States. Therefore, fraternization was not only permitted, it was encouraged. The Sixteenth Armored Division liberated Pilsen, world famous for its pilsener beer. Advanced units of the Fourth Armored Division entered the suburbs of Prague, but were ordered to withdraw by General Eisenhower, leaving the capital city to the Soviet Union in accordance with agreements made at Yalta (February 1945) by Stalin, Churchill, and Roosevelt.

From Branau, we advanced against occasional scattered resistance, losing a few men to rifle and machine gun fire from the distant wooded hills. When this occurred, the cavalry would dash off in their reconnaissance cars with their .50 caliber machine guns blazing. As they bounced across the fields, they reminded us of wild west cowboys going after the Indians in our old western movies.

Soon after crossing into Austria, we were amazed to see the snow-capped mountains in the distance. The Alps appeared to be only ten to fifteen miles away; actually they were forty to fifty miles further. When we got closer we used a captured German Navy to look at the mountain goats high in the Alps. The range finder was a beautiful piece of equipment. It was about four inches in diameter and forty-eight inches long. It looked like a telescope with the eyepiece in the center of the tube and viewfinders on either end. Mounted on a tripod, it had a range of twenty to twenty-five miles and was originally built to be used on a battleship. I am not exactly sure when or where it came into our company's possession. However, we did capture the Zeiss-Ikon optical plant near Erfurt and perhaps it went into somebody's loot bag while we were there. It had probably been stashed in the ammunition trailer with the cook tent since that time. I am almost certain we did not capture a

German battleship after we drank all the champagne in Bad Durkheim, but if we had, none of us would remember anything about it.

We did not see any Austrian cities that appeared to have been bombed or shelled, nor did we meet any resistance in or near inhabited places. Also, the Austrian people seemed to have fared better than the Germans during the war. Their farms were well stocked, they had plenty of food, and they were healthier and better clothed than the German civilians. Toward us, the Austrians were cordial but wary. Many expressed relief at being occupied by the United States rather than the Russians. They had no way of knowing that by secret agreement, their country had already been given to the Soviet Union at Yalta.

According to one "historical" account, "The attacks through Austria were largely a matter of hopping on trucks and watching the scenery roll by for the 317th infantrymen. Although isolated points of resistance were met and reduced." (*The Thundering Herd, 317th Regimental Newspaper*. 26 Sept. 1945. The writer was a member of regimental headquarters who never get near the front lines.)

Where this writer saw any trucks is beyond me and the only hopping we saw was by the enormous Austrian jackrabbits. As a matter of fact, we cleared the last seventy miles of the war in the same manner as the first 250 across Luxembourg and Germany, walking through mud, snow, and knee-deep water or crawling through the same stuff while machine gun and rifle bullets were singing over our backs. When we were lucky enough to ride, our chariot was the top of a Sherman tank.

Near Voecklabruck, Austria, we finally got the chance to show our stuff and prove our excellent marksmanship. Our company, supported by tanks, was advancing single file, ten to fifteen yards apart, along a highway in a valley between two hills. Suddenly, a medium-size deer, which had been disturbed by the enemy, darted from the woods about 200 yards away on our right. The excited animal ran straight toward our column and crossed the highway—almost colliding with Knobby—then scampered up the other hill into the woods. At first sighting, one of our men fired at it so naturally the rest of us joined in. Collectively, we fired at least 800 shots and every one of them missed the deer. The Germans in the woods were probably laughing themselves silly at our deer hunt. After the war, we all proudly wore our sharpshooter medals.

Near Bad Ischl, units of the Third Cavalry, in reconnaissance cars, and the Seventy-first Infantry, on tanks, raced past us and liberated another Nazi concentration camp at Ebensee, Austria. We arrived about six hours later and found that Ebensee was just as bad as Buchenwald. It was not as large and did not have gas chambers for mass killing or ovens with which to incinerate the bodies. However, by the large number of bodies stacked like cordwood, and the size of the lime pits, it was apparent that the Nazis had been killing day and night in an attempt to destroy as much evidence as possible before we arrived. Fortunately for some, the Third Cavalry arrived just in time. Early that morning, the Germans had herded about 6,000 inmates into a railroad tunnel and were preparing to blow up both ends in order to bury the prisoners alive. They were saved by only minutes.

The concentration camp at Ebensee contained about 12,000 inmates who were alive when we liberated it and we counted approximately 4,000 dead bodies and skulls. This camp differed from Buchenwald in that these inmates were Austrian, German, Italian, Czechoslovakian, and a few other European nationalities. These "Enemies of the State" were teachers, preachers, senators, representatives, government officials, and just average citizens.

Under Nazi Germany's thought control, hate crime laws any person who disapproved of any action taken by members of the Nazi Party was called a Communist or Jew lover and was subject to imprisonment. The Secret Police (Gestapo) arrested thousands of good, patriotic German citizens who they only suspected of having thoughts in opposition to Hitler's government. In fact, in order to control the thoughts of the people, Hitler banned many foreign and domestic newspapers shortly after his rise to power in 1933. Any citizen caught with an illegal newspaper was sentenced to a concentration camp for three to six years. However, once in prison, the person was classified as an enemy of the state and therefore, was not subject to release at the end of their term.

Many examples were made in order to instill fear into the hearts of the general public. A case in point occurred in the city of Stettin in 1936, when 280 factory workers were arrested after a paid Gestapo agent accused them of reading an illegal newspaper. After a mock public trial in a "People's Court," they were all shipped to the infamous Dachau concentration camp and records do not indicate that any of them were ever released.

In this police state, neighbor informed on neighbor, children informed on parents, students informed on teachers, and parishioners informed on preachers until everyone in the entire country lived in terror of a knock at the door in the middle of the night.

There were few, if any, Jews at Ebensee. However, these people, like those at Buchenwald, were dignified, intelligent, and without joy at being liberated, because they too expected nothing more from the United States of America than what they had received from the Nazis.

In later years, we, the soldiers who liberated the concentration camps, rightfully placed the primary responsibility for the Holocaust on the leaders of the Nazi regime. However, after being an eyewitness to the results of bad political leadership, we never again fully trusted our own elected officials.

We passed through the Seventy-first Division at Ebensee and proceeded to attack south, southeast toward Graz, Austria. Our next encounter with the enemy occurred near Leizen, seventy miles south of Linz. With my squad in the lead, Company B was advancing cautiously, single file, along a two-lane road. Suddenly, Little, the point man, halted and reported he was hearing strange noises and picking up a strong smell of something similar to dead horses. Knobby and I, as his radioman, responded to the head of the column.

Resuming the march, we soon came around a bend in the road and were face to face with what appeared to be an army of civilian refugees filling the road and countryside from hill to hill. As we approached, the smell of their open fire cooking was worse to us, than dead horses, and the reported strange noise turned out to be a foreign language that none of us had ever heard before. Then, we saw some of the men appeared to be armed with old, rusty rifles. To our surprise, we learned that they were the Imperial Guard of the Royal Hungarian Army. What we had taken for civilian rabble was, in fact, officials of the Hungarian Government who were escaping from the advancing Russian Army with their families. (The Hungarian Field Army, serving under German Field Marshal Friedrich von Paulus, had been destroyed at Stalingrad, Russia in December 1942.)

As soon as the Hungarian officers became aware of who we were, they informed us, through an interpreter, that they were allies of the Germans and insisted we take their surrender. Captain Bettlinski and Lieutenant Jones wanted no part of them, so Knobby reported our plight to battalion headquarters. In response, Colonel Hayes replied, "We do not want to guard and feed them, tell them to burn their weapons and keep walking toward the rear." In a very short time, we realized that the battalion commander had overestimated the military intelligence of the Royal Hungarian Army. Neither the colonel nor we had any idea they would be dumb enough to leave their rifles and pistols loaded when they set fire to them. However, as soon as we heard *pop, pop, pop, crack, crack, crack*, we fully understood the extent of our error, and went flat on our stomachs and stayed there until the fires cooled down.

The Hungarians were a very friendly and pleasant people. They did not ask for anything, but appeared to be short of food so we gave them most of the rations we were carrying. Apmann, speaking

German, told their general that they would be well fed and cared for when they reached our prisoner of war camp.

Boy, were we dumb!

By packing the Hungarians off to the rear, once again, we missed our chance to be famous. (By the time the reporters arrived in Buchenwald, Generals Patton and Eisenhower were there, so naturally we were ignored as liberators. Then, at Kassel, *Life* magazine arrived with New York's own "Fighting Sixty-ninth" a week after we had taken the city from die-hard SS troops.) As it turned out, two weeks later, the capture of the Royal Hungarian Army's Imperial Guard hit the front page of the *Chicago Tribune* and almost every other major newspaper in the United States.

Two days after we refused to take them, their surrender was accepted by Eightieth Division Headquarters. However, while they were being processed as prisoners of war, Hungarian-born, Master Sergeant William J. DeHuszar, of the intelligence section, uncovered a startling fact: not only were they the Imperial Guard of the Royal Hungarian Army, they were carrying the State Treasury of Hungary, including their total gold reserves when they tried to surrender to Lieutenant Knoll and me.

It seems after we left them without weapons, they became nervous and buried everything of value. According to Associated Press published reports in the *Chicago Tribune*, 21 May 1945, "The treasure trove dug out of the mountains included 4,000,000 pengos, 130,000,000 dollars at the present (1945) rate of exchange, 29,000 kilograms of gold bullion worth $30,000,000, complete sets of banknote plates for printing all Hungarian currency, plus other wealth representing most of the capital interest and individual deposits of Hungary removed from Budapest before the Russians captured that city on 13 February 1945. Also in the mountainside were more than 1,000,000,000 (German) reichmarks, $159,000 in American currency, and six cases of priceless art treasure." General McBride notified Third Army Headquarters of the find and General Patton responded by ordering that everything be secured and packed for shipment to the United States. Most of the treasure, including the gold bullion, was returned shortly after the war to the duly constituted Communist government. However, the Royal Jewels, including St. Stephen's one-thousand-year-old Byzantine crown, which was studded with gems and decorated with miniatures depicting religious scenes, were kept by the United States for over thirty years. In 1978, as a goodwill gesture, President James Earl Carter Jr. ordered them removed from our gold vault at Fort Knox, Kentucky, and returned to the Government of Hungary.

On the morning of 8 May 1945, Company B was advancing cautiously across a field of grain. Knobby was on the point, not meeting any resistance, with Waldrip as his radioman, and I was about 200 feet behind them carrying an SCR 300 radio for our new forward observer. Lieutenant Lazar, our old FO, and his radioman had been injured the day before in a jeep accident. Suddenly, the green lieutenant asked Captain Bettlinski to halt the column, saying he wanted to register his guns. Actually, we all knew he was just showing off and wanted to see some shells explode. Anyway, he gave me a fire order and I transmitted it to the cannon company but instead of the usual reply, "On the way," we received:

"Halt in place! Fire only if fired upon" . . . our war in Europe was over!

Chapter XVI
"Report to Russian Army Headquarters"

At the European war's end, midnight, 8 May 1945, there were still over 2,000,000 German troops in the field. The American and Russian Armies had met at a number of points but we, on the front line, had no reason to believe that a die-hard Nazi SS unit might not attack just for the glory of dying for the Fuehrer. Also, considering the distance separating our division from the Russian Army, it was altogether possible that an isolated enemy unit might not receive the news of the German surrender. Therefore, we dug in, set up machine gun nest and mortar positions, establishing a final defense line. Our specific orders were not to allow anyone, soldier or civilian, to pass through our line and we were not allowed to accept any surrenders. Everyone and everything in front of our MLR belonged to the Russian Army. On 10 May 1945, the Third Cavalry Reconnaissance Platoon moved through our lines and began searching for the Russian Army. After a few days without incident, our MLR was reduced to outpost and roadblocks. This allowed most of us to come out of our foxholes. Near Leizen, Austria, we found a group of buildings, which from all appearances had been recently occupied by the Royal Hungarian Army. Therefore, our first post-war task was to make our new home habitable. In order to do this, we had to burn everything except the buildings. From the size of our bonfires, it's a wonder we did not melt the snow off the top of the nearby Alps.

As soon as the last shot was fired in Europe, General McBride volunteered for service with General MacArthur in the theater of war. Naturally, not wanting to get lonely, he decided to take us with him. So, at our first assembly, Captain Bettlinski informed us that we would soon be redeployed to fight the Japanese Army in the Pacific. The captain went on to say that the general did not want us to become dull and careless, so we would immediately begin to train for jungle warfare.

For the first time since Camp Blanding, we were given an established routine: assembly, sick call, mess call, field training, and best of all, off-duty time. In combat nothing is routine; assembly is simply keeping a sharp eye on the point man and maintaining your distance from the other men in the squad so that one well-placed mortar round does not kill everyone, sick call is a yell for the medic, mess call is a cold can of C-rations, field training is seeing how quickly and how deeply you can dig when the fire fight starts, and there is no such thing as off-duty time. Also, on the front line, privacy, modesty, and personal hygiene do not exist. Toothpaste, shaving cream, and even soap, at times, were luxuries we learned to do without. An occasional Saturday night bath was accomplished with a steel helmet half full of cold, muddy water. However, each K-ration meal included a packet of a very essential items. We were the only combat soldiers in history to be supplied with toilet tissue. Latrines and bath houses were twenty to forty miles behind the front. Therefore, all strictly personal functions were very public and needs were met in full view of other members of the platoon.

The training at Leizen was unlike Blanding in that the officers and men were more relaxed and informal. In fact, when the company assembled for morning roll call, Knobby, in front of the platoon, would salute the captain, who was almost 100 feet away, and sing out his report. However, we in the platoon, being much closer, could tell what Bettlinski took for, "All present and accounted for," was actually, "What in the world are we standing out here for?"—or words to that effect.

Off-duty time was spent playing baseball, walking in the foothills of the Alps, writing letters, or just catching up on some of the sleep we had lost over the past few months. Somewhere we had acquired a phonograph and one record, but after hearing "Honeysuckle Rose" a few hundred times it ceased to be entertaining.

There were two very fascinating things in this section of Austria: peat and jackrabbits. The peat could be dug right out of the hillside. Then, when it had been dried for a day or two, it would burn like wood. The jackrabbits, with big long ears, were as large as beagle hounds and they would not run until we were almost close enough to touch them. We were still fully armed at all times, so naturally on one of my walks in the hills, I decided to bring back a jackrabbit for supper. Hitting something that big, even with an inaccurate .30 caliber carbine and my aim was no great accomplishment. However, after carrying the "twenty pound" (probably more like eight) animal about one-half mile, I tossed it in a ditch. I don't like little rabbits for food, much less one that tastes like horse meat. Actually, we had no use for the jackrabbit; since the war had ended, we were getting three good meals a day, which included pies, cakes, ice cream, and Cokes.

At the roadblocks and outpost, we had not encountered any enemy troops, but we still remained ready for combat; we wore steel helmets and carried fully loaded weapons at all times. Also, we remained dressed, including boots, except when bathing or changing clothes. In fact, we felt a little nervous and uneasy because Third Army Command was aware that we were in the Russian zone of occupation. Therefore, they did not bring up our heavy support guns or equipment.

Within a few days, the advance party, a general staff, and about 200 reconnaissance troops of the Russian Army arrived and occupied their side of the line. Naturally, we had to throw a big party for them, and they had to try to outdo us with a bigger one. The Russians sent over one of their Cossacks to serve as an orderly to General McBride and to reciprocate he returned the courtesy. I would like to think I was chosen for my looks and military bearing, but actually I just happened to walk into the company command post as the first sergeant said, "Yes Sir" into the field telephone. Turning to me, the first man he saw, he barked, "Clark, report to battalion headquarters, they want a man for a three-day detail." If he had known what the detail consisted of he would have taken it himself. At the battalion CP, I was given a shoe polish kit, a white coat, and a few quick instructions, then driven over to the Russian headquarters.

The Russians were tired and dusty from their long drive in open jeeps. I was immediately impressed by their quick acceptance and courtesy. However, I was surprised that the Russian officers would not eat until they were assured that their men were being fed and quartered in buildings. (Any American officer, from Lieutenant Knoll to General McBride, would have known that their soldiers were carrying enough rations for three days, and any sergeant could have found quarters for his men.)

The general to whom I was assigned was an army commander, equal in rank to General Patton. His name was Malinowsky. The commander's uniform was made of a coarse, heavy material and his boots were thick, hard leather, which made them easy to polish. He had a chest full of medals that appeared to be riveted to the cloth.

Shortly after I arrived, he lay down to rest. A few minutes later, I noticed he was breathing hard and appeared to be choking, so I stepped out in the street and called to an American colonel. The colonel responded immediately with an American doctor and two Russian officers. Thanks to the doctor, he was soon breathing normally. However, I heard the interpreter tell the colonel that the general did have a "slight" medical problem that had been aggravated by the dusty ride. As they started to leave, the colonel turned to me and said, "Watch him like a hawk, and if he so much as sneezes, I want to know it immediately." Fortunately, he did not have any more problems in my presence.

At the formal meeting of our two armies, the Russian honor guard faced one company of our troops in front of a hastily-erected reviewing stand in the town square. General Malinowsky's speech was short, but very appropriate; he said, "The soldiers and officers of the Soviet Army greet the soldiers and officers of the American Army. The soldiers and officers of the Soviet Army salute the soldiers and officers of the American Army." General McBride's response was just as short, but I was standing between two officers who were speaking Russian, so I could not make out what he said.

Unfortunately General McBride's party for the Russians did not proceed exactly as planned. He had intended to serve them a very formal dinner. However, to his surprise he discovered that his guests were very informal, preferring vodka and bourbon to fish and beef. Also, he was astonished to learn that the Russian officers, including General Malinowsky, seldom sit down and, unlike American officers, they do not expect nor want to be served. The affair turned out to be more of a medieval feast than a formal dinner party. Only about fifteen to twenty American generals and colonels were the guests of General McBride, so it was interesting to see full bird colonels peeping in the windows as the party progressed.

After the dinner, the tables were removed and the entertainment began. As General Malinowsky's orderly, I was permitted to remain and watch what appeared to be a U.S.O. troupe. There was a swing band, dancers, singers, and a group of Chinese acrobats. Although the Russians continued to talk and drink during the show, it was apparent by their applause that they thoroughly enjoyed every act.

The following day, General McBride and his staff met with the Russians to work out arrangements for our departure. General Malinowsky expressed amazement that we were not guarding a large nearby German armor repair and storage depot containing hundreds of tanks and pieces of equipment. Because we had captured it and it was in our possession, he inquired as to how long the American Army would need in order to remove it. General McBride quickly replied, "The war is over and we have absolutely no use for that pile of junk. We have no intention of guarding it while we are here and we are not taking any of it with us when we leave." The Russian was elated at the general's answer, and immediately proposed a toast to our great friendship. This was followed by a toast to Stalin, Roosevelt, Churchill, Eisenhower, and everyone else he could think of, including the brave American and Russian soldiers. However, as soon as the meeting broke up, trusting as he was, he placed Russian guards all around the captured German depot. Neither General McBride nor our United States Government had the slightest idea that most of these tanks would be repaired and, in less than six short years, would be used against American troops in Korea.

On reporting back to the company, I answered sick call and visited the doctor at the battalion aid station. Apparently after more than three months in a foxhole, I had developed more than just a persistent cough. The medical officer took one quick look at me and I was on my way to the field hospital at Bamberg, Germany. I received excellent care at Bamberg, but the rest helped more than the medication. It was a real treat to sleep on white sheets and drink pure water that did not taste like kerosene.

Chapter XVII
Patton's Best General: Horace L. McBride

Returning to duty with the company, I was pleasantly surprised to find that we were now stationed in the beautiful Bavarian Alps. Our new home was Fussen in Allgau, Germany (population 10,000). Company B headquarters was located just two miles from one of the most fascinating buildings in the world, Neuschwanstein, or "the Storybook Castle." It was the pride of King Ludwig II, "the Crazy King" of Bavaria, who died in 1886. With old Ludwig no longer there, I had no desire to visit. It was very impressive from a distance, but I never thought it would be worth the walk just to see the inside of an unoccupied building.

Again I walked into the command post at exactly the right minute. As luck would have it, the company was out on a field problem and battalion headquarters had requested a man for special assignment. The duty officer, not knowing what the detail would be, barked, "Clark, report to the battalion CP" and, being an old combat soldier, I knew better than to question an assignment. As a military axiom goes, "The army can't make you do anything, but it can make you wish you had."

At battalion headquarters, I was informed that the army was establishing an Information and Education school in Fussen where everything from auto repair to French would be taught. My special assignment was to live in the school, the Hotel Bahnhof, as "charge of quarters" (CQ) and inspect the building every weeknight after it had been cleaned by the German cleaning ladies. Also I would sign for an occasional delivery of supplies. This gave me a lot of free time to read, write letters, and to walk along the banks of the Lech River and think of home.

The ground floor of the hotel was occupied by our large kitchen, two dining rooms (one for officers, one for enlisted men), the major's office, and a foyer. The second floor was classrooms. The only residents of the building, the mess sergeant and I, lived on the third floor. Naturally, as the charge of quarters, I chose a nice big corner room with a beautiful view of the Alps. The personal belongings of the hotel owner, including thirty to forty pair of skis, were stored in the attic and basement. Unfortunately, we discovered the skis after the war in Europe had ended. Before 8 May 1945, they could have been considered captured German war equipment and sent home as souvenirs.

There was a nice photograph of the town of Fussen hanging in the officers' dining room. However, I knew if it disappeared, questions would be asked, because I was not the only one who admired it. Opportunity knocked when I picked up a stack of old magazines at the company CP for our day room. Right on top was a *Life* magazine cover, the exact size of the picture frame, which was graced with a full color photo of President Roosevelt. The following morning, not one officer complained about the missing picture of Fussen, or, for that matter, even asked why it had been replaced.

The people of Fussen (Tyrolians) were not typical Germans or Austrians. According to liberated American prisoners of war who had been held in or near the town, most of the natives were anti-Nazi. In fact, many Fusseners secretly fed and cared for our men at great peril to themselves. The owners of the bakery and the newspaper (*Fussener Zeitung*) had taken exceptional risks during the last two years of the war. Consequently, when we arrived, we made sure that these friendly enemies did not lack for any of the necessities of life. The baker received plenty of flour, sugar, and other supplies and we kept the newspaper busy with orders for stationery, unit newspapers, and souvenir editions.

The Burgomaster was also an honorable man. He and his family spoke English very well and were of great assistance in communicating with German civilians who worked for me at the school. Fraternization was still forbidden by the army, but official contact was allowed. Therefore, due to our business association, I was able to have dinner with his family numerous times in the town castle. The 300-year-old building was originally built as the residence of the Bishop of Augsburg. I declined an invitation to stay overnight, because its stone walls and floors caused it to be cold, drafty, and damp, even in the warm months of June, July, and August. I much preferred my quarters at the resort hotel.

We were allowed to patronize the many shops that were open in Fussen as long as there was no social contact. The barber, print shop, bookstore, laundress, and other merchants were required to accept German or American (invasion) currency. However, every one of them preferred to barter for cigarettes, soap, candy, gum, or coffee. It was surprising to discover that many things we considered common necessities were actually luxuries that these people had not enjoyed for many years.

We were permitted to have our personal laundry done locally by German civilians or we could send it to the Army Quartermaster Laundry unit and expect to receive about one-half of it back in six to ten days. Naturally, we chose to find a washerwoman. In my first experience with a laundress, I left a large bar of army-issued (the same old Octagon brand we manufactured at Colgate) laundry soap with my clothes. When I returned the following day to pick them up, they were folded neatly with the slightly used soap bar lying on top of them. The lady was amazed when I said, "You are welcome to the soap, I don't need it." She protested, saying, "Nein, nein," then went on to explain in broken English that soap was very valuable and she could not accept something worth that much for just one small stack of laundry. I left the fifty marks, invasion currency, on the table and insisted she keep the soap. No doubt she was the happiest laundress in Fussen, because one American mark was worth ten German marks on the open market.

On 2 September 1945, life began again in Fussen.

The two atomic bombs dropped on the Japanese home islands ended the Pacific War. Suddenly we realized our fighting days were over. We would not be the final assault force against the Imperial Japanese Army. We turned in our steel helmets, hand grenades, and explosives, keeping only our personal protection rifle, carbine, or pistol and a few rounds of ammunition. Training was relaxed and more soldiers became students at the school.

Nonfraternization rules, a farce from the beginning, were revised. Fines, $65 for social contact, could now be paid in German marks. Also, infractions of this rule would no longer be placed in the soldier's personnel file. The fine could easily be obtained by selling a pack of cigarettes. Soldiers were welcome in German taverns, but German girls were not allowed in noncommissioned officers' (NCO) clubs or day rooms. The NCO club in Fussen was the most popular place in town, with its German band, German beer, and American Coca-Cola. The beer was tasteless and contained only two percent alcohol, so most of us stayed with Coke.

De-Nazification began suddenly with a startling twist. American soldiers and German citizens awoke to find every building in town plastered with posters depicting the horrors of the concentration camps, captioned, "Whose Fault?" The implication was that every German shared the guilt and responsibility for these excesses, which in a sense was true. Immediately, American Military Government established rules and guidelines in order that this individual and collective guilt could be erased. In effect, these edicts barred all Germans who had ever been members of the Nazi Party from holding any position above that of a common laborer until they had been de-Nazified. General Patton was one of the first American commanders to condemn these decrees. They were unenforceable, he said, because most honest Germans would readily admit they were guilty of party membership. Apparently the de-Nazification rules were written by the same group of people who gave us nonfraternization. However, in a very short time, de-

Nazification became the larger farce, because any officer, from second lieutenant to general could and did de-Nazify the best-looking German girls for "secretaries."

Like most German towns, Fussen's main square was graced with a large, thirty foot statue of the Kaiser. During the war, these objects had provided a great amount of pleasure to our tankers who enjoyed blasting them off their pedestals. However, Fussen was occupied after 8 May 1945, so their Kaiser survived. Naturally, he posed a temptation to two teenage soldiers who would have liked to place some plastic explosives around his ankles and blow him sky high. But alas, the war was over, so one night about midnight, Bernard Huck and I scaled him like mountain climbers and placed a real World War I German spiked helmet on his head. The local citizens did not think it was funny, but no one attempted to remove it as long as we were in Fussen. Ironically, the joke was on us, because today a spiked helmet is valued at more than $500.

Major General Horace L. McBride, our wartime commanding general, was promoted to command the XX Corps. Naturally, this man, in our opinion, was the best general in the United States Army. According to reports in the *New York Times*, his command post was always located more forward than any other division commander. Perhaps this was one reason he was chosen by General Patton to lead the American counterattack against the German Army in the Battle of the Bulge. General McBride was about five feet, seven inches tall and weighed around 140 pounds. He was in his mid-50s but looked older. We never saw him frown but he was not ashamed to cry especially when his artillery commander and close friend, Brigadier General Edmund W. Searby, was killed in action.

In previous wars, we read about generals having their horses shot from under them; "Hairless Horace" was no exception. He seldom required his front line company, battalion, or regimental commanders to come back to his division command post; instead, he went forward to theirs. Therefore, he was often under enemy fire so it was no surprise to him or to us when his driver rushed into the First Battalion CP and announced, "General, a German 88 just destroyed your jeep." To this, looking calmly toward Colonel Hayes, he said, "That's O.K. I'll take his." When he got back to his rear headquarters a week later, he picked up a new jeep and sent the major's back up to the front. The general was very close to his troops. In fact, he even allowed Corporal Pettingill to draw a comic strip in the division newspaper using him as one of the characters. He could have easily passed for General Halftrack in the Beetle Bailey strip.

Chapter XVIII
Respite

With World War II finally over, President Harry S. Truman ordered his military commanders to demobilize the Armed Forces of the United States. Consequently, one of the first steps in reducing the size of the army was a process called redeployment. Unfortunately, the same bureaucratic brains who gave us nonfraternization and de-Nazification were assigned the task of planning and carrying out redeployment and demobilization. Their solution was a point system, which took into consideration age, marital status, number of children, and length of service.

This point system would have been fair, if all things had been equal up to this point. However, while we were fighting, nothing was considered too expensive for us. Now with the killing stopped, in order to save money, politicians decided that married soldiers with children would be sent home first, and rear echelon troops, who had spent years in a relatively safe environment, went next. Combat riflemen, who for the most part were eighteen years old with less than one year of service, were not even considered eligible for return to the United States. Therefore, we had another year to spend overseas.

On the day the war ended in Europe, American Army units occupied most of Germany, large portions of Czechoslovakia, and Northwest Austria. The almost straight American front line extended from Tangermunde, forty miles north of Magdeburg, Germany, to Leizen, Austria, seventy miles south of Linz. Consequently, in order to comply with the Yalta Agreement we had to evacuate about two-thirds of this captured territory. Of the cities taken by the Eightieth Division, Kassel went to the British; Eisenach, Erfurt, Weimer, Jena, and Gera were handed over to the Russians, who also got all of Czechoslovakia and Austria. This realignment of armies caused considerable crowding in some areas, but we were fortunate to be almost forgotten in the Alps.

With redeployment, the army educational system was canceled and the school closed. We were informed that the Eightieth was to be deactivated immediately, becoming a paper or ghost unit. This meant older, high point, men would be transferred to other units for transportation home and we, the younger ones, would be assigned to the occupation army. In order to accomplish these transfers smoothly, my unit, the First Battalion, moved into Garmish-Partinkirchen, Germany, with elements of the Tenth Armored Division.

Garmish, a beautiful winter resort city of 20,000, lies on a flat plain surrounded by enormous mountains. On the east, the Wank rises to 5,240 feet; to the south, the Kreuzeck to 5,420 feet; to the southeast, the Alpspitze to 7,248; and to the southwest on the Austrian border, Germany's highest mountain, the majestic Zugspitze, reached 9,782 feet.

The fighting phase of the war did not reach this area of Germany. Therefore, there was no bomb or shell damage and many of the tourist attractions were still in operating order. One of the most fascinating of these, without a doubt, was the Wankbahn, a pair of small, fifteen-man capacity cable cars that traversed between Partinkirchen and the top of Wank Mountain. Naturally, many of us teenage soldiers wanted to try everything, so we boarded the gondola for the twenty minute trip to the summit. However, at the last minute, some of the bravest combat riflemen took one look at the size of the cable and refused to get in, leaving our car with only seven riders. I am not sure the spectacular view from the top of the mountain was worth the trip. Honestly, I must admit one ride in a cable car the size of a hot air balloon basket is enough for a lifetime. Fifty years later, I still have nightmares of being stranded on top of the mountain with no way down. In fact, I was so scared going up, I turned down two opportunities to reenter the swinging little box for the trip back down the cable.

Our unit was assigned to maintain law and order in the area. Actually, all we did was ride around town or out in the foothills in a jeep or command car sightseeing. Occasionally, we would visit with the men of the Tenth Armored Division who were guarding the prisoner of war compound on the outskirts of Garmish. This open air compound held nearly 30,000 potentially dangerous SS troops. Many of these fanatics surrendered only after the Nazi government of Admiral Karl Doenitz had been taken into custody by the Allies at Flensburg, on the Danish border, on 23 May 1945. These prisoners, like all others, were treated in accordance with the Geneva Convention governing the treatment of prisoners of war. However, due to their nature and the crimes attributed to them, security was very tight.

The prisoners were confined to small, barbed wire enclosures and were housed in tents. The outer compound was surrounded by double fences topped with barbed wire and machine gun towers about every 200 feet. Tanks, half-tracks, and battle-dressed troops were on constant patrol and the entire camp was lighted at night with large, 12,000,000 candlepower searchlights. Machine gunners were ordered to fire occasional bursts between the outer fences just to unnerve the prisoners and to show we would, if necessary, shoot prisoners who tried to escape.

This camp also held some of the major war criminals who were awaiting trial before the International War Crimes Tribunal. SS Chief Heinrich Himmler's niece was being held there in a special cell, because she stripped naked and tried to seduce one of the guards soon after her capture. When I saw her, she did not look enticing. She was a big blond, weighing about 190 pounds, with short, straight hair; her face was very mannish and her eyes cold and hard. I was amazed at how closely she resembled Ilsa Koch, the Bitch of Buchenwald.

Our regiment was spread out over a large area of the Bavarian Alps, just north of the Swiss border. The regimental command post was located at Murnau, our personnel section in Oberammergau, home of the world-famous Passion Play, and our rest camp at the playground of Royalty, Walchen See. Due to our status as a redeployment staging unit in the process of being dissolved, we had few military duties and were not required to drill, train, or stand inspections. We were called out for assembly only twice while we were located at Garmish. Free time and jeeps and reconnaissance cars were in abundance for transportation. Therefore, we spent many days touring our "little bit of Switzerland," as the area was described by Captain Robert A. Walker who commanded the rest center. Captain Walker was justly proud of his elaborate resort and treated us like millionaire tourists on vacation. In addition to all types of sports and games, sailboats, motorboats, and rowboats were free for the asking, and there was no time limit as to how long we spent out on the beautiful Alpine lake.

Also, while stationed at Garmish-Partinkirchen, we were treated to the biggest entertainment event of our lives, an exciting U.S.O. show, "Radio City Music Hall Revue." The three and a half hour show featured Hollywood star Alan Jones with the fabulous Rockettes and the Music Hall Corps de Ballet from New York City. Waldrip and I were lucky enough to get good, fourth row center seats. These were actually better than the first three rows, because soldiers seated there became a part of the act during the vaudeville routines. The Rockettes were very good, actually acclaimed by many as the world's best, and the rest of the cast were all professional entertainers making it an enjoyable show we would never forget. Our short month in Garmish passed quickly. The once mighty Eightieth Infantry Division became smaller and smaller each day, as attrition took its toll. Finally, in early October of 1945, orders came through assigning me to the 508th Military Police Battalion at Munich, Germany.

I was not happy with my new unit designation. Of all the jobs in the army, being a military policeman did not rank high on my list. I really had hoped to become a part of the United States Army's new constabulary force, which was being formed to replace conventional combat units. The constabulary would be issued distinctive uniforms and considered elite troops. They would patrol the American zone of occupation in fast reconnaissance vehicles and, in case of civilian unrest, would be supported by quick response special troops.

Unfortunately, less than one year after the shooting stopped, the role of the United States Army in Europe changed dramatically. From an occupation army policing a defeated country, we again became a combat army confronting a powerful enemy. Our old German enemy was no longer a threat to the United States, but our old Russian friend suddenly became an adversary. Consequently at the first indication of Premier Joseph Stalin's saber rattling, General of the Army, Dwight D. Eisenhower immediately scrapped the constabulary force and returned the United States Army to a war-like stance, with infantry and armored divisions at the ready supported by air wings.

Chapter XIX
Munich: Beautiful But Dangerous

During World War II, almost all city police officers in Germany were members of the Nazi Party. Therefore, as Allied Armies captured cities and towns, the local police force was disarmed and disbanded. Then, when combat troops moved out, civil order was restored and maintained by military police (MP) units. This system was very effective while the war was still in progress and martial law was in effect. However, with the cessation of hostilities, there came an urgent need to restore a civilian police system.

In order to understand the problem of law enforcement faced by both the United States Army and German authorities, it is necessary to recognize three basic laws:

(a) Combat law. To a combat soldier, every person in front of him or under his control is considered an enemy. Therefore, if the individual soldier perceives the slightest threat (violation of combat law), he immediately punishes the violator.

(b) Martial law. All civil rights cease to exist. All violations of military orders are considered a serious threat to good order and violators are severely punished by military authorities as the situation warrants.

(c) Civil law. Law violators are accorded all the benefits of a Civil Code of Law. Under the American justice system, all persons are presumed innocent until proven guilty in a court of law.

The European War had been over less than six months in October 1945, when I arrived in Munich. The city was, at that time, was under a combination of combat and martial law. However, American military government was making an attempt to restore some German civilian control. The local jail had been returned to German hands, and civilian hospitals were operating without military supervision. A few German police armed with rifles were being used during daylight hours directing traffic. However, the dangerous task of maintaining law and order in this city of 1,500,000 people fell to the men of the 508th Military Police Battalion, which numbered about 600.

The 508th, being a rear echelon unit, was filled with high point, long service men. Therefore, as soon as the war ended, they were among the first to be sent home. Consequently, Captain Tief and First Sergeant DeCamp were faced with the almost impossible task of making military police officers out of former combat soldiers and green replacements from the United States.

A soldier experiences a wide range of emotions. Lying in a cold, muddy foxhole is miserable, not exciting. Riding atop a thirty ton tank expecting to be blown to bits any minute is frightening, not exciting. Crawling through dragon's teeth, tank traps, with a bag of plastic explosives is nerve-racking, not exciting. Being a nineteen-year-old military policeman in Munich, Germany, is all of the above, plus excitement every minute of the day. In fact, much of the time, service on the streets of Munich was just as dangerous as in any front line rifle company.

When we arrived in Munich, we were surprised to learn that we were under another nonfraternization policy. Military police, we were informed, do not associate with soldiers from other units. We lived in a one block long, two-story brick building and were quartered four men to a room. Our dining room would have been a credit to any fine hotel and our meals were served on china plates by German civilians who also did the dishes.

A trip was made every day to the former Dachau Concentration Camp by a special detail that picked up German prisoners of war who cleaned and maintained the buildings in our compound. I got very well acquainted with Siegfried (Siggie), a former SS storm trooper who cleaned our room. He had fought in Africa, Italy, France, and Germany. He had nothing but contempt for German soldiers who lied and said they had only fought on the Russian front. Siggie said, "War is war, sure I fought against American soldiers; they were good fighters, I've got nothing to be ashamed of."

Duty was varied. We did street patrol in radio jeeps, eight hours on, sixteen hours off, usually four to six days in a row then three days off. Also, each company maintained two or three twelve-man quick response teams, called riot squads. The riot squad was actually the forerunner of the modern police Special Weapons And Tactics (S.W.A.T.) teams. We answered every call prepared to face any situation. With our red lights flashing and sirens screaming, we could respond to any location in Munich in a matter of minutes. When assigned to the riot squad, we were on orders to remain in the guardroom, fully dressed, carrying a .45 caliber Thompson submachine gun at all times. When the alarm sounded, as it often did, we would jump in the truck and be on our way in less than one minute. Our Thompson submachine gun gave us ample fire power to restore order. However, the Thompson is a very touchy weapon and, on one occasion, I jumped out of the riot truck at the scene of a disturbance and accidentally slammed the bolt forward. By the time both feet hit the ground, I had fired the twenty round magazine. Luckily, I was one of the first men out of the truck, so I did not hit any of our squad. Discretion being the better part of valor, I flattened out on the street and crawled under the truck to reload.

After a riot squad tour of duty, we were given forty-eight hours off, which we needed, to rest and relax. There were also fixed posts to be manned, traffic duty, walking patrols, and occasionally, we would be called on to assist the Army Criminal Investigation Division (CID) in apprehending a dangerous criminal. At first glance this duty gives the appearance of being routine, but MP service in Munich was never boring, dull, or routine. In fact, it was very unusual to complete an eight hour tour of duty without being involved in a dangerous situation. Also, it was a common occurrence to be involved in an incident where weapons were used and people were killed or wounded.

All patrols operated out of a central Military Law and Order (MLO) command post, which served as the police headquarters and radio base station. Motor patrols consisted of two or more men armed with .45 caliber pistols and/or Thompson submachine guns. Both weapons gave us tremendous, but inaccurate, fire power. Therefore, most of us always carried a personal, accurate .38 caliber pistol—mine was a Belgium Browning.

About two hours into our very first patrol, we were ordered to report to the MLO for special instructions. Here, for the first time, we learned that German prostitutes, in order to ply their trade legally in Munich, had to be registered. Also, in order to stay in the good graces of the authorities, they were required to report to clinics weekly for venereal disease checkups. Those who became infected or failed to report were put on a list and it was our job to find them and bring them in. This proved to be one of our easiest laws to enforce, because all German civilians were required to carry and show on demand an identification card. However, it still sounds unbecoming to admit that I ran all over Munich looking for prostitutes, especially those with venereal diseases.

Most German civilians were cooperative at curfew and passed check points. The mere mention of Cornelius Strasse, the location of the Munich City Jail, was enough to send fear into their hearts. Everyone was well aware that it had little food, cold floors to sleep on, and bad-tempered German jailers. Prostitutes also knew we could charge them with "suspected VD," which meant we would transport them to the women's hospital. There they would be tested, then sent to Cornelius Strasse for up to two weeks until results were obtained.

Trouble could come at any time. Johnny Reo and I were patrolling the beautiful English Garden by the art museum when we came upon a disturbance. Two German women, who appeared to be prostitutes (why else would they be out after dark in a park) were arguing with four or five black soldiers. After checking the women's ID cards and the soldier's passes, we allowed them to leave separately. However, a short time later, we encountered the same group again, still having words. The sergeant took me aside, while Reo watched the group, and explained that the women had taken their money and then refused their advances, saying they did not want to have anything to do with blacks. We immediately told the women they were under arrest for taunting American soldiers, and advised the sergeant to leave the area with his men, which he did without protest.

Now we faced another problem: one of the women refused to get in the jeep. Reo and I were both from the old school and thought we should always be nice to the ladies, so I called the MLO and explained our situation. The provost officer was very emphatic, "Clark," he said, "if she acts like a man, treat her like a man." She heard the transmission and, before I could hook the radio back on the dash, she was in the jeep with her friend. After that incident, I had no more qualms about arresting women.

As a part of our regular patrols, we were required to check all the beer houses in our sector. To say the least these "tavern checks" were not easy. First, one MP patrolman had to stay with the jeep because an unattended vehicle in Munich was stolen in seconds. This meant we entered alone, in our uniform of white gloves, white pistol belt, MP arm band, and glistening helmet liner with a big red "A" in the center; needless to say, we stood out like a sore thumb. Second, very few other soldiers when they are stone sober care for military police, so it is easy to imagine their feelings when they are roaring drunk.

Usually we got some nasty jeers as we made a quick survey for soldiers reported absent without leave (AWOL), government property being offered for sale, prostitutes on our wanted list, or other easy-to-observe violations. We had nightsticks in the jeep, but they were never carried on tavern checks. Their appearance, we were told, indicated to the drunks that we were looking for a fight. More than once, I wished the person responsible for the no nightstick rule could have accompanied me on a routine tavern check.

The Swartzwald Madel (meaning Blackforest Girl) was one of the nicest, quietest clubs in our sector, but anywhere there are drunks, there is the potential for trouble. Fortunately for us, on one occasion, we followed standard procedure to the letter. Reo parked near the entrance, got out of the jeep armed with the Thompson submachine gun, and posted himself about six feet from the door of the club. My job was to step inside, take a quick look around, and step right back out. As I opened the door, we both saw a soldier just inside standing on a table, waving a pistol, and yelling. Standing in the open door, I made a perfect target. There was no chance that he was going to allow two MPs to enter, so I let the door close behind me and approached him slowly as though nothing was wrong. Surprisingly, he let me walk right up to the table. When I said quietly, "Come on down and let everybody have a good time," he bent down to stare at me. Then he made a big mistake; he looked away to see if there were any more MPs around. My hard plastic helmet liner cracked like a shot as it caught the left side of his face. Luckily, for me, he hit the floor on one side of the table and his gun landed on the other. I drew my .45 and backed up in a corner just as Reo and two other MPs entered. Reo had called the riot squad, which arrived about ten minutes later. Needless to say, the Swartzwald Madel was closed for the night. We took our drunk to the MLO and called his unit to pick him up—the standard procedure for a minor infraction.

Very few of our encounters had happy endings. In fact, a simple pass check could, and often did, turn nasty. One afternoon shortly after coming on duty, we spotted a suspicious-looking civilian walking in the same direction as we were driving. Kimbell pulled to the curb and I called out, "Come here." The man, instead of complying, turned and ran in the opposite direction. Just as I started to get out of the jeep, Kimbell spun the vehicle around, throwing me into the street. Without weighing the consequences, I drew my .45 and fired. Immediately the suspect whirled around. Thinking he had turned to shoot back, I fired again and he went down. Amazingly, at a distance over 100 feet, I had hit him both times. The first shot went through his right hand, causing him to spin. The second shot hit half way between his right elbow and shoulder. Such marksmanship can only be attributed to the inaccuracy of the Army .45 and the fact that I fired, combat style, without taking aim.

At the end of my tour of duty, I reported the incident to First Sergeant DeCamp. He commended me for, "Shooting first and asking questions later." DeCamp reminded me that under martial law, when the subject failed to comply with the lawful order "Come here," he committed a serious offense. According to the first sergeant, my job was not to determine why he ran, but to make sure that anyone who broke the law in my sector would be quickly and severely dealt with by the United States Army.

However, when I arrived at the MLO the following morning to file a report of the shooting incident, I received a big surprise. The duty officer advised me that I had not been involved in any arrest the night before where shooting had taken place. Knowing full well I could not take that report back to Sergeant DeCamp, I requested to see the provost marshal. The provost, a captain, could easily tell that I was more afraid of my first sergeant than I was of him, so he relented. I was then allowed to see a Counter Intelligence Corps (CIC) agent. He explained that the prisoner was a major Nazi war criminal who had been turned over to the OSS. Therefore, his capture would not be admitted and there would be no Army report of any kind; I could forget the entire incident. The fact that it was a U.S. Civilian Government OSS investigation satisfied DeCamp and I never heard any more about the case.

Chapter XX
Military Policeman On Duty

Munich was a hotbed of black market activity. Cigarettes, at twenty American Military Currency dollars a pack, were the basic medium of exchange. Shoes, blankets, food, soap, and especially American whiskey brought excellent prices or trades. On the German side, many works of art from museums and artifacts looted from churches were available to the right buyer. On one occasion, based on a tip to CID, we raided a house near Freising, twenty miles north of Munich, and recovered an enormous golden cross that had been stolen from the Benedictine Church located in that city.

There were also some very clever German con men operating in Munich. One case in point involved a number of complaints to the MLO that the army canteen was not returning photographs. An investigation showed that many soldiers were turning in film that had been purchased on the black market. Actually it was not film at all, just the wrapper, spool, and box that had been taken from the PX trash bin. The con man had rewound the spools, minus film, and there was no way to tell good from bad without unwrapping, and this would have exposed good film to light, thereby ruining it.

Our PX rations were more than adequate. Every week each soldier was allowed to purchase soap, sundries, and two cartons of cigarettes. Whiskey and gifts were available on a fair distribution, priority basis. Being a nondrinker, except for an occasional weak German beer when the water was exceptionally bad, and a nonsmoker, I could have easily engaged in the black market. However, I was there to enforce the law, not break it, and I had no desire to serve time in an army jail then receive a dishonorable discharge.

Usually I purchased my full ration at the PX and then resold it for the same amount to one of my buddies who was a heavy smoker. However, on one bitterly cold, snowy afternoon, as I was returning from the PX, I saw a German civilian, a man about sixty, walking slowly with his head down. From all appearances, he did not have a friend in the world. I decided to change his attitude, so I called out, "Hans, come here." Surprised, he crossed the street and said, "Ya." I smiled and handed him a carton of cigarettes, and said, "Cheer up." He had no idea what I meant and protested, "Kein gelt," indicating that he had no money. Then, to confuse him even more, I handed him the other carton and walked away. A short distance down the street, I turned and looked back—he was still standing in the same spot staring at the crazy American soldier who had just given him the equivalent of a year's pay.

When we became better acquainted with the German people, Bavarians in particular, we understood their plight. They had been led into a devastating war, many actually believing they had a just cause, while over 1,000,000 others had been thrown into concentration camps for opposing the Nazi regime. Today, I can really empathize with the loyal, hardworking, patriotic German citizen of the 1940s. In the past fifty years, I have seen young American men die in useless battles of three undeclared wars. From the frozen slopes of North Korea, the rice paddies of Vietnam, and the jungles of Central America, we have returned our dead. These brave men died in vain. History has judged Adolph Hitler and his henchmen, and history will not be kind to dictatorial American Presidents who have signed executive orders committing our sons to slaughter nor cowardly United States Congressmen and Senators who, to their shame, have chosen not to uphold the Constitution by impeaching such a President.

As Christmas approached, First Sergeant DeCamp, brother of radio and film star Rosemary DeCamp, suggested we collect money for toys and clothes for the children of the civilians who worked in our compound. In just two days, a carton about two feet square that had been placed in the hall outside the orderly room was overflowing with German and American Military currency. Also, a larger carton nearby was filled with candy, gum, and coffee.

In late October, Captain Tief assembled a Task Force (TF), which included an MP company (ours), a CIC detachment, and an infantry battalion to carry out a highly secret operation. In our briefing, the captain explained that over 5,000 officers of the Yugoslavian Army, former German prisoners of war, were being quartered in the Bavarian Motor Works (BMW) plant in Munich. According to the Geneva Convention, they were to be returned to their homeland at the cessation of hostilities. However, their country was now under control of Communist Dictator Josip Broz (Tito) and they had fought on the side of the Allies, under their King Peter, to whom they were still loyal. Since being released from German prison camps, they had rearmed themselves and were now planning to return home to overthrow Marshal Tito. Our government could not allow this to happen, because President Truman had agreed at the "big three" (Stalin, Churchill, and Truman), meeting in Potsdam in July 1945 that the United States would not interfere with the Yugoslavian Communist Government.

At about four in the morning, the infantry battalion surrounded the buildings; our company, armed with Thompson submachine guns, made a quick entry into the plant, disarmed the officers, and the CIC arrested the commander and his staff. The operation went very smoothly. However, the officers were disappointed that our government would support a communist dictator who was as bad or worse than the Nazi one we, with their help, had just defeated.

After the raid, I became good friends with some of the officers and would stop and visit when my patrol was in their area. They were clean, intelligent, and law-abiding. Now classed as displaced persons not subject to repatriation, they were now refugees without a country.

Suddenly, for the first time since Camp Blanding, we were rudely awakened by the blast of whistles and banging on doors. From all the noise, we would not have been surprised to learn that World War III had been declared. However, we were not so fortunate. Once assembled, Sergeant DeCamp informed us that General Patton was en route to Munich and we would have the honor of blocking all streets along his route, so he could pass quickly through the city. If he had asked, I could have told the sergeant I had already seen the general twice, and although I admired his tactics, I would just as soon have stayed in bed.

From my cold, wet post on Odeons Platz, near the Feldherrenhalle, I threw General Patton a snappy salute but from 100 feet away; I doubt he even took notice. Too bad we were not on duty on the outskirts of Mannheim, Germany, less than one month later on 9 December 1945, when General Patton was fatally injured in what was otherwise a minor traffic accident.

Since we all had a mean streak, one of our most enjoyable tasks was enforcing curfew. Munich was laid out with a series of cartwheel streets around a hub called a Platz. This made it easy to block off an entire section at a time. I especially liked to pull duty on Marien Platz in front of the City Hall, because there were few taverns in the area and we had less drunks with which to contend. However, there were Allied Civilian hotels nearby, and most civilians detested military police. Of course, there was no love lost, because we felt they were all draft dodgers and slackers while we were fighting the war. One newspaper reporter got very nasty when we checked his German girlfriend's ID card. Then seeing we meant business, he calmed down and asked, "Isn't there anything I can do for her?" To this Reo replied, "Sure, you can help her into the truck." On another occasion, a smart aleck American civilian snapped at me, "I'll have you know that I rank even with a captain." To which I replied, "Shut up and get in the truck. I can take anybody up to a brigadier general."

The most astounding thing we discovered in checking soldier's passes and civilian IDs was the wide age difference. Even though there were plenty of younger German women readily available many of our young soldiers and officers picked up women in their late fifties and early sixties. One explanation could be they thought older women might have fewer boyfriends, so there was less chance of venereal disease with the older ones. Actually, we picked up about an equal number of old and young women with venereal diseases, so their chances were about the same.

With all the rubble and bombed-out sections of the city, Munich was a very dangerous place. There were certain areas that the military police did not venture into after curfew. Criminal Investigation Division (CID) and Counter Intelligence Corps (CIC) men were even more at risk than us, because they had to infiltrate the black market in order to know when some big deal was taking place.

On one occasion, we were alerted by CID that a truckload of cigarettes would be moving through our area. We immediately established roadblocks with orders to search all vehicles. Within an hour after we were in place, a military police riot squad truck approached with siren screaming; ordinarily it would have been allowed to pass, but not this time. Inside, instead of a riot squad, we found a full truckload of American cigarettes. The driver and his companion, both military police sergeants from another company, were arrested on the spot.

In the comics, only Beetle Bailey and Sad Sack goof-off and are given undesirable duty as punishment. However, this does not always hold true in the real world. In the army, every soldier is subject to doing something very stupid. When this occurs, one thing is certain; the first sergeant will be right there to make him accountable for his actions.

Johnny Reo and I were always first class military policemen; we were never late for patrols, had good reports from the MLO, and neither of us smoked or drank. However, one beautiful, winter day we were assigned to the riot squad and restricted to the guardroom. We knew we could see the riot truck from the front gate, so we saw no good reason to stay cooped up all day inside the building. However, we had no sooner arrived at the gate house when a jeep turned into the compound. Just our luck, the driver was First Sergeant DeCamp and his passenger was Captain Tief. From the expression on DeCamp's face, we knew we should return to the guardroom immediately.

The following morning, our names were on the daily report to see Sergeant DeCamp. The first sergeant was very cordial and said nothing about the incident at the gate. He first looked at Reo, then me and said, "We have some prisoners of war cleaning the ceiling in the dining room, I don't think they know how to do a good job, do you?" Immediately both of us replied, "No, Sir." Then he said, "Why don't you go down in the morning and show them how it should be done?" Without any hesitation, we agreed. At six the next morning, after a quick breakfast, we were up on the tables, with buckets and rags, receiving some strange looks from the prisoners of war. About nine, DeCamp came in, looked up and said, "I think they can finish it themselves, don't you?" Again we agreed, got down, and went to the showers. To be absolutely truthful, this was not the only time I deserved extra duty; it was just the only time I was required to perform it.

By December 1945, the 508th Battalion was filling up with military police veterans who had reenlisted and returned from the United States. Also, Allied Military Government was turning over more and more responsibility to the German Civilian Authorities. Therefore, many of us old men with less than six months to serve were transferred to other units. I really hated to leave Munich just as the beautiful lady was returning to life. The opera house had reopened and yes, I went. I sat with a full bird colonel and neither of us understood a word, but the music was outstanding.

Because I had a military police, Military Occupation Specialty (MOS) number (677), I was lucky enough to be assigned to another military police unit. Surprisingly, this unit turned out to be a horse of a different color.

Chapter XXI
"Tarnish on the Blade"

After the beauty and excitement of duty in Munich, our first and lasting impression of Wurzburg was very depressing. We arrived in the almost totally destroyed city to the sight of women, aged fourteen to seventy, clearing away rubble, brick by brick.

However, this was only our first disappointment. Although we would still wear the crossed pistols and carry the right MOS number, our duties would be entirely different from those in Munich. The letters, G.O.D., W.D.T.C., in our new address gave us a clue to the type of duty we could expect to find at this post. These ominous letters stood for Guardhouse Overhead Detachment, Wurzburg Disciplinary Training Center. Actually, the United States Army had just introduced us to one of the most undesirable tours of duty in the military service—cadreman at a military prison.

"Sergeant Clark reporting for duty, Sir!"

Major Flynn glanced up and with more of a wave than a returned salute answered, "Sit down, Clark." For the next three hours, I learned of the problems facing the detachment commander. First, all his junior officers were ninety day wonders, straight from Officers Candidate School at Fort Benning, Georgia. They had been trained as combat rifle platoon leaders but, according to him, knew nothing about a Discipline Training Center. Next, all of his old men who had reenlisted, had transferred to other more desirable units. Finally, he had orders from general headquarters in Washington to fully staff his command. This meant, among other details, that he would be required to appoint a firing squad and hangman detail. Naturally, I volunteered to serve as sergeant of the guard on both. Fortunately, while I was assigned to the DTC, we were not called on to perform this duty. However, I have often wondered how Sergeant John Woods felt when he tripped the trapdoor in the Nuremberg City Jail for the ten condemned Nazi War Criminals on 16 October 1945. (At least he got his name in the history books.)

With the end of hostilities on the European Continent on 8 May 1945, France, a sovereign state, was no longer obligated to serve as an Allied base of operations. Consequently, the United States began consolidating its forces into the occupation zone agreed to at Yalta. The American Army prisoners incarcerated in the DTC at Marseilles, being the most unwelcome guests in the country, were the first to be asked to leave. Our task at Wurzburg was to construct and staff a maximum security military prison. The site of our new facility was a bombed-out airport on a hill overlooking the city. Unfortunately, we were forced to immediately accept a token number of twenty prisoners, even though we were totally unprepared (no cells, barbed wire, or sufficient guards) to properly care for them. This was to satisfy an army regulation which stated, "A DTC must house prisoners in order to draw supplies from an army depot."

At first, prisoners were kept in basement rooms under our barracks, a two-story concrete and steel building which had been only slightly damaged by Allied air attacks. The small, eight-foot by eight-foot cells were sparsely furnished with only an army cot, one blanket, and a five gallon bucket. There was no heat, running water, or electricity in their rooms and light entered from a barred grating in the window well. The inmates were allowed outside only once each day to empty the bucket that served as their commode. We were armed with the M-1 .30 caliber carbine, a twenty-round, semiautomatic weapon. One particular prisoner enjoyed taunting his guard until he met me. Defiantly he asked, "What would you do if I ran?" Calmly I replied, "I would shoot you, why?" This was the right answer, since he was not a prisoner of war but an American who had committed a criminal act.

After a few days of guard duty, the major assigned me to duty as sergeant of the guard at the prison compound. In this capacity, I came into contact with a new type of prisoner, the Detained Officer, commonly referred to as "Meatheads." These were United States Army officers who had been court-martialed and found guilty of crimes, but under the Articles of War could only be stripped of their rank by the President of the United States, under whose pleasure they served. They had "put tarnish on the blade" and, while awaiting a final decision from President Truman, they were under a form of house arrest at the DTC and were not afforded any rights or privileges of their rank. However, they were assigned duties, according to their abilities, under the supervision of the Sergeant of the Guard.

Actually, many of the detained officers at Wurzburg had served in combat with honor and distinction but when the war ended, they found it impossible to return to being "officers and gentlemen." Now they were in prison for acts which were not only condoned, but encouraged, in wartime. Also, due to the shortage of field grade and general officers caused by rapid redeployment shortly after the war, many lieutenants and captains were placed in positions in which they had no training or expertise.

Typical of this group was First Lieutenant Hugh Edwards. (Real names of detained officers are not used.) Lieutenant Edwards, a combat engineer, was one of the first American officers to enter Berlin, Germany after VE Day, 8 May 1945. The task of his unit was to quickly establish checkpoints and roadblocks between the American and Russian zones of occupation.

As soon as he arrived in Berlin, Edwards became involved with a German woman, in spite of nonfraternization laws to the contrary. Of course his association could have been justified if she had only served as an interpreter, but alas, she did more. The zones were secured in less than three months and, when his unit was replaced by military government, Edwards was reassigned to Bamberg, Germany (population 70,000) as the town mayor.

After a few days in his new job, Lieutenant Edwards became concerned about the welfare of Ilsa, his girlfriend, in Berlin. Truthfully, he should have forgotten Ilsa, because he already had a wife in the United States and a companion, a nurse, at the local military hospital. In his capacity as military governor, he had control of all army supplies in the city, many of which were being distributed to German civilians and displaced persons. Therefore, he saw no good reason why he should not load a jeep full of these goods and return to Berlin.

Ilsa was happy to see him and the supplies, but what she really wanted was good American money. Equipment is expendable in wartime, so Edwards solved this problem like any good combat soldier; he simply sold his jeep to the "Russians" on the black market, intending to report it stolen. However, the Russians turned out to be United States Army CID men who arrested him on the spot.

At his trial later that same month, he overheard one of his judges, a full bird colonel, say, "Let's make an example out of this one." Consequently, justice was swift and sure. The entire proceedings before a brigadier general, two colonels, and three majors lasted less than four hours, including a ten minute deliberation by the judges, before the guilty verdict was rendered. Edwards was so outraged that when he left the courtroom via the provost marshal's office, he laid his raincoat on the desk and upon leaving, walked out with the clerk's typewriter under his arm. This was a normal reaction, using army logic, because he knew he would need it in order to type his appeal to Washington, thus the old army axiom, "A good soldier is never short."

Supplies began arriving and Major Flynn expected the utmost from his staff of detained officers. They were to transform the muddy airfield into a reception center for inmates as soon as possible using a work force of more than 500 German civilians, displaced persons, and prisoners of war. The first compound was to contain five prefabricated buildings, each measuring twenty by forty-eight feet. These were to be surrounded by inner and outer fences with machine gun watchtowers erected on all four corners. The entire area was to be covered by searchlights, turning night into day.

Captain Black, formerly of the United States Army Air Force, filled the post of superintendent of buildings; Lieutenant Edwards was charged with layout and construction; and Captain Rodgers, an infantryman, served as the supply officer. All three were very competent. Work progressed rapidly, because labor was plentiful and many of the civilians were expert in their professions. Of course, the good nourishing meal furnished them at noon caused them all to be more willing to please us. Also, as long as they were employed by the American Army, they were exempt from being pressed into service by German authorities to clear rubble from the city of Wurzburg.

With construction running well ahead of schedule, in January 1946, I decided to go on sick call and have a couple of sebaceous cysts removed from my shoulder. This should have taken about an hour at the Army field hospital in Wurzburg, where Lieutenant Edwards' girlfriend was a nurse, but the army is always unpredictable. The surgeon took one look at my face, shoulders, and back and transferred me to the 116th General Hospital in Nuremberg, Germany.

The surgeons at the 116th removed the two cysts that had been bothering me. Then during the next month, they removed approximately twenty more that concerned them. Actually I believe they just wanted to practice minor surgery and a sebaceous cyst is about as minor as you can get. To remove the cyst, the surgeon makes a small slit in the outer skin, then clips around the sac until it is free. However, if he is not careful or the scalpel slips, it will pierce the sac making it impossible to remove whole. When this happens, the scar will refill for years. These cysts formed when oil glands in the skin became blocked by dirt while I was in combat and could not properly care for my skin. It is impossible for combat soldiers to maintain personal hygiene.

Luckily, I was never examined very closely at the 116th, so I missed the hospital's specialty. Under the pretense of cleanliness, the surgeons insisted that every patient, no matter what his illness, be circumcised. In fact, one operating room was set aside for this purpose and the procedure was performed on an assembly-line basis.

The War Crimes Tribunal was in session at the Palace of Justice in Nuremberg during my hospital stay, and the 116th served as the medical facility for the war criminals. Our most frequent patient was Julius Striecher, the infamous "Jew baiter." Streicher was found guilty of crimes against humanity and, at 2:18 A.M. on 16 October 1946, strangled to death when the hangman's knot failed to serve its purpose. Security was not very tight and many of the hospital patients visited and talked to the war criminals, but I had no interest in those I considered to be vile, filthy Nazis. Also, the Palace of Justice was nearby and tickets to observe the trial were readily available. In fact, according to those who attended, the visitor's gallery was never more than half filled because the proceedings were dull and boring. Headsets were provided and, by turning the dial, one was able to hear a simultaneous translation of the words being spoken in court. The four judges, American, British, French and Russian, sat at one end of the rectangular, sixty-five by one hundred foot, courtroom. The accused, twenty-one haughty and unrepentant Nazis, occupied the prisoners' dock, which was encompassed on three sides by United States military policemen. I had lots of time to write letters, read books, and go sightseeing, but after hearing eyewitness accounts of the trial, I had no desire to waste an afternoon looking at a group of mass murderers.

Granted there was not much left of Nuremberg to see. The city had been about eighty percent destroyed by bombing and shelling. Parts of the old walled city and Albrecht Durer's house were still standing and were historically significant, but in contrast to the beautiful sights in Munich, the city as a whole was dull and ugly.

In fact, a true story concerning one of its largest squares attests to the "beauty" of the city. Each year prior to the war, during Adolph Hitler's reign, Nuremberg, played host to an enormous rally on the anniversary of the founding of the Nazi Party. On one such occasion, the citizens of the city honored their Fuehrer by renaming Market Platz, "Adolph Hitler Platz." Hitler, who had lived in such beautiful cities as Vienna and Munich, was disgusted that such a smelly, filthy place would carry his name. However, in order not to offend the city fathers, he accepted the dubious honor. On returning to Berlin, he made his feelings known to his inner circle. His deputy, the ever faithful Rudolph Hess, arrived at a satisfactory solution. All the Fuehrer had to do was invite his friend, the Italian dictator, to a meeting in Nuremberg. Then as a goodwill gesture, rename the marketplace, "Benito Mussolini Platz." Consequently, in return for his "Pact of Steel," the Italian dictator received heaps of rotting produce and large piles of horse manure.

Returning to Wurzburg, I found the prison stockade almost completed. Captain Black and Lieutenant Edwards were elated to have me back. The command had grown and a full bird colonel, Colonel O. H. Olmstead had replaced Major Flynn. The colonel, who had served as the finance officer in General Eisenhower's Headquarters, and I got along well from the beginning. He did not associate with detained officers, therefore, I became his "Adjutant."

It was difficult, and sometimes dangerous, adjusting to green recruits, officers, and enlisted men who were arriving from the United States. I was quartered with the Guardhouse Overhead Detachment in the headquarters building near the prison compound. It was a large three-story structure with rooms on either side of a long hall. In each room were four beds, lockers, and a large desk at the window. Being an old combat man, I thought nothing of leaving my fully-loaded pistol lying on my bed while I sat at the desk to write letters. However, I had not counted on the stupidity of one of my new roommates. Fresh from the States and fascinated by my Belgium Browning .38, he picked it up, pulled the hammer back, and squeezed the trigger. The bullet missed my head by about three inches and lodged in the window facing. To this day, I do not fully load my pistol. At least when I hear the receiver being pulled back I will have time to react.

A few days later, I again felt like a fugitive from the law of averages. The latrines were at the end of the long hall, and it was not uncommon for a guard coming off duty to leave his Thompson submachine gun outside the door when he used that room. As it happened, just as I opened my door and prepared to step into the hall, one of the new recruits picked up a fully-loaded Thompson to look at it and blasted twenty rounds the length of the building, some hitting within a foot of where I was standing. Many people fail to understand when I remark, "Anything after age nineteen is gravy," but then they never served with a bunch of trigger-happy idiots at the DTC.

Luckily, United States Army Headquarters in Washington, D.C. saved the day and my life, by designating the city of Wurzburg, Germany, as the site of a military community. A section of Wurzburg was to become a small American city containing wives and families of American occupation troops. This meant I would again be placed on special duty off the post. My new home was in the former teachers' college in Wurzburg. It was a large L-shaped building, one wing two city blocks long and the other three blocks in length. There were quite a few offices in the building, but only the mess sergeant and I were assigned sleeping quarters. My room was slightly smaller than the colonel's office, but I really did not need a silver (wooden) eagle with a twelve foot wing span on my bedroom wall.

My new title, Utility Sergeant, was very appropriate, because I was responsible for everything except the kitchen, which naturally belonged to the mess sergeant. First, and most importantly, I was accountable for seventeen detained officers. Next, being in charge of the motor pool, I controlled the jeeps, command and reconnaissance cars, and all the gasoline. Lastly, I reported directly to the colonel. In fact, I carried a little card which stated, "I will assume responsibility for property signed for by Sergeant James R. Clark." It was signed, "O. H. Olmstead, Colonel Commanding Wurzburg Military District." This came in very handy for bluffing at supply depots because, like the WDTC, we could not legally obtain supplies until we actually had families in quarters.

The colonel was very understanding and really knew how to appreciate an expert, commonly referred to as a "dog robber," who can and will acquire necessary supplies and equipment when they are needed. On one occasion, he came up to the work site where German laborers were digging a trench for a new phone line by hand. Looking quizzically he asked, "Will this be finished in three days?" At the rate we were going, it would take at least three weeks, but knowing what he meant, I replied, "Yes, Sir." The following day, he stopped again to observe our progress and appeared to be pleased. However, he did not inquire where I had obtained a twenty-seven ton ditch digger. However, he did compliment the equipment operator, an engineer sergeant, who was working for two cartons of cigarettes.

During the war and immediately afterwards, it was an accepted practice to evict the occupants of any building needed for quarters or any other military purpose. With this, I am in total agreement. However, in my opinion the procedure used by the United States Government in acquiring houses for the Wurzburg Military Community was not justified as "military necessity." Considering the war had been over almost a year, the action taken bordered on criminal.

Planned as a secret military operation, a task force was formed, consisting of an infantry battalion (800 men), a military police company (180 men), and special troops. At the designated time of three o'clock in the morning, an area containing fifty-four undamaged houses near the teachers' college was surrounded and sealed off by the infantry. Then two riflemen, one military policeman, and a member of the WMC staff with an interpreter occupied each unit. The occupants were herded into one room and guarded by the riflemen while all the contents such as furniture, bedding, dishes, rugs, and curtains were inventoried and confiscated. The occupants were then given a receipt and advised that they could remove only their personal items and clothing from the premises. They were escorted out of the area by the military police and not allowed to return. These furnished houses would now serve as quarters for American families who were en route to Wurzburg from the United States.

Psychologists have determined that if hostages are kept in captivity for any length of time, they will begin to sympathize with their captors. This same behavioral change occurs in combat soldiers when they are placed in occupation duty too long. To me, these Wurzburg citizens were no longer enemies but fellow human beings. Many years later, this feeling was compounded when I discovered that the destruction of their city was not a military necessity. Actually, Wurzburg was destroyed by carpet bombing on 16 March 1945, as a punitive action in order to comply with the Yalta Agreement made by President Roosevelt, Prime Minister Churchill, and Generalissmo Stalin.

Granted, the fanatical Nazis did commit heinous crimes against humanity. However, their dastardly deeds of seizing private property did not justify our action at Wurzburg almost a year after peace had been declared. Nor did their practice of bombing undefended cities excuse our leaders when they took vengeance on the German population.

Lieutenant Edwards and the German architect did a beautiful job transforming the ground floor of one wing in the headquarters building into a commissary for the WMC. Instead of removing walls, they simply created a series of wide arches from room to room.

Edwards and I became good friends. I even wrote to President Truman on his behalf. The President, a World War I artillery captain, was very sympathetic, and set aside the lieutenant's conviction and allowed him to leave the service with an honorable discharge. My letter may not have had any bearing on President Truman's decision, but at least it did not lessen the lieutenant's chances.

While I was busy getting the houses ready for families that had already left the United States, I had forgotten that I was still assigned to the guardhouse overhead detachment. Even though I reported to a full colonel, I was still on the roster of the guard company. When I received word to report to Lieutenant Weston, who had just taken command of the company, I assumed that my orders had come through for my return to the States.

Marching into the orderly room, I threw my best salute and barked, "Sergeant Clark, reporting Sir." The young lieutenant frowned and replied, "You are not standing reveille and retreat with the company." To which I replied, "No Sir." With as much authority as he could muster, he snapped, "Beginning tomorrow morning, you will report for reveille and retreat." Remembering the proper answer, I said, "Yes Sir." Another salute, then executing an about-face that would have made General Patton proud, I took one step toward the door. Not understanding my actions, the lieutenant suddenly had second thoughts and stopped me by asking, "Who told you that you did not have to stand company formations?" Again the proper reply, "Colonel Olmstead, Sir." Now realizing that he had almost been suckered by an old sergeant, he stammered, "Continue your schedule as it is now until you hear from me." As expected, I never saw or heard from the commander of troops again.

Among the first dependents scheduled to arrive was Colonel Olmstead's wife and, while we were waiting for the train from Frankfort, Germany, he unburdened his troubles on me. First and foremost, he would never forgive the Germans for not holding just one more week. As it happened, he was scheduled for promotion to brigadier general on 10 May 1945, and when the war ended on 8 May 1945, all colonels were frozen in grade—now he would never get his star. Then, there was the matter of his adjutant, who by then should have been a major or lieutenant colonel, but due to his lousy performance, was still, and would always remain, a captain. The colonel, referring to this captain's personnel file, said, "His efficiency reports are more like deficiency reports." Also, he was very depressed because, he lamented, "I don't even own a set of dishes over here." Shortly after the war, he had gone back to the States on leave, where he expected a great reception. However, he soon discovered that soldiers, even former colonels, were not in demand in the civilian job market.

The colonel brightened up considerably when the train arrived. Mrs. Olmstead appeared to be about ten years younger than her husband. However, being a staff officer under General Eisenhower would add ten years to anyone's life. While orderlies loaded the baggage, the colonel gave his wife a short tour of the train station. Then we placed the colonel and his lady in the rear seat of the command car, a 1942/45 Chevrolet sedan, for the short ride to the military community.

Luckily, I was aware of the arrival of Mrs. Olmstead. According to a very funny story, mistakes could, and did, often happen. Supposedly, one officer's orderly was away on leave when his wife arrived. Naturally, on his return, he resumed his regular duties. Consequently, bright and early, he went into the officer's bedroom, jerks back the covers, slaps the officer's wife on the fanny, and announces, "O.K. Babe, back to the village." If this had actually happened, I can't imagine who would be in the most trouble, the orderly or the officer.

Chapter XXII
Tourist in Switzerland

With the Wurzburg Military Community completed and the officers' families settled in, I was allowed to take a short leave. Two trips were available: one a tour of Rome, Italy, where the Pope would bless me, or a tour of Switzerland. I had already been blessed by surviving the war so, naturally, I chose Switzerland.

In order to get from Wurzburg, Germany, to Basel, Switzerland, we had to stop over in Strasbourg, France. The train station was crawling with pimps, boys ten to fourteen years old touting the traits and qualities of their sisters, and the prostitutes themselves, who in one breath, would tell the soldiers what they would do and in the next proclaim in English, "Me clean, Joe." Actually, the opportunity for venereal disease was not a matter of choosing the right prostitute; every one of them was infected with one variety or another. After one or two propositions, word was passed that the big, ugly sergeant wearing the silver rifle pin was not to be approached because of his nasty disposition. Of course, they had no way of knowing that I had dealt harshly with prostitutes since I was thirteen years old. In my Nashville, Tennessee neighborhood prostitution was a way of life. In fact, in one family, two cousins were members of the profession, one a streetwalker and the other a brothel girl. A common argument among relatives centered on which cousin was the biggest whore. Personally, I could never determine any difference. Suffice it to say, I did not have any desire to patronize either of them, nor for that matter any thereafter.

At the border control point, we were immediately transformed from American soldiers to American tourists. The Swiss customhouse officials waved most of us through, checking only an occasional bag that appeared to be large or heavy. Swiss law was very strict in regard to black market trading, and they came down swiftly and hard on violators. Our transportation and lodging were prepaid by the U.S. Army and we were allowed to exchange only a limited amount of money.

Our group was assigned two very knowledgeable Swiss guides for the tour. However, we found little need for them, because all the people we came into contact with were friendly and helpful and most of them spoke perfect English. Switzerland was beautiful and immaculate. The shops were well stocked and every merchant we dealt with was fair and honest. At this time, American servicemen were the majority of their tourists, so we traveled on first class trains and stayed in all the best hotels. Food was excellent and plentiful. We had only to set our shoes and dirty laundry outside our hotel room door at bedtime in order to awaken and find clean, pressed clothes and shined shoes the next morning.

I paired with a captain as a roommate for the duration of the tour. We got along well because he was refined and cultured. The tour was not regimented; our time was our own, only cities visited and departure times were fixed. The electric trains departed exactly on time and traveled quietly and smoothly at terrific speeds. We always crossed above or below the tracks, never over them, because the trains came into and through the stations at sixty to one hundred miles per hour.

Our first day was spent in Basel, which was Switzerland's second largest city. It was amazing to walk around in a civilized society and not be approached by prostitutes, thieves, or vagrants. However, I felt very uneasy without my loaded pistol. It had to be left in Wurzburg because the Swiss were very touchy about foreign soldiers carrying guns in their country. Basel was in the French-speaking section of Switzerland, but English was their second language. Most of the people also spoke German, and our guide was fluent in nine languages.

From Basel, we proceeded to Berne for a short stop, then on to Fribourg for an overnight stay. At three the following afternoon, we boarded a deluxe tour bus for a forty minute ride through beautiful farmland to the city of Bulle, in the foothills of the Alps. The mountains of Switzerland were very impressive and, unlike the German and Austrian Alps, were alive with activity. From the edge of the city, we could see chalets far up on the slopes. Even higher on the solid rock faces, the barrels of enormous guns jutted out like thorns on rose bushes. After a quick tour of the city, we boarded a luxurious train for a trip through the mountains. As we approached our next destination, I could see a big, impressive building on the face of the mountain overlooking Lake Geneva. When I pointed it out to our guide, I asked, "Who's castle is that?" Without hesitation, he replied, "That is the Grand Hotel, where you will be staying for the next two days."

As soon as we arrived, I realized my error in assuming that it was only a castle; I had never seen a castle that could compare with it. The Grand Hotel was truly "fit for a king." The captain and I were given an enormous three-room suite. The main dining room was unbelievable with linen tablecloths, fine china, and crystal chandeliers. From all appearances, the hotel staff was sharpening their skills for richer tourists, who would visit in post war years, because we were treated like royalty.

The highlight of my tour (and of my life) came when I discovered that I could place a collect telephone call to my darling Audrey. The process was quite complicated. First the call had to be placed hours ahead because of limited phone lines. Then after arrangements were made, I was to be given a definite time to be by the phone. However, we hit a snag when the New York operator called back and informed the Swiss there was no such place as Martinsburg, Indiana. My heart fell but taking one more chance, I advised her to forget Indianapolis and ask the Louisville, Kentucky operator for the little town only twenty miles from her location. My guess worked and in a short time, New York came back and assured me that my call was scheduled for 6:00 A.M. Swiss time. On the other side of the Atlantic, the Louisville operator had alerted Martinsburg. The operator there called Audrey and invited her to take the call at the switchboard, when it came in at midnight, instead of over the party line at home. With American and Swiss efficiency, the connection was made on the exact minute. Her voice was clear and beautiful and we talked for twenty minutes. (The cost was $80, but it was worth a million.)

From Glion, I spent a day in Geneva, the wristwatch capital of the world. Naturally, I could not resist the temptation, so I bought two; a dainty little "record" for Audrey, which she still has, and a large fancy "Silvavia," which I only kept long enough to resell as soon as I returned to Wurzburg.

One of the most fascinating places in Europe, Chateau de Chillion, was in walking distance of the Grand Hotel. Down in the damp dungeon, with a little imagination, you could see the "prisoner" in chains and closing your eyes you could hear his groans from the rack. A sound that has haunted the old fortress for three centuries. (Lord Byron was a powerful writer.)

We were surprised to see so many men in civilian clothes carrying rifles. Then our guide explained; the Swiss do not have an army, every citizen is the army. The men are called up for a certain period each year and must take part in special training and maneuvers. When they return home to resume daily life, they take their arms, ammunition, uniform, and supplies with them, so they can answer the call to arms on a moment's notice. The basic vehicle in the Swiss Army is not the tank, it's a bicycle. As our guide explained, "You do not need a tank when one or two soldiers can blow up a mountain and bury a German division." The Swiss concept of gun control also explained their low crime rate. When every citizen has a loaded army rifle in his home, only a fool would attempt to break in and try to do him harm.

We departed Glion at 2:20 P.M. and arrived in Sierre at 4:04. The weather was perfect, so we walked out to the vineyards in the Rhone Valley and sampled some of the sweet grapes. Back in town, we cooled off with rich, thick ice cream which was made with milk from real Swiss cows.

At ten A.M. the following morning, I sensed that we were in for a surprise because the engine attached to our train was enormous. Not until we were en route to Lucerne did we learn that we were not going over or around the mountain, we were going straight through it. The Brigue-Lotschburg tunnel was only nineteen kilometers (twelve miles) long, but at one point, while we were under Mount Balmhorn, there were two miles of rock on top of us. When we popped out in the refreshing sunlight, you could hear a big sigh of relief from everyone on board. We stopped at Spiez for lunch at a nice restaurant overlooking the lake, then enjoyed a three hour sightseeing tour. At 3:30 P.M., we boarded a smaller train for the journey to Lucerne.

If the Grand Hotel in Glion above Lake Geneva had been fit for a king, then the Switzerhof at Lucerne was a queen's palace. Our suite was on the fourth floor, center front, and overlooked Lake Lucerne. From our windows, we could see the clear blue water dotted with sailboats and large pleasure cruise ships. The plush green foothills came right down to the water's edge. At a distance, these same hills seemed to blend into the mountains, which rose to majestic snow capped peaks about ten miles away.

The city itself could only be described by one word, splendor. Every building was picture postcard perfect, freshly painted, and in excellent repair. The avenues were wide and the bridges were works of art. (Although Munich, Germany was my favorite city in Europe, if I could afford to go first class, I might change my mind and choose Lucerne, Switzerland.)

As the axiom says, "All good things must come to an end." So after two more wonderful days of rest and relaxation, we boarded a luxurious train for the border control point at Basel. Fortunately, we did not stop over in France on our way back to Wurzburg. Therefore, I can only assume the prostitutes and pimps are still plying their trade, in and around the train stations, in the same manner their ancestors did after the wars of 1870 and 1914.

I was not overly excited about returning to my post at the Wurzburg Military Headquarters. I knew with the community job completed, I would probably be assigned as first sergeant of the troop command and really did not relish the task of baby-sitting a bunch of green recruits. Also, I did not look forward to working with officers of Lieutenant Weston's caliber. I was tired, frustrated and more homesick than ever. Going home had become something I dreamed about at night, thought about during the day, but accepted the fact it was never going to happen.

Suffice it to say my mood changed considerably when I picked up my first orders from the charge of quarters on my return to duty.

They read:

HEADQUARTERS
WURZBURG DISCIPLINARY TRAINING CENTER
APO 227 US ARMY 31 May 1946 SPECIAL ORDERS NUMBER 104

The following named EM, 2913 DTC O/H Detachment are Reld Fr asgmt thereat and trfd in gr atached un-asgd to 56th QM Base Depot, APO 169, U.S. Army WP o/a 3 June 1946 to Giessen, Germany reporting upon arrival to the Commanding Officer for further instructions.

Travel by rail and/or motor vehicle ATZD. TND TCNT 60-114 P 432-02 A212/50425. (AUTH: VOCG, CBS 31 May 46 NAMEASN MOS D.O.B. Clark, James R. 35905849 677 2 May 26 By Order of Colonel McClune S.C. Strohecker Captain, Infantry Adjutant

In United States Army language these orders simply said, "Pack up Clark, you are going home."

At that point in time, I ceased to belong to Uncle Sam. The rest of my life would be dedicated to my beautiful wife, Audrey. So I wrote on 31 May 1946:

WMC
My Darling Wife,

Dearest this letter will be short, sweet, and maybe the last time I need to write for a while. I returned from Switzerland 11:00 A.M., this morning and at 1:45 P.M. I was told to pack my bags that my shipment leaves the DTC at 9:00 A.M. Monday June 3, 1946. My trip should take 25 to 30 days.

Goodnight my darling, God bless you and stay near the phone.

Your loving husband Ray
I love you darling.

Appendix A
Prison Camps Established in Nazi Germany

1. Prison camps for British and American military personnel captured in the course of the war and civilian internees stranded in Germany and occupied countries at the outbreak of hostilities. Established by International Law in accordance with the Geneva Convention, these camps were subject to inspection by the International Red Cross. These prisoners were, as a rule, treated humanely. However there were exceptions; notably, Adolph Hitler's "Top Secret Commando Order" issued on 18 October 1942 which stated, "From now on all enemies on so-called commando missions in Europe or Africa challenged by German troops, even if they are in uniform, whether armed or unarmed, in battle or in flight, are to be slaughtered to the last man." Later that same day Hitler issued a supplementary directive to his commanders explaining, "It must be made clear to the enemy that all sabotage troops will be exterminated, without exception, to the last man . . . Under no circumstances can (they) expect to be treated according to the Geneva Convention . . . If it should be necessary for reasons of interrogation to initially spare one man or two, then they are to be shot immediately after interrogation."

This order by the German Leader and others issued by his Field Commanders brought unlawful death to thousands of American and British military personnel. A few specific examples will be sufficient to document these dastardly deeds.

On the night of 22 March 1944, two officers and thirteen men of the 267th Special Reconnaissance Battalion of the U.S. Army landed behind German lines in Italy. They were all in uniform and carried no civilian clothes. Captured two days later they were executed by firing squad on 26 March, on direct orders of General Anton Dostler, Commander, Seventy-fifth German Army Corps.

Fifteen members of an American-British force, including a war correspondent of the Associated Press, parachuted into Slovakia in January 1945 and were subsequently captured. They were all executed at Malthausen concentration camp (near Linz, Austria) on the orders of Nazi War Criminal, Ernst Kaltenbrunner. This same camp was the site of the brutal murder of forty-seven American, British and Dutch flyers in September 1944.

One of the most flagrant violations of the Geneva Convention occurred on 17 December 1944 near Malmedy, Belgium when seventy-one captured American soldiers were brutally slaughtered on orders of Nazi SS Colonel Jochen Peiper.

2. Prison camps for French, Dutch, Danish and Belgian Prisoners of War. These captured soldiers were held as hostages and no attempt was made to adhere to the Geneva Convention on their behalf. They were arbitrarily sent to German slave labor and concentration camps. Also, when an act of violence or sabotage occurred within their country they were selected at random and executed, usually at a ratio of fifty hostages for one German death.

In all, 29,660 French hostages were executed by the Germans during World War II. This figure does not include 40,000 more who "died" in French prisons while in custody of the German Army.

3. Prison camps for Russian and Polish prisoners of war. Military prisoners of these countries fared very badly at the hands of their captors. Hundreds of thousands were executed by German field commanders and over two million were shipped to Germany as slave laborers. In fact, Field Marshal Wilhelm Keitel, head of the German armed forces was convicted at the International War Crimes Tribunal of ordering Russian and Polish prisoners of war branded like cattle. For this and other horrible crimes, he was hanged at Nuremberg, Germany on 16 October 1946.

Some of the most hideous medical experiments in Nazi concentration camps were reserved for captured Russian officers who were in good physical condition. One series of these tests was conducted by Dr. Sigmund Rascher at the German Air Force decompression chamber in Munich, Germany. A Russian officer brought from nearby Dachau concentration camp was placed in the chamber and air was pumped out so that oxygen and air pressure of high altitude could be simulated. At the International War Crimes Tribunal, one eyewitness described the procedure in these words:

> *I have personally seen through the observation window of the decompression chamber when a prisoner would stand in a vacuum until his lungs ruptured . . . They would go mad and pull out their hair in an effort to relieve the pressure. They would tear their head and face with their fingers and nails in an attempt to maim themselves in their madness. They would beat the walls with their hands and head and scream in an effort to relieve the pressure on their*

> *eardrums. These cases usually ended in the death of the subject.*

Those who were not killed in the experiment were left to die unattended from ruptured lungs and other complications as they were of no further use to the Nazi doctors.

In testimony at Nuremberg, another of Dr. Rascher's experiments is described by one of his staff. Walter Neff says,

> *It was the worst experiment ever made. Two Russian officers were brought from the prison barracks. Rascher had them stripped and they had to go into the vat naked. Hour after hour went by, and whereas usually unconsciousness from the cold set in after sixty minutes at the latest, the two men in this case still responded fully after two and a half hours. All appeals to Rascher to put them to sleep by injection were fruitless. About the third hour one of the Russians said to the other, "Comrade, please tell the officer to shoot us." The other replied that he expected no mercy from the Fascist dog. The two then shook hands with a "Farewell, comrade." Finally, after five hours in thirty-six degree Fahrenheit water, they froze to death.*

Ironically, the person who held ultimate responsibility for these and other horrible experiments was Dr. Hubertus Strughold, Director of Nazi Germany's Aeromedical Research Institute in Berlin before and during World War II. Like many Nazi officials with high ranking friends in the American government, he was able to emigrate to the United States shortly after the war. He has been here ever since working with the United States Air Force at what is now the School of Aerospace Medicine.

4. Slave labor prison camps. The inmate population (estimated by most historians to be seven to nine million) in these prisons consisted of male and female civilians who had been seized in countries which were occupied by the German Army. They were shipped to large industrial centers in Germany with only the clothes they were wearing at the time of their capture. Arriving at their destination in cattle cars, they were segregated men to one camp, women to another. During their imprisonment they were supplied only with sufficient food and shelter to keep them healthy enough to work long hours at hard labor. Slackers or those who became unable to produce to the satisfaction of their overseer were sent to concentration camps. On the other hand, if they were overzealous, they would be chosen as cadre (straw bosses) at concentration camps.

Nazi Dr. Gutkelch, in a report to Alfred Rosenberg, commissioner for the central control of questions connected with the East-European region (head of the slave labor program) describes a slave laborer train of "newly recruited" Russian workers which was bound for Germany. "In this train women gave birth to babies who were thrown out of the windows during the journey. Persons having tuberculosis and venereal diseases rode in the same car. Dying people lay in the freight car without straw and one dead was thrown on the railway embankment."

Dr. William Jaeger, senior doctor for the Krupp works described the condition of Russian and Jewish women when he arrived at their camp. In testimony at Nuremberg, he said,

> Upon my first visit, I found these (eight hundred) females suffering from open festering wounds and other diseases. I was the first doctor they had seen . . . There were no medical supplies . . . They had no shoes and went about in their bare feet. The sole clothing of each consisted of a sack with holes for their arms and head. Their hair was shorn. The camp was surrounded by barbed wire and closely guarded by SS guards. The amount of food in the camp was extremely meager and of very poor quality. One could not enter the camp without being attacked by fleas . . . I got large boils on my arms and the rest of my body from them.

In reporting on the conditions in eight other camps inhabited by Russian and Polish slave laborers, Dr. Jaeger recalled:

> The clothing of the Eastern (European) workers was likewise completely inadequate. They worked and slept in the same clothing in which they had arrived from the East. Virtually all of them had no overcoats and were compelled to use their blankets as coats in cold and rainy weather. In view of the shortage of shoes many workers were forced to go to work in their bare feet, even in winter.
>
> Sanitary conditions were atrocious. At Kramerplatz only ten children's toilets were available for the 1,200 inhabitants . . . Excretion contaminated the entire floors of these lavatories . . . The Tartars and Kirhhiz suffered most; they collapsed like flies (from) bad housing, the poor quality and insufficient quantity of food, overwork, and insufficient rest.
>
> These workers were likewise afflicted with spotted fever. Lice, the carrier of the disease, together with countless fleas, bugs and other vermin tortured the inhabitants of these camps . . . At times the water supply at the camps was shut off for periods of from eight to fourteen days.

Reporting on a Krupp slave labor camp at Essen, Germany for French prisoners of war, Dr. Jaeger surmised that they were treated much better than those from the East whom the Germans considered less than human. Of the camp at Essen, he said,

> *Its inhabitants (the French) were kept for nearly a half year in dog kennels, urinals and old baking houses. The dog houses were three feet high, nine feet long, six feet wide. Five men slept in each of them. The prisoners had to crawl into these kennels on all fours . . . There was no water in the camp.*

5. Concentration camps for "Enemies of the State." These prisons contained national and state legislators, distinguished persons, labor leaders, judges, preachers, writers, military officers as well as ordinary citizens who had offended the Nazi regime. During the Nazi's first six years of power (1933-1939) concentration camps were established in Dachau, near Munich; Oranienburg, near Berlin; Duerrgoy, near Breslau; Boergermoor in northwestern Germany (later called Bergen-Belsen); Mauthausen, near Linz; and Buchenwald, near Weimer. According to official German records, the prison population in these camps stood at 21,000 in 1939. However, by 1942, the inmate count had more than doubled and nine more camps were under construction. New arrivals increased dramatically as the German Army advanced into Russia. In Fact, in a letter dated 28 December 1942, Heinrich Himmler, SS Chief, ordered the army to reduce the number of deaths in transit. According to a report he had received, of 136,870 new arrivals between June and December 1942, 70,610 were already dead, an additional 9,267 were executed on arrival and 27,846 were unfit to work and were sent to the gas chambers. This left less than 30,000 for the slave labor camps. The work of guarding the concentration camps and carrying out the brutal sentences of flogging, torture and execution which were everyday occurrences was given to Himmler's SS Death's Head Units (*Totenkopfverbande*). These sadistic criminals enjoyed such documented acts as setting fire to the long beards of old men and shooting young mothers with babies in their arms.

Many inmates of the concentration camps were subjected to horrendous medical experiments. At Dachau, nude prisoners were thrown onto frozen ground, then doused with cold water in order to determine how long it would take them to freeze to death. This was done on the premise that the German Air Force could learn how long an airman could survive in the North Sea if his plane went down. Also, arms and legs of inmates were given compound fractures, then left untreated until gangrene caused death. This on the pretext of determining how long a wounded soldier could survive without being treated. Camp Commander Ilsa Koch at Buchenwald and Joseph Kramer at Bergen-Belsen gladly participated in Professor August Hirt's skull type study. Hirt, head of Anatomical Institute of Strasbourg asked that they supply him with undamaged heads in hermetically sealed tin cans which he would measure and photograph, then skin and strip to the skull so he could scientifically study different races. German records show that one hundred and thirty were supplied by Kramer, while Koch only forwarded eighty and had more than fifty on hand when the 317th Regiment of the Eightleth Infantry Division liberated Buchenwald in early April 1945. I personally saw some of the tins with and without heads.

The most ghastly and unmerciful experiments were carried out on the "rabbit girls" at the infamous Ravensbrueck women's concentration camp. They were subjected to lethal injections of typhus and jaundice. Also, they were used as human guinea pigs in sadistic sterilization procedures and experiments.

6. Extermination camps. On 31 July 1941, Hermann Goering transmitted an order from Adolph Hitler to Reinhard Heydrick, head of the SS Security Service. This order titled "Final Solution of the Jewish Problem," commands:

> *I herewith commission you to carry out all preparations with regard to . . . a total solution of the Jewish question in regard to those territories of Europe which are under German influence . . .*
>
> *I furthermore charge you to submit to me as soon as possible a draft showing the measures . . . already taken for the execution of the intended final solution of the Jewish question.*

At this time (July 1941) extermination camps were already in operation at Belzec, Treblinka, Wolzek and Auschwitz. However, realizing the enormous task of killing an estimated eleven million Jews (Heydrick quoted: 131,000 left in Germany, five million in U.S.S.R., three million in Ukraine, two and a quarter million in Poland, three quarters of a million in France and a third of a million in England), Heydrick assembled the heads of fifteen ministries in the Berlin suburb of Wannsee on 20 January 1942. Known in history as the Wannsee Conference, it set in motion the greatest mass slaughter in modern times.

All of the thirty plus concentration camps either were or evolved into death camps where millions of tortured, starved inmates perished.

Rudolph Hess, commandant at Auschwitz, gives a vivid description of Treblinka, where records account for over two million prisoners who entered, with only forty known survivors. At the International War Crimes Tribunal, Hoess testified,

> I visited Treblinka (in June 1941) to find out how they carried out their extermination. The camp commandant at Treblinka told me that he had liquidated 80,000 in the course of half a year. He was principally concerned with liquidating all the Jews from the Warsaw Ghetto.
>
> He used monoxide gas and I did not think that his methods were very efficient. So when I set up the extermination building at Auschwitz, I used Zyklon B, which was a crystallized prussic acid which we dropped into the death chamber from a small opening. It took from three to fifteen minutes to kill people in the death chamber, depending on climatic conditions.
>
> We knew (when) all the people were dead because their screaming stopped. We usually waited about a half hour before we opened the doors and removed the bodies . . . Another improvement we made over Treblinka was that we built our gas chambers to accommodate 2,000 people at one time whereas, at Treblinka, their ten gas chambers only accommodated 200 people each.

Rudolph Franz Hoess was born in 1900, the son of a shopkeeper in Baden-Baden, studied for the priesthood (as did Adolph Hitler), and joined the Nazi Party in 1922. He was implicated in the murder of a school teacher in 1923 and received a life sentence but was released in 1928. He joined the SS in 1932 and in 1934 became a member of a Death's Head Unit. Thus, he spent most of his adult life as a prisoner or jailer. At the International War Crimes Tribunal at Nuremberg, Germany in 1945, he freely boasted that he had exterminated two and a half million persons and had allowed another half million persons to starve to death. Turned over to the Polish people by the Allies, Hoess was tried, convicted and hanged in March 1947 at Auschwitz, the scene of his horrible crimes.

Appendix B
Timeline

9 November 1923	Hitler's attempts to overthrow the government in Munich. Fourteen of his storm troopers were killed.
30 January 1933	Hitler appointed Chancellor by President Hindenburg.
February 1933	Concentration camp opens at Dachau.
6 March 1933	N.S.D.A.P. (Nazis) win 287 seats in the Reichstag.
March 1933	Over 100 Reichstag members imprisoned by Hitler in Dachau as Enemies of the State.
21 March 1933	Reichstag votes to give Hitler dictatorial powers.
23 March 1933	Eugenio Narduzzi, first death recorded in Dachau. Published in the *New York Times* by Pierre von Paasem.
3 April 1933	Reichstag passes a law forbidding Jews from most professions: teachers, lawyers, judges, etc.
10 May 1933	Nazis burn thousands of books.
30 June 1934	Hitler and his storm troopers kill more than 6,000 German citizens including former Chancellor Schliecher and Hitler's priest.
2 August 1934	German President Hindenburg dies and Hitler becomes supreme leader of Germany.
15 September 1935	Laws go into effect making Jews subjects, not citizens, of Germany.
16 July 1937	Buchenwald concentration camp opens for Jews who are told to leave Germany without their possessions. (No country will take them.)
9 November 1938	Night of Broken Glass; Nazis rampage against Jews all over Germany.
1 September 1939	Germany attacks Poland. World War II begins.
24 June 1942	Lidice, Czechoslovakia destroyed. All men killed, women and children shipped to concentration camps.

Appendix C

Nuremberg Tribunal—Major War Criminals Trial
November 1945—16 October 1946

Age In 1946

Martin Bormann	Death in Absentia	
Hermann Goering	Death—Committed Suicide	52
Joachim von Ribbentrop	Death—Hanged 1:10 A.M., 16 Oct. 1946	63
Wilhelm Keitel	Death—Hanged	63
Ernst Kaltenbrunner	Death—Hanged	43
Alfred Rosenberg	Death—Hanged	52
Hans Frank	Death—Hanged	46
William Frick	Death—Hanged	69
Julius Streicher	Death—Hanged	61
Fritz Saukel	Death—Hanged	48
Alfred Jodl	Death—Hanged	56
Arthur Seyss-Irquart	Death—Hanged 2:45 A.M., 16 Oct. 1946	54
Rudolph Hess	Life—Committed Suicide, 17 Aug. 1987	52
Walter Funk	Life—Released 1957	56
Eric Raeder	Life—Released 1955	70
Baldur von Schirach	20 Years—Released 1966	39
Albert Speer	20 Years—Released 1966	40
Konstantin von Neurth	15 Years—Released 1954	72
Karl Doenitz	10 Years—Released 1956	55
Hjalmar M. G. Schact	Acquitted	69
Franz von Papen	Acquitted	66
Hans Fritsche	Acquitted	46
Robert Ley	Committed Suicide While Awaiting Trial	

Bibliography

Allen, Colonel Robert S., *Lucky Forward.* New York: Vanguard Press Inc., 1947.

Department of the Army, *The Army Almanac.* Washington, D.C.: U.S. Government Printing Office, 1950.

Dodd, William E. and Martha, Editors. *Ambassador Dodd's Diary*, New York: Harcourt Brace and Company, Inc., 1941.

Greenfield, Kent Roberts, Editor. *Command Decisions.* Washington, D.C.: Department of the Army, ca. 1960.

Greenfield, Kent Roberts, General Editor. *The United States Army in World War II, The Last Offensive.* Washington, D.C.: Department of the Army, ca. 1960.

Griffin, Lieutenant Colonel Robert A. *The School of the Citizen Soldier*, New York: D. Appleton-Century Company, Inc., 1942.

Hieden, Konrad. *Der Fuehrer.* Boston: Houghton Mifflin Company, 1944.

Paassen, Pierre van. *Days of Our Years.* New York: The Dial Press, 1946.

Shirer, William L. *The Rise and Fall of the Third Reich.* New York: Simon and Schuster, 1960.

Tansill, Charles Callan. *Back Door to War—The Roosevelt Foreign Policy 1933-1941.* Chicago: Henry Regnery Company, 1952.

Vagts, Dr. Alfred. *Hitler's Second Army.* Washington, D.C.: Infantry Journal, 1943.

White, Margaret Bourke. *"Dear Fatherland, Rest Quietly."* New York: Simon and Schuster, 1946.

Williams, Mary. Compiler. *The United States Army in World War II, Special Studies, Chronology, 1941-1945.* Washington, D.C.: Department of the Army, 1960.

Index

Aachen, Germany, 36
Absent Without Leave (Awol), 131
African, 3
Adolph Hitler Platz, Nuremberg, Germany, 142
Aleutian Islands, 12, 26
All Purpose Capsule (APC), 80
Allen, Colonel Robert S. 59, 60
Allied Forces, 14, 32, 36, 72, 103, 125, 134
Alps Mountains, 108, 109, 115, 116, 120, 124, 126, 148
Alpspitze Mountain, Germany, 124
Amberg, Germany, 104
America First Committee, Pro-Nazi Organization, 2
American, 98, 102, 104, 113, 115, 121, 123, 124, 128, 129, 131, 132, 135, 139, 140, 142, 143, 145, 147, 148, 149
American Press, 5
American Public, 6, 14
American Red Cross, 51
Anzio Beachhead, Italy, 14
Apmann, Sergeant Eric, 67, 68, 77, 78, 89, 96, 106, 112
Arkansas, 12
Associated Press, 104, 113, 153
Atlanta, Georgia, 21
Attu Island, 26
Auschwitz, 103, 158, 159
Austria, 28, 51, 109, 110, 112, 115, 116, 124, 153
Austrian, 110, 111, 124, 148
Autobahn, 87
Axis Powers, 32
Bad Durkheim, Germany, 80, 83, 84, 105
Bad Ischl, Austria, 171
Balmer, Corporal _____, 74, 75
Bamberg, Germany, 77, 105, 106, 119, 140
Banks, Colonel C. G., 30
Basel, Switzerland, 147, 148, 150
Battle of the Bulge, 123
"Battle of Honor," 104
Baverian Motor Works (BMW), Munich, Germany, 134
"Beast of Bergen-Belsen," Captain Joseph Kramer, 103
"Beetle Bailey," 123, 136
Belgium, 3, 28, 36, 61, 97, 154
Benito Mussolini Platz, Nuremberg, Germany, 142
Berlin, Germany, 104, 140, 142, 155, 157, 158
Berne, Switzerland, 148
Bettlinski, Captain Walter, 63, 64, 66, 85, 90, 107, 112, 114, 115, 116
Big Three, 104, 134
Birdwhistle, Corporal _____, 66
Bishop of Augsburg, 121
Bitburg, Germany, 66, 68, 69
"Bitch of Buchenwald," Ilsa Koch, 99, 101, 103, 126
"Black," Captain _____, 141, 142
Black Market, 133, 136, 140, 147
Blitzkrieg, "Lightning War," 2, 3
Blondheim, Eleanor Lansing Dulles, 98
Blondheim, SS General David, 98
Bollendorf, Germany, 59
Borden, Indiana, 26
Bradley, General of the Army Omar Nelson, 36
Branau, Austria, 109
Brees, Lieutenant General Herbert J., 8, 9
Brigue-Lotschburg Tunnel, Switzerland, 150

British, 124
British Air Force, 54
British Army,
  Second Army, 36
  Twenty-first Army Group, 36
British Army Weapons,
  Maxim Gun, 33
  Three Pound Gun, 46
British Navy, 45, 47, 51, 52
  Battleships: *George V*, 52; *Lord Nelson*, 52
  Channel Steamers, Castle Ships, 51, 52, 54, 55
  Mine Sweepers, 52
  Troopships: HMS *Pasteur*, 45, 46, 48, 50, 51, 61
Broz, Communist Dictator Josip (Tito), 134
Buchenwald, Germany, 101, 102, 103, 104, 110, 111, 113
Budapest, Hungary, 113
Bulle, Switzerland, 148
Byron, Lord George Gordon, 149
Camp Blanding, Florida, 21, 22, 23, 24, 25, 29, 34, 38, 39, 40, 43, 56, 58, 60, 68, 70, 88, 106, 108, 115, 116, 135
Camp Hood, Texas, 21, 40
Camp Jackson, South Carolina, 7
Camp Polk, Louisiana, 21, 40
Camp Shanks, New York, 44, 45, 61
Canadian First Army, 36
Carter, President James Earl, 113
Carthage, North Africa, 54
Central America, 134
Charlemagne, 105
Charlestown, Indiana, 12
Chateau de Chillion, Switzerland, 149
Chattanooga, Tennessee, 21, 43
Chemnitz, Germany, 104
Cherbourg, France, 7
Chicago, Illinois, 5, 11, 19
Chicago Tribune, 104, 113
Chinese, 1, 118
Churchill, Prime Minister Winston S., 104, 108, 118, 134, 145
Civil law, 128
Civil War, 92
Clark, Alva D., 9
Clark, Audrey M. (Lovell), 43, 61, 62, 65, 149, 151
Clark, Sergeant James Ray, 10, 13, 17, 24, 28, 30, 31, 34, 42, 55-59, 62, 63, 64, 65, 66, 68, 69, 75-76, 77-79, 80, 81, 82, 84-86, 87-89, 90-96, 101, 103, 106, 107, 112-114, 117, 118, 120, 123, 125, 126, 128, 129, 130, 132, 133, 135-139, 141-146, 147, 148-151
Coca-Cola, 52, 122
Colgate and Company, 12, 122
Combat law, 128
Committee to Defend America by Aiding the Allies, 5
Communist, 111, 113, 134, 135
Concentration camp, 101-103, 110, 111, 112, 122, 134, 154, 155, 157, 158, 160
Cooper, Governor Prentice, 10
Coral Sea, 12
Cornelius Strasse, Munich, Germany, 130
Costello, Colonel Norman, 96
Crematorium, 95, 102
Crerar, General Henry D. G., 36

164   The Fiery Furnaces of Buchenwald

Crystal Lake, Florida, 24
Cumberland River, 11
Czechoslovakia, 109, 124
Czechoslovakian, 111
D-Day, 6, 10, 14
Dachau, Germany, 5, 6, 101, 111, 129, 154, 157, 160
Danish, 125, 154
DeCamp, First Sergeant _____, 128, 132, 134, 135, 136, 137
DeCamp, Rosemary, 134
DeHuszar, Master Sergeant William J., 113
Democrats, 20
Dempsey General Miles, 36
De-Nazification, 122, 123, 124
Detroit, Michigan, 11
Deutsch Madels, 2
Devers, General Jacob L., 36
Diekirch, Luxembourg, 57, 58, 59, 72
Dingolfing, Germany, 108, 109
Displaced persons, 135, 140, 141
Dodd, William, American Ambassador to Germany (1933-1938), 6, 102
Doenitz, Admiral Karl, 125, 161
"Dog Robber," 144
Doolittle, General James H., 12
Dover, Captain George J., 30, 35, 38, 40
Dragon's teeth, 72, 78, 129
Dresden, Germany, 104
Drum, Lieutenant General Hugh A., 8, 9
Dulles, Allen Walsh, 98
Dulles, Eleanor Lansing, 98
Dulles, John Foster, 98
Durer, Albrecht, 142
Ebensee, Austria, 110, 111, 112
"Edwards," First Lieutenant Hugh Conlan, 140, 141, 142, 145
E. I. DuPont Company, 11, 12
Eifel Hills, Germany, 63, 65, 67
Eisenach, Germany, 124
Eisenhower, General of the Army Dwight D., 19, 36, 103, 104, 108, 113, 118, 127, 143, 146
Eisenhower, President Dwight D., 9, 19
"Enemies of the State," 111, 157, 160
England, 1, 4-5, 14, 25, 49, 50, 51, 55, 61, 104, 158
English, 50, 98, 101, 104, 124, 142
English Channel, 3, 10, 50-52
English Garden, Munich, Germany, 130
English pilots, 5
Erfurt, Germany, 77, 87, 88, 90, 91, 108, 124
Ethiopia, 3
Europe, 3, 40, 44, 88, 104, 114, 115, 121, 124, 127, 149, 150, 153, 158
European, 3, 5, 111, 115, 128, 138, 156
Fales, Major General Edwin, 24, 40, 108
Feldherrnhalle, Munich, Germany, 135
Flensburg, Germany, 125
Florida, 21, 22, 23, 25, 31, 37, 38, 41, 43
Flynn, Major _____, 138, 140, 143
Ford Motor Company, 4
Fort Benjamin Harrison, Indiana, 16, 17-19
Fort Benning, Georgia, 10, 19, 21, 138
Fort George G. Meade, Maryland, 42, 44
Fort Knox, Kentucky, 113
Fort Lewis, Washington, 19
Fort McClellan, Alabama, 58
Fort Myers, Virginia, 19

France, 1-2, 7, 15, 26, 36, 45, 46, 49, 50, 51, 52, 54, 55, 61, 69, 71, 77, 80, 128, 138, 147, 150, 158
Frank, Hans, 6, 161
Fraternization, 105, 109, 121
Frazier, Brigadier General Thomas A., 10
Freising, Germany, 133
French, 36, 44, 52, 54, 62, 93, 98, 120, 142, 148, 154, 156, 157
French First Army, 36
French Navy, 47
Fribourg, Switzerland, 148
Fuehrer, Adolph Hitler, 3, 96, 104, 108, 115, 142
Fussen in Allgau, Germany, 120-122, 123, 164
Fussener Zeitung, 121
Gaddie, Sergeant _____, 67, 71, 75, 78, 80, 93
Garmish-Partinkirchen, Germany, 125, 126
Gatling, Richard J., 33
Gay, Major General Hobart J., 108
"General Halftrack," 123
Geneva Convention, 98, 125, 134, 153, 154
Geneva, Switzerland, 149
George VI, 52
Gera, Germany, 104, 124
German Aircraft,
  Junker 87 Stuka Dive Bomber, 2
  Storch, Observation Plane, 82
  Messerschmidt ME-109, Fighter/Bomber, 82
German Air Force,
  Pilots, 50
  "Bed Check Charlie," 82
German American Bund, 4
Germany Army, 3, 28, 36, 56, 72, 79, 80, 83, 86, 123, 153, 154, 155, 157
Germany Army Units,
  Seventh Army, 7
  LXXXII (Eighty-second) Corps, 73
  Volkstrum, 92
German Navy,
  Submarine, 14, 46, 47
  Battleship, 110
  Range Finder, 109
German Weapons,
  Armor, 118
  Cannon, 88 mm, 64, 81, 82, 88, 93-96, 108
  Grenade, Concussion ("Potato Masher"), 78, 87, 90
  Nebelwefer, Multi-barrel Rocker Launcher, 60, 65, 66, 70, 96
  Pistol, 9 mm, Luger, 28
  .38 caliber Walters (P-38), 28
  7.65 mm Czechoslovakian, 28
  .380 caliber F. B. Radom, 28, 85, 130, 143
  .38 caliber 1917 model "Machine Pistol," 86
  Tank, Mark IV "Tiger," 65, 66, 72, 92
  Mark VI "Royal Tiger," 65, 87, 88
  V-1 Rocket, 4
  V-2 Rocket, 4
Germans, 2, 5-6, 25, 34, 61, 85-86, 87, 88, 89, 90, 93, 96, 100, 101, 110-111, 115, 120-122, 127-129, 130, 133-135, 137, 140, 144, 145, 146
Germany, 1, 2, 4, 5, 6, 9, 32, 36, 59, 61, 63, 77, 102, 104, 110, 111, 125, 128, 129
Giessen, Germany, 151
Glauchau, Germany, 104
Glion, Switzerland, 149, 150
Goebbels, Paul Joseph, Nazi Propaganda Chief, 6, 97

Goering, Reichmarshal Hermann, 4, 6, 97, 158, 161
Gotha, Germany, 87
Grant, General Ulysses S., 14
Gray and Dudley Manufacturing Company, 11
Graz, Austria, 112
Greimerath, Germany, 71
Guam Island, 12
Gulf of Mexico, 11
Hahm, General Frederick, 73, 80
Harlaching Forest, Germany, 6
Hayes, Colonel James H., 56, 79, 83, 89, 92, 107, 112, 123
"Heinies," 90
Hess, Rudolph, 6, 102, 105, 106, 142, 161
Hill 403, Germany, 63, 64, 70
Himmler, Heinrich, Chief of Nazi Secret Police (Gestapo), 6, 97, 126, 156, 157
Hitler, Adolph, Nazi Chancellor and Reichfuehrer, 2-4, 6, 78, 97, 98, 105, 107, 109, 111, 134, 142, 152, 158, 160
Hitler Youth, 2
Hoare, Samuel, British Foreign Minister, 3
Hobbs, Major General Leland S., 7
Hodges, General Courtney, H., 36
Holland, 36
Hollywood, California, 5, 126
Holocaust, 103, 112
Hoover, Sergeant Byron, 79
Hotel Bahnhof, Fussen, Germany, 120
Howell, Private Freddie, 57, 58, 65, 66
Huck, Sergeant Bernard J., 123
Hungarian Field Army, 112
Hungarian Government, 112, 113
Hungarian Imperial Guard, 112, 113, 115
Hungarians, 112, 113
Hungary, 113
Hunt, George Walter, 12-13
Huns, 5
Indianapolis, Indiana, 13, 149
International War Crimes Tribunal, 4, 100, 103, 126, 142, 154, 159, 161
Ireland, 49
Italian Army, 3
Italian Citizens, 6
Italian Fascists, 2, 3, 155
Italians, 25, 34, 111
Italy, 3, 9, 14, 32, 129, 147, 153
Jackson, President Andrew, 8
Jacksonville, Florida, 22, 24, 35, 43
Japan, 5, 9, 12, 32
Japanese, 25, 34, 122
Japanese Imperial Army, 1, 3, 115, 122
Japanese Imperial Fleet, 14
Japanese Submarines, 12
Jeffersonville, Indiana, 13, 16, 18
Jena, Germany, 104, 124
"Jerries," 5
Jews, 6, 100, 102, 111, 156, 158, 159, 160
"Jew Baiter," 142
Joint Chiefs of Staff, British-America, 14
Jones, Alan, 126
Jones, Major General Alan, 44
Jones, First Lieutenant, _____, 65-66, 84, 85, 90, 93, 107, 112
Kahr, Gustav von, 6
Kansas, 5

Kaiserslautern, Germany, 28, 79, 80
Kassel, Germany, 77, 86-87, 107, 113, 124
Kentucky, 44
Kimbell, Sergeant _____, 132
Klausner, Erich, 6
Knoll, First Lieutenant Frederick "Knobby", 57-58, 61, 65, 66, 67, 84, 89-90, 110, 112-114, 116, 117
Koch, Ilsa, "Bitch of Buchenwald," 99, 101, 103, 126, 158
Korea, 10, 119, 134
Kramer, SS Captain Josef "Beast of Bergen-Belsen," 158
"Krauts," 5, 78
Kreuzeck Mountain, Germany, 125
Krueger, Lieutenant General Walter, 9
Kuhn, Fritz, Head of German American Bund, 4
Kyll River, Germany, 69
Kyllburg, Germany, 69
Lake Geneva, Switzerland, 148, 150
Laval, Pierre, French Foreign Minister, 3
Lazar, Lieutenant _____, 87, 91-92, 96, 108, 114
Lech River, Fussen, Germany, 120
Le Havre, France, 45, 54-55
Leizen, Austria, 28, 51, 112, 115, 116, 124
Liepzig, Germany, 104
Liessem, Germany, 69
Life magazine, 87, 113, 121
Lindbergh, Colonel Charles A., 4
Linz, Austria, 112, 124, 153, 157
Lister, Dr. Joseph, 39
Little, First Sergeant _____, 65-67, 74, 75, 112
Liverpool, England, 50, 51
Lomax, Colonel Arthur Eugene, 9, 10
"Loot Bag," 63, 65, 93, 96, 109
Los Angeles, California, 5
Louis, Joe, Heavyweight Champion, 45
Louisville, Kentucky, 149
Lovell, Audrey May, 13
Lucas, Major General John P., 14
Lucerne, Switzerland, 150
Ludwig, King of Bavaria, 120
Lund, Sergeant Melvin S., 58, 60, 63, 66, 67, 74-76
Luxembourg, 36, 55, 57, 59, 61, 71, 110
"M-1 Thumb," 92
MacArthur, General of the Army Douglas, 12, 14, 19, 42, 115
Magdeburg, Germany, 124
"Maggie's Drawers," 27
Mahin, Major General Frank, 12
Mainz, Germany, 83-84
Malinowsky, Field Marshall, 117-118
Malony, Major General Harry J., 73
Mannheim, Germany, 135
Marien Platz, Munich, Germany, 135
Market Platz, Nuremberg, Germany, 142
Marseilles, France, 139
Marshall, General of the Army George C., 9, 19
Martial law, 128, 132
Martinsburg, Indiana, 26, 148
Maurice, Emil, 6
Maxim, Hiram Stevens, 33
Messerschmidt, Willie, 4
Meuse River, France, 36
Midway Island, 12
"Military Necessity," 144, 145
Mississippi River, 11
Montgomery, Field Marshal Bernard, 36, 54

Morris, Major General H. H. Jr., 73
Mortain, France, 7
Moselle River, France, 93
Mount Balmhorn, Switzerland, 150
Mount Washington Cemetery, Washington County, Indiana, 26
Munich, Germany, 5, 6, 25, 39, 127, 128-131, 133, 134, 135, 136, 137, 138, 142, 150, 154, 157, 160
Murnau, Germany, 126
Mussolini, Benito, Fascist Dictator of Italy, 2-3, 142
McBride, Major General Horace L., 64, 68, 73, 80, 82, 83, 87, 88, 91, 92, 103, 104, 106, 113, 115, 117, 118, 119, 123
McClune, Colonel _____, 151
McNair, Lieutenant General Leslie J., 14
Nanking, China, 1, 2
Nashville Bridge Company, 11
Nashville Tennessean, 12
Nashville, Tennessee, 7, 10-12, 43, 44, 147
National Guard, 7, 10, 18, 19
National Socialist, 105
Nazi, 91, 128, 132, 134, 135
Nazi Gestapo, Secret Police, 6, 111
Nazi Government, 101, 105, 106, 112, 125
Nazi Regime, 5, 112, 134, 157
Nazi SS, "Werewolf" Division, 108
Nazi Storm Troopers, SS, 2, 7, 28, 69, 79, 82, 85, 87, 96, 109, 113, 115, 125, 129, 156, 157, 158, 159, 160
Nazi War Criminal, 4, 96, 97, 126, 132, 138, 142, 153, 161
Nazis, 101, 103, 104, 142, 144, 160
Neidervellmar, Germany, 87
Neiderweiler, Germany, 69
Neuschwanstein Castle, 120
New Albany, Indiana, 108
New Guinea, 14
New York City, New York, 5, 46, 48, 113, 126, 149
New York Times, 6, 9, 123, 160
"Next of Kin," 17, 69
Nonfraternization, 122, 124, 129, 140
Normandy, France, 3, 26
North Africa, 12, 14
North Sea, 36, 157
Noswendel, Germany, 76
Nuremberg, Germany, 4, 97, 100, 106, 107, 138, 140, 142, 154, 155, 156, 159, 161
Nussbaum, Germany, 63
Oberammergau, Germany, 126
Odeons Platz, Munich, Germany, 135
Ohio River, 11
"Old Hickory," 7, 8
Old Hickory, Tennessee, 11, 12
Olive Branch Cemetery, Washington County, Indiana, 26
Olmstead, Colonel O. H., 143, 144, 146
Olmstead, Mrs. O. H., 146
Okefenokee Swamp, Florida, 22
Omaha Beach, France, 7, 10
Owenton, Kentucky, 58
Pacific Coast, 5
Pacific Ocean, 4, 5
Palace of Justice, Nuremberg, Germany, 142
Panama Canal, 5
Paassen, Pierre von, 5, 6

Papen, Franz von, 96, 97, 98, 100, 161
Paris, France, 3, 55
Patch, General Alexander M., 36
Patton, General George S., 8, 12, 14, 15, 19-20, 36, 59, 60, 68-69, 83, 100, 103, 104, 107, 108, 109, 113, 117, 122, 123, 135, 145
Paulus, Field Marshal Frederick von, 112
Pearl Harbor, Hawaii, 4, 5, 12
Pekin, Indiana, 13, 26, 62
Pershing, General of the Armies John J., 14
Peter, King of Yugoslavia, 134
Pettingill, Corporal _____, 123
Philippines, 5, 12, 18
Pilger, Sergeant _____, 58, 59, 71
Pilsen, Czechoslovakia, 109
Poland, 2, 158, 160
Police State, 111
Pont-a-Mosson, France, 93
Potsdam, Germany, 134
Prague, Czechoslovakia, 104, 109
Pruem River, Germany, 69
Quirk, Colonel J. T., 69
Radio City Music Hall Revue, Corps De Ballet, 126
Rampy, Sergeant _____, 57, 58, 65, 71
Rape of Nanking, China, 2
Regensburg, Germany, 77, 108
Reo, Sergeant Johnny, 130, 131, 132, 135, 136
Republicans, 20
Rhine River, Germany, 63, 64, 67, 68, 69, 72, 77, 80, 83, 84, 86, 90
Riot Squad, 129, 130, 132, 136
"Rodgers," Captain _____, 141
Rohm, Ernst, 6
Rome, Italy, 2, 147
Roosevelt, President Franklin D., 3-5, 6, 7, 8, 10, 11, 102, 104, 109, 118, 121, 145
"Roosevelt's Butchers," 109
Russian, 93, 104, 110, 117, 118, 124, 127, 129, 140
Russian Army, 72, 104, 112, 115, 117
Russians, 51, 104, 110, 113, 117-118, 124, 140, 155
Saar Basin, Germany, 77
Saarburg, Germany, 71, 73, 80
Saboteurs,
  German, 12
  Italian, 12
"Sack of Rome," 2
"Sad Sack," 136
St. Lo, France, 7
Saint Stephen's Byzantine Crown, 113
St. Wendel, Germany, 78, 79
Sarreguemines, France, 36
Saturday Evening Post, 62
Sauer River, Germany, 59, 60
Schliecher, Elisabeth von, 6
Schliecher, German Chancellor Kurt von, 6, 160
Schmidt, Wilhelm, 6
Schmidt, Willie, 6
Searby, Brigadier General Edmund W., 123
Seine River, France, 54
Selassie, Haile, Emperor of Ethiopia, 3
Sherman, General William T., 14
Short, Major General Walter C., 8-9
Siegfried Line, Germany, 58, 59, 61, 64, 69, 72, 73
Siegfried, "Siggie," 129
Sierre, Switzerland, 150
Simbach, Germany, 109

Simpson, General William H., 36
Slave Labor Camp, 77, 87, 95, 100, 101, 102, 154, 155, 156, 157
South Pacific, 26
Southampton, England, 50, 51, 52
Southwest Pacific, 14
Soviet Union, 104, 109, 110
Spain, 2
Speer, Albert, 4, 161
Spiez, Switzerland, 150
Stalin, Soviet Dictator Joseph, 104, 109, 118, 127, 134, 145
Stalingrad, Russia, 112
Starke, Florida, 22, 24
Statue of Liberty, 46
Stempfle, Father Bernard, Adolph Hitler's Father Confessor, 6
Stettin, Germany, 111
Strasbourg, France, 36, 147, 158
Stricker, Corporal Raymond, 65, 82
Striecher, Julius, 142
Strohecker, Captain S. C., 151
Swartzwald Madel, Munich, Germany, 131, 132
S.W.A.T. Team, 129
Swiss, 61, 147, 148, 149, 150
Switzerland, 3, 36, 60, 98, 126, 147, 148, 150, 151
Tangermunde, Germany, 124
Tassigny, General Jean de Latte, 36
Tennessee, 7, 8, 9, 10, 11, 12, 21, 43, 44, 147
Tennessee State Militia, 10, 11, 25
Thionville, France, 69, 71
Tholey, Germany, 77
Tief, Captain _____, 128, 134, 136
Tokyo, Japan, 12
Troy, Asia Minor, 54
Truman, President Harry S., 124, 134, 139, 145
Tyrolians, 121
Unexploded Bomb (UXB), 51
United Service Organization (U.S.O.), 118, 126
United States of America, 1, 3-5, 25, 28, 87, 109, 110, 111, 113, 124, 137, 143, 145, 146
  Congress, 3, 7, 10, 103, 134
  Department of State,
    Secretary of State, 98
    German-American Affairs Desk, 100
  Government, 4, 5, 14, 34, 44, 119, 144
  War Department, 8, 20
    Office of War Information (OWI), 14
United States Aircraft,
  Boeing B-17, Flying Fortress, 5
  North American B-25, Mitchell, 12
  North American P-51, Mustang, 84
  Piper L-4, Cub, 72, 82
  Republic P-47, Thunderbolt, 64, 72, 73, 87
  Vultee L-5, Sentinel, 82
  Vultee P-66, Vanguard, 11
United States Air Force, 4, 141, 155
  Eight Air Force, 14
  Ninth Air Force, 14
  XIX Tactical Air Force, 72, 73, 87
United States Armed Forces, 124
United States Army, 10, 11, 12, 14, 18, 23, 30, 36, 61, 85, 87, 102, 105, 108, 118, 123, 124, 127, 128, 132, 138, 140, 141, 151
  Articles of War, 25, 139
  Battalion Aid Station Hospital, 80, 119

Ceremonial Troop, 19
Chief Historian, 73
Clearing Station Hospital, 87
Combat Aid Men (Medics), 40, 78, 84
Combat Engineers, 58, 72
Combat Infantrymen, 124
Command Post (CP), 85, 89, 120, 123, 126
Constabulary Force, 127
Counter Intelligence Corps (CIC), 132, 134, 135, 136
Criminal Investigation Divison (CID), 130, 133, 136, 140
Demobilization, 124
Detained Officer ("Meathead"), 139, 140, 143, 144
Disciplinary Training Center (DTC), 138, 139, 143, 144, 151
Duty Officer, 120, 132
Field Manual, 26, 37, 38, 41
Finance Officer, 143
Forward Observer (FO), 72, 81, 82, 92, 96, 108, 114
Ground Forces Replacement Depot (AGFRD), 42
Guardhouse Overhead Detachment (GOD), 138, 143, 145
Induction Center, 17
Infantry Replacement Center (IRTC), 21, 24, 40
Main Line of Resistance (MLR), 8, 87, 89, 108, 115
Medical Officer, 119
Military Academy (USMA), 14
Military Community, 143-145, 146, 147, 151
Military Currency, 133, 134
Military District, Wurzburg, Germany, 144
Military Government, 105, 122, 128, 137, 140
Military Law and Order (MLO), 130, 131, 132, 133, 136
Military Occupation Specialty (MOS), 42, 137, 138, 151
Military Police (MP), 44, 87-88, 127, 131, 134-137
Occupation Army, 125, 127
Office of Strategic Services (OSS), 96, 98, 132
Officer Candidate School (OCS), 10, 14, 17, 41, 138
Order of Battle, 73, 80
Pentagon, 19
Post Exchange (PX), 133
Provost Officer, 131, 132, 140
Public Relations Officer (PRO), 69
Redeployment, 124, 126
Selective Service Draftee, 18
Staff Officer, 146
Standard Operating Procedure (SOP), 17
Supreme Headquarters Allied Expeditionary Force (SHAEF), 104
Task Force (TF), 109, 134, 144
Washington General Headquarters (GHQ), 19, 37, 138, 143
Washington Guards, 44
Zone of Occupation, 127, 140
United States Army Units
  Air Corps, 4, 8
  First Army, 9, 36
  Second (II) Corps, 14
  Third Army, 15, 19, 20, 36, 68, 69, 83, 91, 104, 106, 108, 109, 113, 117

Third Cavalry Group, 109, 110, 115
Sixth Army Group, 36
Twelfth Army Group, 36
Twentieth (XX) Corps, 68, 72, 103, 108, 123
First Armored Division, 8
Second Armored Division, 19
Fourth Armored, 36, 69, 104, 109
Sixth Armored, 86, 87, 91, 104
Seventh Armored Division, 36
Tenth Armored Division, 73, 79, 86, 125
Sixteenth Armored Division, 109
Fifth Infantry Division, 64, 69
Twenty-sixth Infantry Division, 71
Twenty-ninth Infantry Division, 10
Thirtieth Infantry Division, 7-8, 9
  120th Infantry Regiment, 7
  Company H 317th Infantry Regiment, 9
Sixty-ninth Infantry Division, 87, 113
Seventy-first Infantry Division, 110, 112
Eightieth Infantry Division, 36, 57, 71, 73, 80, 86, 91, 104, 106, 107, 113, 123, 124, 126, 158
  317th Infantry Regiment, 56, 71, 109, 110
  Regimential Combat Team, 109
  First Battalion, 64, 84, 106, 112, 117, 120, 123, 125
  Company A, 64, 68, 91-92
  Company B, 68, 73, 87, 90, 91-92, 110, 112, 114, 120
  Company C, 68, 91-92
  Cannon Company, 92, 114
508th Military Police Battalion, 127, 128, 137
2913th Guardhouse Overhead Detachment, 151
116th General Hospital, 141, 142
Fifty-sixth Quartermaster Base Depot, 151
United States Army, Weapons and Equipment,
  Atomic Bomb, 15, 122
  Bazooka 4.2 Rocket Launcher, 24, 58, 65, 66, 85, 91
  Command and Reconnaissance Car (C&R), 144
  Gas Mask, M-1 1918, 32, 33
  Gas, Poison Mustard, 33
  Gatling Gun, 33
  Grenade, Thermit, 55, 65, 67, 96
  Half-Tracks, 125
  Lister Bag, 39
  Proximity Fuse, 60, 72
  Radio, SCR 300, 65, 84, 90, 91, 106, 107, 114
  Radio, SCR 536, 65, 67, 84, 89, 90
  Radio SCR 610, 84
  Sam Browne Belt, 9, 39
  Tank Destroyer, 74, 78, 79, 91, 92, 107
  Tanks, 125
    Sherman 30 ton, 69, 90, 93, 96, 110, 129
    Sherman 30 ton with Rocket Launchers, 69, 83
  40 mm Automatic AntiAircraft Gun (BOFORS), 82, 83
  8 inch Cannon, 81
  76 mm Cannon, 74, 79
  90 mm Cannon, Assault Gun, 83, 90, 91
  105 mm Howitzer, 10, 64, 81, 83, 107, 108
  155 mm Cannon, 10, 60, 81, 83, 87, 108
  240 mm Cannon, 60, 81, 83, 108
  .30 caliber, Heavy Machine Gun, 24, 31-32, 79, 81, 83
  .50 caliber Machine Gun, 10, 79, 83, 109
  81 mm Mortar, 10, 24, 31, 83
  .30 caliber M-1 Garand Rifle, 24, 25, 26, 39, 65, 74, 81, 82, 85, 88
  .30 caliber M-1 Carbine, 116, 139
  .30 caliber Browning Automatic Rifle (BAR), 24, 39, 74-75, 81
  .45 caliber Colt Automatic Pistol, 24, 27-28, 39, 130, 132
  .45 caliber Thompson Submachine Gun, 24, 39, 40, 81, 129, 130, 131, 135, 143
United States Marines, 10
United States Merchant Marine, 9
United States Navy, 5, 10, 11, 12, 14, 48, 83
  Aircraft Carriers, 5; Hornet, 12
  Battleships, 5; Iowa, 52; Missouri, 52; Nevada, 54; Texas, 54
  Cruisers, 5
  Destroyers, 5, 11, 12, 46, 47, 48, 52
  Landing Craft, Infantry (LCI), 53
  Landing Craft Vehicle Personnel (LCVP), 83
  Submarines, 12
Utley, Clifford M., Director of Chicago Council of Foreign Relations, 6
Vandals, 2
Victor Emmanuel III, King of Italy, 3
Vietnam, 10, 134
Vinci, Leonardo da, 105
Vire Canal, France, 7
Virginia, 44
Voecklabruck, Austria, 110
Wadern Forest, Germany, 71
Wake Island, 12
Walchen See, Germany, 126
Waldrip, Sergeant Clyde A., 65, 82, 85, 90, 107, 114, 126
Walker, Captain Robert A., 126
Walker, General Walton H., 68, 69, 73, 103, 108
Waldholzbach, Germany, 73, 74, 76
Wank Mountain, Germany, 125
Wankbahn, 125
War Fathers, 106
Washington D.C., 9, 44, 72, 73, 97, 100, 103
Washington, General George, 23
Weimer, Germany, 124, 157
Weisbaden, Germany, 28, 84
West Point, New York, 14
Weston, Lieutenant, 145, 150
Weyland, Major General Otto P., 73
White, William Allen, 5
Wilhelm II, Kaiser, 87, 123
Wilhelmshore (Kaiser Wilhelm Forest), Kassel, Germany, 87
Woods, Master Sergeant John, 138
Woodside, Captain James A., 91
World War I, 2-3, 10, 32, 33, 34, 86, 123, 145
World War II, 4, 7, 9, 10, 12, 13, 14, 19, 43, 71, 73, 80, 92, 97, 98, 105, 124, 128, 154, 155, 160
Wurzburg, Germany, 138, 139, 141, 142, 143, 144, 145, 147, 148, 149, 150
Yalta, Russia, 104, 109, 110, 124, 139, 145
Yugoslavian Army, 134
Zeiss-Ikon, 109
Zugspitze Mountain, Germany, 125